THE BLACK SPIRITUAL MOVEMENT

T0168164

The Black Spiritual Movement

A RELIGIOUS RESPONSE TO RACISM

Second Edition

HANS A. BAER

The University of Tennessee Press • KNOXVILLE

To Lenore, Eric, and Andrea

First edition copyright © 1984 by The University of Tennessee Press / Knoxville
All Rights Reserved. Manufactured in the United States of America.

Preface to the second edition copyright © 2001 by The University of Tennessee
Press / Knoxville

Paper, 2nd edition: 1st printing, 2001.
This book is printed on acid-free paper.

Library of Congress Cataloging in Publication Data

Baer, Hans A. 1944–
    The Black spiritual movement : a religious response to racism / Hans A.
Baer.—2nd ed.
        p. cm.
Includes bibliographical references and index.
ISBN 1-57233-146-1 (pbk.: alk. paper)
        1. Afro-American Spiritual churches. 2. United States—Race relations.

BX6194.A464 B34 2001
277.3'082'08996073—dc21   2001027908

Contents

Preface to the Second Edition

The first edition of *The Black Spiritual Movement* (1984) was the first book-length study of African American Spiritual churches in the United States. It was reviewed in at least fifteen journals and one African American newspaper, *The Sun* in New York City. In the same year as its publication, Michael P. Smith (1984:28–68) published a photographic account and journal of various aspects of African American cultural life in New Orleans, including of the Spiritual churches in New Orleans. Since then, anthropologists Claude F. Jacobs and Andrew J. Kaslow (1991) published a book on Spiritual churches in New Orleans and journalist Jason Berry (1995) published a book on the Black Hawk motif in Spiritual churches. A few other scholars have published short pieces on aspects of the African American Spiritual movement.

Anthropologists and other social scientists who conduct ethnographic research, particularly sociologists, have over the past two decades increasingly recognized that the ethnographer's personal experience constitutes a central component of the research process. In contrast to earlier ethnographic accounts, which generally did not discuss the researcher's methods and problems in detail, the "unmasking" of fieldwork has become a popular matter, which, according to James Clifford (1986:3), has evolved into an "emergent interdisciplinary phenomenon." As John L. Wengle (1988:viii) argues, "Whatever the ultimate cause for this increase in self-reflexive interests may be—for surely any general explanation would need to consider the increase in self-reflexive interests apparent in the other (human) sciences today—anthropologists are currently more open and willing to discuss their field experiences publicly than ever before."

Despite the existence of a notable literature on the dilemmas of ethnographic research, social scientists who conduct ethnographic research on religious groups have only recently begun to discuss the unique problems that they have encountered (Robbins et al. 1973; Lofland 1977; McGuire 1982; Wagner 1983, 1990; Barker 1984; Rochford 1985; Richardson et al. 1987; Van Zandt 1991; Davidman 1991).

According to Crapanzano (1976:69), ethnography constitutes "a symptom of a particular confrontation"—between the ethnographer and his or her subjects. I examine the dilemmas of this confrontation through the use of what Van Maanen (1988) terms a "fieldwork confessional" that focuses on the manner in which I gained entrée into Black Spiritual churches, the reactions of their adherents to my presence as a participant-observer, and the reactions of selected members of the movement to my description and analysis of their respective congregations. My fieldwork on the Spiritual movement was carried out while teaching at several institutions and during a one-year stint as a postdoctoral fellow in the Medical Anthropology Program at Michigan State University and has served as an important component of collaborative work with Merrill Singer on African American religion (Baer and Singer 1981, 1988, 1992).

My primary research strategy in conducting research on the African American Spiritual movement was participant-observation. As a participant-observer, I not only observed the lives and activities of the Spiritual people but participated, at least in part, in their round of activities. From the beginning of my research, I kept a log of my observations and conversations with the Spiritual people. I also routinely took notes at religious services, upon which I later elaborated, and while interviewing subjects. While formal interviews with members of Spiritual churches provided me with useful information, I feel that an even more important source of data was casual conversation in people's homes, before and after religious services and study classes, and during church dinners. As Crane and Angrosino (1984:157) observe, "Most anthropologists freely admit that a surprisingly large part of their information—sometimes the *best* information" comes from informal or impromptu interviews.

My experiences as an "academic gypsy" during the early part of my academic career provided me with the opportunity to study Spiritual churches in several places, namely Nashville, southeastern Michigan (Detroit, Flint, and Saginaw), the New York–New Jersey megalopolis, Hattiesburg (Mississippi) and North Little Rock (Arkansas). After I "discovered" my first Spiritual congregation in October 1977, I visited the eleven Spiritual congregations in Nashville over the next twenty months, at least whenever time permitted a break from my heavy teaching load at George Peabody College for Teachers. My research focused upon the Temple of Spiritual Truth (pseudonym), a storefront near the central business district, but I also visited all of the other Spiritual congregations in the city at least twice. During the period of 1977–87, I visited forty-two Spiritual congregations in sixteen cities and twelve states and attended over one hundred religious services as well as many other events, including study classes and suppers in Spiritual congregations.

During my first year of teaching at George Peabody College, I contemplated the possibility of conducting fieldwork on the Church of Christ, given that Nashville—the site of David Lipscomb College (now University)—is a major center of this fundamentalist-conservative sect. After attending services at several white Church of Christ congregations, I decided to look for a more "exotic" topic. I began to consider the possibility of conducting research on some aspect of African American religion due to the large number of Blacks residing in Nashville. Although I had done some reading in this area, I had never even visited a Black church and was not sure how I as a white person would be received if I were to do so. One of my African American students assured me that I would be welcomed if I were to visit his congregation, which was also affiliated with the Church of Christ. After visiting his congregation, I attended the Sunday morning service at a Black Baptist congregation where I also received a warm welcome.

Upon noticing that the four churches listed under the category "Spiritualist" in the telephone directory were located in Black neighborhoods, my curiosity prompted me to visit one of them in October 1977. The members of this congregation, whom I met in a house church, informed me that they referred to their congregation as "Spiritual" rather than "Spiritualist." I was particularly struck by the presence in the sanctuary of two crucifixes and the observance of various Catholic rituals, such as kneeling before the altar or reciting the "Hail Mary," which I associated with my religious socialization into Roman Catholicism rather than Protestantism. I also wondered how African Americans in a city that is sometimes described as the "Protestant Vatican" because various Protestant groups have their headquarters, publishing houses, or educational institutions there would have come to incorporate Catholic elements into their religion. When I discovered a paucity of information on Spiritual churches in the literature on African American religion, I decided that I had discovered a topic worthy of ethnographic research.

Although I sometimes was able to contact the pastor of a particular Spiritual congregation before visiting it, more often than not this was very difficult to do. In many cases, the telephone number of the congregation that I wished to visit was not listed in the telephone directory. Furthermore, even when a number was listed, it was often impossible to reach anyone at the church except when services were being conducted. At any rate, once I made contact with the pastor or other leaders of a Spiritual church, I always identified myself as an anthropologist and a professor or research fellow with an interest in the Spiritual movement. Unfortunately, people who are the focus of social scientific research often find the endeavors of researchers, including ethnographers, to be strange and incomprehensible. While undoubtedly many Spiritual people viewed my efforts in a somewhat similar manner, others were quite cognizant of my goals from the very beginning. On the occasion of my first visit to the Temple of Spiritual Truth (pseudonym), Bishop Frank Jones (pseudonym) asked me whether I was a minister. When I replied that I was a college professor, he noted that I must be "analyzing" his congregation. Fortunately, he added that it was good for someone to do this sort of thing.

My unexpected arrival at various Spiritual churches was apparently a somewhat disarming event for some members. At least in the case of the smaller Spiritual churches, the appearance of a white person is rare, if not a nonexistent, occurrence. Upon my arrival, I was sometimes asked if I was a minister or a preacher. Although I never was asked whether I was a police officer or a detective, on several occasions it was believed that I might be. According to an elderly Spiritual male medium, any stranger, regardless of skin color and particularly if a male, who appears at a Spiritual church is likely to be suspected of being a law enforcement officer. I saw that this might often be true when on one occasion a strange middle-aged Black man entered a storefront congregation after the Sunday morning service and asked to see the pastor. The woman with whom I had been speaking looked at him suspiciously and asked him who he was and what was the purpose of his visit. Such reactions to strangers are not due so much to fears that the members of a particular congregation have violated the law but rather because Spiritual people are well aware that their churches are often reputed to provide spiritual advise in playing the "numbers" racket—an illicit lottery. In one instance, the pastor of a Spiritual church in Flint openly admitted to his congregation that he initially suspected that I might be a law enforcement officer. After he asked me to introduce myself to the congregation, which was celebrating his first anniversary as its "Royal Elect Ruler, Prophet, and Savior," the pastor noted that he wanted to be interviewed for this event but the local newspaper had declined to do so. Instead, he regarded my visit as a substitute of sorts, stating: "God sent the doctor. I did not know who he was when I saw him. I thought he was the police." Needless to say, the congregation responded with hearty and empathetic laughter.

On another occasion, however, King Louis H. Narcisse, D.D., the now deceased founder-leader of the Mt. Zion Spiritual Temple association, did not receive my visit with the same level of enthusiasm. Although I had visited the "East Coast Headquarters" of the association in Detroit on two previous occasions and had been well received by the members, when he visited the church himself, he viewed my presence with considerable apprehension. After the service, King Narcisse closely interrogated me in the presence of his congregation about my reasons for visiting the temple. He spoke about sinister "forces" that were attempting to harm religious groups and asked me if I had ever heard of either the Communist Party or the Central Intelligence Agency, very likely suspecting that I might be connected with these organizations. For a half-hour or so, Narcisse quizzed me on what I had learned about Spiritual churches and tried to engage me in a theological debate. I found my encounter with him so uncomfortable that I even contemplated running out of the church. In retrospect, I regret that I did not ask him for permission to revisit the temple because I believe that Narcisse was one of the neglected "gods of the Black metropolis" (Fauset 1971).

In my role as participant-observer, I attempted to participate in religious services and activities as fully as possible without being obtrusive or converting to any of the churches. On occasions when I did hold back from participating in certain rituals, I was often urged to do so. While I made concerted efforts to be explicit about my role as an anthropologist, many Spiritual people viewed my research as a spiritual quest for truth. In a similar vein, members of the Children of God told Van Zandt (1991:10) that the Lord was using him to provide the outside world with an objective account of their group, and that God would make him a member upon completion of his study. Anthropologist Frances Kostarelos (1995:xvii). describes the reaction of members of an African American evangelical Baptist storefront congregation on the West Side of Chicago as follows: "Over the years the church members explained my presence and field work in their church according to their way of thinking. From their perspective, a young white women devoting herself to a Black church in a run-down and dangerous neighborhood was the work of God."

Based upon their ethnographic study of a Pentecostal sect, Robbins, Anthony, and Curtis (1973) note that any empathetic stance on the part of the ethnographer is likely to create a dilemma, particularly in the case of conversionist sects. Members of the Jesus Commune (pseudonym) exerted considerable pressure on Richardson, Stewart, and Simmonds (1978) to join the sect. McGuire (1982:22) reports that the Catholic Pentecostals among whom she conducted fieldwork were also "disturbed by the presence of a researcher who appeared to understand, yet was not compelled by that understanding to believe." Other social scientists have experienced efforts by members of the religious sects that they studied to convert them as well (Lawless 1988:xviii; Wagner 1990:220; Davidman 1991:54). Gordon (1987) maintains that the expectation that field researchers make a religious commitment exerted by proselytizing or conversionist sects creates two basic problems: (1) subject distress and (2) the threat of eventual termination from the research project. Indeed, Whitehead's (1987:43–44) ethnographic research on the Church of Scientology was terminated by two church officers because she had not shown evidence of a stronger commitment beyond that of her method of "cultural learning."

Due to the dilemmas that had arisen as a result of having admitted to the Levites, a Mormon sect based in Utah (Baer 1976, 1988b), that I was an agnostic, I generally told the members of the churches I visited that I had been reared as a Catholic but also often admitted that I was a lapsed one. While some Spiritual people were apprehensive about my motives for visiting their congregations, their definitions of my role also often changed over time. Mediums in their prophecies sometimes indicated that, even if I was not aware of it, the Spirit was directing my efforts toward higher goals than the scholarly ones that I had stated. When on one occasion I reiterated my scholarly objectives to Bishop Frank Jones, he vigorously insisted that my endeavors also had a higher spiritual dimension. I suspect that my willingness to participate in religious activities may have unwittingly misled some Spiritual people to believe that I was undergoing a process of religious conversion. A case in point was my "testimonies" before various congregations. While initially I was reluctant to do so, after a while I decided that, rather than being one of the few individuals not testifying, and because I was often asked to do so anyway, I came to use these junctures in the service as an opportunity to thank people for their assistance in my research. After one such instance, an elder in the Temple of Spiritual Truth complimented me upon my spiritual progress.

In his ethnographic study of Nichiren Shoshu, David Snow (1980:116) notes that, while he was quite explicit about his objective of learning about the sect from a sociological perspective, he "felt somewhat like the 'con artist'" when he was called upon to give testimonies. Melinda Bollar Wagner reports similar experiences in her fieldwork on Spiritual Frontiers Fellowship (SFF):

> Although the group leaders and most members knew I was a student of the group, they insisted from time to time that I was undergoing spiritual growth, just as they were. If I did not protest, I would be uncomfortable. If I protested too much, it would make the group uncomfortable, which would in turn make me uncomfortable. This is the epitome of the anthropological double-bind. The field worker wishes not to disturb or influence the people he is studying, yet he wants them to know he is studying them. The problem is magnified when working within one's own culture. (Wagner 1983:199–200)

In contrast to Wagner, who actually belonged to SFF during the course of her fieldwork, I suspect that the greatest handicap in my ability to gather information on Spiritual churches was my refusal to join any one of them. Although little overt effort was made to convert me during the course of my fieldwork, Bishop Frank Jones repeatedly urged me to join the Temple of Spiritual Truth over a period of several months. While I was flattered and tempted by his offer, it created an awkward dilemma for me. I was well aware that some anthropologists have undergone initiation rites or have joined religious or secret sodalities in indigenous societies as part of their ethnographic work. I asked myself whether I was willing to make the same commitment and to assume the same obligations that Roger Bastide (1978), a renowned French anthropologist, did when he joined an Afro-Brazilian sect. I finally decided that, in light of my own agnosticism, it would have been unethical for me to feign conversion to a belief system that I did not personally accept. Bishop Jones eventually ceased his efforts to convert me.

It appears, however, that I came to be regarded as a sort of honorary member of the Temple of Spiritual Truth when, after acknowledging the presence of several visitors, including a former wife, at a religious service by asking them to speak, Bishops Jones noted that he would not ask me to speak because I was "all but a member." In the fall of 1978, I accompanied some twenty-six members of the temple on a visit to two Spiritual churches in Indianapolis. Since I was the only white person disembarking from the bus, Bishop Glenda Jackson (pseudonym), the assistant pastor and wife of the pastor, felt compelled to explain my presence to one of the pastors of our host churches by noting, "he is one of our members." In a similar manner, Wagner in her ethnographic research on a Christian school was introduced by one of the teachers to someone as "sort of on staff" (quoted in Wagner 1990:223).

The subjects of ethnographic research increasingly read accounts of their groups and respond to them in writing (Clifford 1986:117). Some Spiritual people read *The Black Spiritual Movement* and reacted to it in diverse ways. As Van Maanen (1988:35) asserts, "Ethnographies of any sort are always subject to multiple interpretations. They are never beyond controversy or debate." Given that I visited many Spiritual congregations in many parts of the country, I was not able to obtain a systematic view of the members' response to my research. Two years after the first edition of this book appeared (Baer 1984), I received a telephone call from the Reverend Paul Southerland, the pastor of the Redeeming Church of Christ on the South Side of Chicago. He told me that he had purchased eighty copies of my book and was selling them to members of his congregation. Rev. Southerland invited me to visit his church in order to "dialogue" with his congregation. Given that I had never visited any Spiritual churches in Chicago—the city with the greatest number of Spiritual churches in the country—I welcomed the opportunity to visit the Redeeming Church of Christ. Rev. Southerland represents a new breed of ministers within the Spiritual movement and refers to his congregation as the "church of tomorrow." He had been reared in the Alpha and Omega Church, a large Spiritual congregation in Detroit affiliated with the Metropolitan Spiritual Churches of Christ. He lamented that the Reverend Clarence Cobbs, the flamboyant head of the Metropolitan Spiritual Churches of Christ (MSCC) and the pastor of the Church of the Deliverance on the South Side of Chicago, had not permitted him to write his master's thesis on the association. Southerland served for seven years as the pastor of the Spirit of Tabernacle in the Bronx. After the pastor of Redeeming, who had established a splinter association following Cobbs' death in 1979, died himself in 1984, Southerland was elected pastor of the church. As part of his endeavor to streamline the Spiritual movement, he was in the process of establishing an "academic program" at Redeeming and encouraged his members to read and discuss *The Black Spiritual Movement* as part of this endeavor.

In May 1986, I spent several days visiting Redeeming Church of Christ and other Spiritual churches, including the First Church of Deliverance, in Chicago. Rev. Southerland arranged for me to present two talks on my research to his congregation. Uncertain as to what to expect, I presented a general overview of the contents of my book, which many in the audience had read. During the discussion period, I received a flood of criticisms concerning specific points in the book about Spiritual churches. Most of my critics argued that their congregation does not engage in many of the rituals or subscribe to many of the beliefs that I described in my book. One person argued that an outsider such as myself could not possibly understand the Spiritual movement. Peshkin

(1986:18) encountered a similar response when a minister told him
that his Jewish background precluded his being able to discern the
significance of Christian schools. In my own case, I responded that
my book represents a general overview of a very diverse movement
with many associations and congregations in it. I also stated that
I had uncovered the "tip of the iceberg" in my overview of the
Spiritual movement. Feeling somewhat defensive, I argued that I
had never been in their church before and had not written specifically about it and asked the audience if it would have been better
if I had not written a book about the Spiritual movement. Various
members of the audience toned down their criticism of my book,
and a member praised it for forcing Spiritual people to see how
others view them. Rev. Southerland chose not to enter the debate
but told the audience that he had been proud of the manner in
which they had discussed my book. After the discussion period,
several members told me that they had enjoyed reading the book.

Rev. Southerland told me in private that, while "we can argue
with your book, it gives us a chance to see an account of our history." When I told him that I hoped that I had not offended any of
his members, he replied, "Offending is part of growth." On the day
following my first talk, the church secretary, who was a student at a
community college, told me that my critics had been unfair in their
attacks and asserted, "Prior to your book, we [Spiritual people] had
no history."

In my second talk the following evening, I discussed the role of
African American religion as a response to racism and social stratification in the larger society and the status of the Spiritual community within the context of African American religion. I was rather
surprised that, given my experience on the previous evening, no
one in the audience openly attacked my arguments. In fact, an
ambience of mutual agreement pervaded our discussion of the
plight that African Americans have encountered historically and
continue to encounter in American society. Even though various
members of the congregation were surprised to learn that I was
white, I had the sense that our racial differences had at least
been temporarily suspended as a result of our discussion of various political, economic, or structural factors that contribute to the
exploitation of African Americans within the context of American
capitalism and racism. After my talk, a young male member told

me, my book had made him aware that the Redeeming Church of Christ belongs to the Spiritual movement.

When I asked a middle-aged deacon of the church two days later what he thought about my book, he replied, "I agree with everything in it." He noted that he witnessed the diversity within MSCC at its annual conventions and within the Spiritual movement when he visited many Spiritual churches around the country while serving in the military. When he asked someone how my first talk had gone, this person replied that the audience had "torn me up." When the deacon disagreed with his negative evaluation of my book, the man reportedly became angry. The deacon sensed that some people had prepared to attack me again on the occasion of my second talk because they had brought many books to counter my assertions but noted that I had "defused" their arguments in my presentation.

The most interesting response to my book came from a young visiting minister from Baltimore. He said that he had heard a rumor that I was a graduate of Howard University but still had difficulty believing that I was Black because of my name. When he read my discussion of Spiritual churches in New Orleans, which was actually based primarily on the work of others, he concluded that I was Black since a white person is unlikely to know such aspects of the African American experience. He wrestled for a while with my name but finally concluded that I was merely one of many Blacks with unusual names. The young minister confessed that he had been so astonished to discover upon meeting earlier in the day that I was white that he was not sure whether he would be able to deliver his sermon during the evening service. I told him that his belief that I was Black was the highest compliment hat he could have given me as the author of a book on the African American Spiritual movement.

The most gratifying response to *The Black Spiritual Movement* occurred on November 1, 1987, when I revisited the Temple of Spiritual Truth with Gordon Shepherd, a sociology professor at the University of Central Arkansas, on our way home from a meeting of the Society for the Scientific Study of Religion in Louisville. Although Bishop Frank Jones seemed very much like I had last seen him over eight years earlier, he informed that his wife, Glenda, had died three years earlier. Her death appeared to have been a significant factor in the decline of membership at the temple. Bishop Jones, two middle-aged men, and a young woman occupied the elevated sacred area facing the congregation, and three women, a small boy, and the two visiting social scientists sat in the pews. Bishop Jones noted that he was now retired but that the Lord always provided for his needs. He was delighted when I gave him a copy of my book and told him that he was included in it. As he thumbed through the book while sitting in his epis-copal chair, he asked me if he was really included in it. He glee-fully smiled, and I was moved by his enthusiasm. To this day that incident served as a reminder to me that ethnography can serve as a bond between people who come from very different worlds but share a common humanity. Transformation from observing the Other to praxis and liberation, however, is the more critical issue.

Merrill Singer, a colleague who has also done extensive research on religious sects, and I have often pondered on why as non-believers we have been so captivated by religion as a research topic. In my own case, I believe that part of my fascination with religious groups stems from my attempt to come to terms with my gradual break from Catholicism during my twenties. Nonethe-less, while I dropped an adherence to Catholic doctrine, I did not drop the concern for social justice that somehow the good nuns and priests imparted to me in the process of my religious socializa-tion. The 1960s, alienation from my work as an aircraft engineer, and my desire to understand the world and participate in a collec-tive struggle to improve it prompted me to study anthropology.

As a critical anthropologist, I have tended at some level to empathize with the "little peoples of the world," among whom I count the Spiritual people. While I attempted to provide an inside or "emic" perspective on the Spiritual movement, I have empha-sized a social scientific or "etic" perspective. McGuire succinctly captures the dilemma that I faced as a social scientist:

> There is a fundamental difference or perspective, however, between a sociologist and a believer, in that sociologist as sociologist does not accept the believer's taken-for-granted meanings as a given, but rather as an object of study. This perspective sometimes implies that the reason members believe is not only because of the truth value of the belief system. . . . Furthermore, sociology [or anthro-

pology] must necessarily bracket the crucial religious question—to what extent is the action *also* from God. (McGuire 1982:20)

If I had been more of an "insider," as was Ammerman (1987) in her ethnographic study of a fundamentalist congregation, I might have been able to present a more accurate emic view of the Spiritual movement. Yet, even Ammerman (1987:10), who as a "reborn Christian" (but not a fundamentalist per se) and as a member of the congregation's choir, may have also offended some of her subjects since she also analyzes the group from a "secular" sociological perspective. The dilemma that I faced was that many of the Spiritual people wanted me to "go native" by joining their churches. Given my perspective, feigning conversion would have been unethical and exploitative, although I realize it might have provided me with additional insights on the movement. In retrospect, perhaps I should have been more forthright about my philosophical and political views, although I did not systematically conceal them. Perhaps I should have pursued a strategy of what Gordon (1987:269) terms "empathetic disagreement"—that is, "getting close (i.e., creating rapport and maintaining field relationships)" by "'staying distant' (i.e., highlighting differences between observer and observed)."

I became more open about my perspective in the later stages of my research. Ironically, it was the pastor and members of a Redeeming Church of Christ in Chicago—a Spiritual congregation which I had never even heard about—that prompted me to engage in such a dialogue. In August 1987, I had a special opportunity to engage in empathetic disagreement with Dr. Logan Kearse, then President of the Metropolitan Churches of Christ and the pastor of the Cornerstone Church of Christ in Baltimore. While he disagreed with much of the interpretation presented in *The Black Spiritual Movement,* we were able to engage in a lively and open discussion on a topic of mutual interest. In the final analysis, my conversation with him and experiences with other Spiritual people illustrate that the attempt of ethnographers to "inhabit indigenous minds . . . is a permanent, unresolved problem of ethnographic method" (Clifford 1988:47).

Preface to the First Edition

DESPITE its central importance among Black Americans, religion has not received nearly the same degree of attention that certain other Black institutions have received, particularly the family. This apparently prompted one social scientist to lament that "it is a sad fact that we have better descriptions — incomplete as they are — of religious beliefs and practices in West Africa, Brazil and the Caribbean than we have of Black people in the United States" (Szwed 1971:v). Most studies of Black religion, such as those by DuBois (1903), Mays and Nicholson (1933), Dollard (1937), Powdermaker (1939), H. Lewis (1955), Washington (1964), Hamilton (1972), and Frazier (1974), tend to generalize about the mainstream churches, notably Baptist and to a lesser extent Methodist, which claim the allegiance of the majority of churchgoing Black Americans. Only a few scholars have provided us with general overviews of the great variety of more unconventional groups found in the Black community (Jones 1939; Fauset 1971; Washington 1973; G. Simpson 1978). Ironically, the best and most detailed studies of specific Black religious groups tend to be those that deal with unconventional sects, such as Lincoln's (1961) and Essien-Udom's (1962) accounts of the Nation of Islam, Brotz's (1970) and Singer's (1979, 1982) accounts of Black Judaism, and Williams's (1974) ethnography of a Black Pentecostal congregation in Pittsburgh.

This book is an attempt to shed light upon the nature of the specific religious movement in the Black community that encompasses a wide assortment of groups generally known as "Spiritual" churches. In addition to presenting a history and general description of the Spiritual movement, I will place this largely overlooked and misunderstood development within the larger contexts of both Black

religion and American society. In doing so, I hope to counteract some
of the stereotypes about the alleged uniformity of Black religion that
are held not only by the public at large but also by many scholars.
Between October 1977 and July 1979, I studied eleven Spiritual
churches in Nashville, Tennessee. Although my research focused on
one of these congregations, I visited at least twice all the others that
held religious services on a regular basis. In addition, I attended two
"bless services" conducted by a traveling Spiritual prophetess from
Indianapolis, who held a religious service once a month in a Nashville home. Subsequently, I was able to visit seven Spiritual churches
in Detroit, five in Flint, and one in Saginaw, Michigan. (In passing,
it is interesting to note that Detroit, next to Chicago, appears to have
the largest concentration of Spiritual churches — well over one hundred and perhaps as many as two hundred separate congregations —
in the country, even far surpassing New York and New Orleans in
this regard.)

My fieldwork on Spiritual churches included a close examination
of one particular association and several of its congregations. In contrast to other Spiritual groups, members of this association, the Universal Hagar's Spiritual Church, worship their founder, Father
George W. Hurley, as God Incarnate. My investigation of the Father
Hurley sect has included work with its congregations in Michigan,
New York City, and New Jersey.

I have also visited two Spiritual congregations in Indianapolis,
one in Pittsburgh, one in Memphis, and one in New Orleans. In total,
I have visited thirty-five Spiritual congregations (located in twelve
cities and eight states) and have attended about one hundred religious services as well as many other religious and social events in
Spiritual churches.

My primary mode of study has been as participant-observer. In
addition, I have conducted semistructured and loosely structured
interviews as well as had countless conversations with Spiritual people, particularly pastors, elders, and mediums. My work in Nashville and with the Universal Hagar's Spiritual Church permitted an
intensive view of the Spiritual movement; my work elsewhere allowed me to develop a more extensive view.

Most of the fieldwork upon which this book is based was conducted between the fall of 1977 and the winter of 1981. My research

could not have been accomplished without the goodwill and patience of numerous members of Spiritual churches who allowed me to scrutinize their religion. A National Institute of Mental Health Post-Doctoral Fellowship in the Medical Anthropology Program at Michigan State University during the 1979–80 academic year made it possible for me to conduct fieldwork among various Spiritual churches in southeastern Michigan.

I am particularly grateful to Bishops Frank and Glenda Jones (whose real names I will not reveal in order to ensure their privacy), the pastors of my "home church" in Nashville. Despite my persistent refusal to join their congregation, which was due to my inability to make the full commitment that membership in the Temple of Spiritual Truth (also a pseudonym) would have entailed, they tolerated my presence as a "friend" of the church. In fact, on the occasion of one of his anniversaries as pastor, Bishop Frank Jones kindly referred to me as "all but a member." I am also deeply indebted to Reverend G. Latimer, the present leader of the Universal Hagar's Spiritual Church and a daughter of its founder, Father George W. Hurley, for urging members of the association to cooperate with me in my study. Several members greatly facilitated my examination of the history of the church by giving or lending me back issues of *Aquarian Age*, a newsletter that includes many of the writings of Father Hurley.

I am also thankful to John Szwed, Albert Raboteau, Lenore Hirsh Baer, and Merrill Singer for having read earlier drafts of this manuscript either in full or in part. They are, of course, not responsible for the manner in which I incorporated their suggestions or my failure to do so. Members of my family, Lenore, Eric, and Andrea — all of whom accompanied me on various occasions to events in Spiritual churches — have contributed more to my endeavors than they realize. Finally, but not least, I appreciate the support that Carol Orr, Director of the University of Tennessee Press, has given me in this project — both before my fieldwork was actually completed and during the process of writing the book.

My hope is that my efforts here will contribute to a fuller appreciation of the richness of Afro-American religion and the strategies that Black people have adopted in their search for hope and dignity in a society that has treated and continues to treat them brutally.

Perhaps their intense humanity, part of which is described in this work, will inspire more to join in the struggle not only for their liberation but also for that of all peoples who are the victims of oppression and degradation.

THE BLACK SPIRITUAL MOVEMENT

Introduction

BLACK CULTURE is far from monolithic but rather is character-ized by a considerable degree of diversity (Drake and Cay-ton 1945; Drake 1965; McCord et al. 1969; Hannerz 1969; Williams 1980). And just as Black Americans exhibit differences along class, cultural, historical, and regional lines, so do they in their religious orientations and affiliations (Green 1970; Baer and Singer 1981).

Religion is a particularly significant dimension of Black culture to investigate, in large part because in the "dialectic of accommo-dation and resistance," "the protonational consciousness" of Black Americans was "expressed primarily through a religious sensibility" (Genovese 1974:658–59). The development of Black religion, how-ever, has not taken a simple unilinear trajectory but has been ex-pressed in a multiplicity of interrelated streams. This book will focus on one of the most neglected of these streams, the one comprising those groups that generally refer to themselves as "Spiritual" churches. As Wilmore (1972:210) notes, "The period between 1890 and the Second World War was one of luxuriant growth and de-velopment for many forms of Black religion in the United States and Africa that challenged the bourgeois character of the mainline Black denominations and the racist posture of the White churches." The Black Spiritual movement was one of several sectarian developments that emerged during this period as a response to the shifting status of Blacks in American society.

My own discovery of Black Spiritual churches was largely acci-dental, occurring during a teaching stint at a small college in Nash-ville, Tennessee. Although I had read a number of sources that make mention of them, I did not take special note of Black Spiritual churches until I began to explore various possibilities in the study of religious sectarianism in the local area. In the process of visiting Black congregations of various religious persuasions — Baptist, Church of Christ, Holiness, Muslim — I came across several whose members called themselves "Spiritual." Some of these groups were listed in the telephone directory under the heading of "Spiritualist" churches, but I quickly learned that their members generally rejected this label, preferring the shorter term "Spiritual."

The comments of the various scholars who make note of these groups, generally referring to them as "Spiritualist" churches, tend to be cursory (Hurston 1931; Fauset 1971; Tallant 1946; Mays and Nicholson 1933; Washington 1973; Frazier 1974). In his otherwise comprehensive survey of Black religions in the New World, G. Simpson (1978:273) devotes little more than a paragraph to Spiritual churches in the United States. Yet a not insignificant portion of Blacks — particularly lower-class Blacks — have at one time or another been attracted to Black Spiritual churches: according to Drake and Cayton (1945:414), 10.7 percent, or 51 of 475 congregations, in Chicago's Black community fit into this category. Mays and Nicholson (1933:148), in their census of Black churches in seven Southern cities and five Northern cities, found that 3.3 percent and 7.6 percent respectively were "Spiritualist."

Although most Spiritual congregations are small and attract primarily lower-class individuals, some congregations are quite large (numbering in the hundreds) and crosscut socioeconomic lines. Most Spiritual churches — like many small Baptist, Holiness, and Pentecostal congregations — are housed in storefronts, converted residences, and modest church buildings. Of the 114 Spiritual churches in Mays and Nicholson's sample, 97, or 85.1 percent, were located in storefronts, houses, or halls, with the remainder situated in church buildings. On the other hand, some of the larger Spiritual congregations, particularly in big cities such as Chicago and Detroit, may be housed in relatively imposing edifices, not unlike some of the affluent mainstream churches in the Black community.

Other than a few articles that I have written, (Baer 1980, 1981a, 1981b) the most extensive treatment of Black Spiritual churches appears in relatively obscure sources. Considering that much of my own fieldwork was conducted in Nashville, I have been particularly fortunate that Lockley (1936) conducted research on the first Black Spiritual congregation in that city. A thesis by Tyms (1938) includes a chapter on the history, beliefs, and rituals of the Metropolitan Spiritual Churches of Christ, an organization that eventually became the largest Spiritual association in the United States. Daniel C. Thompson (1944), a prominent Black sociologist, began his career by conducting an ethnographic study of the All National Spiritualist Church of God in Atlanta. And anthropologist Andrew Kaslow has written two short articles (1979, 1981) and a special report, with Claude Jacobs (Kaslow and Jacobs 1981), for the National Park Service on Spiritual churches in New Orleans.

The overall objective of this book is to present a general ethnography and analysis of the Black Spiritual movement in the United States. In doing this, I hope not only to expand the body of literature on Black religion but also to rectify some common misperceptions and stereotypes about this example of cultural pluralism among Afro-Americans. Just as is the case in the larger society, one finds certain religious groups that are regarded as unconventional in the Black community. Among the better known are those that reject traditional Christianity and seek a new identity vis-à-vis other religious traditions, such as Islam or Judaism. While not necessarily rejecting many aspects of traditional Christianity, Spiritual churches are also considered a deviant social category. In their study of religious groups in Bronzeville in Chicago, Drake and Cayton (1945:670) found that members of Spiritual (as well as Holiness) churches are "marked down as 'low-status.'" As I will demonstrate later, this stigma has prompted some Spiritual groups to disassociate themselves from others in the Spiritual movement and to adopt more and more of the characteristics typically found among the mainstream denominations in the Black community.

Chapter 1 places the Spiritual movement in the larger contexts of both Black religion and American society, with brief histories of Spiritual churches in the United States and, more specifically, in one southern city. Chapter 2 focuses on the social organization, particularly at the local or congregational level, of the Spiritual movement and describes in some detail various religious events and rituals that I have observed in Spiritual temples. The history, social organization, beliefs, and rituals of the Universal Hagar's Spiritual

Church, one of the oldest Spiritual groups in this country, are detailed in Chapter 3. This is the first extensive discussion of an almost totally neglected Black sect, which was established in 1923 by Father George W. Hurley, a contemporary of Father Divine and — like him — a self-proclaimed god. Chapter 4 deals with the process of syncretism in the Spiritual movement by which elements from various religious traditions — particularly Black Protestantism, Spiritualism, Roman Catholicism, and Voodoo and/or hoodoo — are combined in such a way that they form the ingredients of an essentially new religious tradition. Special attention is given to religious syncretism in the Father Hurley sect, which, in addition to many of the elements found in other Spiritual churches, appears to have incorporated aspects of Garveyism, the Peace Mission, and the Black Islamic and Black Judaic sects. Chapter 5 presents an analysis of the Spiritual movement as one of several possible Black religious responses to the racist and class structure of American society and discusses its compensatory, integrative, manipulative, and psychotherapeutic dimensions. Attention is also directed to the dual nature of the Black Spiritual movement, which juxtaposes elements of accommodation and protest. I interpret the Father Hurley sect as a response to racial stratification that adds messianic nationalism to the thaumaturgical/manipulationist orientation typical of the larger Black Spiritual movement. Finally, I discuss the development of the Spiritual movement from its emergence until the present day.

Spiritual Churches as a Religious Category in the Black Community

Because all religious groups claim to deal with spiritual matters, the term "Spiritual" in referring to a specific category tends to be problematic. Many people, even in the Black community, know nothing or relatively little about Spiritual churches. In my conversations with both Whites and Blacks about my research, I found a tendency to view the term "spiritual" as a label for religious groups in general, or to confuse Spiritual churches with Holiness or Pentecostal (or what are commonly called "Sanctified") churches. Certain groups in the Black American community, however, use the term "Spiritual" as a specific label of self-reference; many include it in the title of a congregation (St. Philip's Spiritual Cathedral)[1] or association (Universal Ancient Ethiopian Spiritual Church of Christ), and call themselves as "Spiritual people," just as members of other religious bodies call themselves as Baptists, Methodists, Pentecostals, Catholics, etc.

As I have already noted, there is a tendency in the literature to refer to Black Spiritual churches as "Spiritualist" churches. My data suggest that the term "Spiritualist" was contracted to "Spiritual" at some point in the evolution of the Black Spiritual movement. According to some of my informants, one reason for this change in terminology was a desire by many Spiritual people to disassociate themselves from the stigma attached to Spiritualism in American society; another may have been a desire to avoid confusion with predominantly White Spiritualist groups.

What makes the classification of Spiritual churches even more cumbersome is that similar groups may choose to assume various other labels, such as "Holiness Science," "Divine Science," or a "Holiness church with a spiritual mind." The tendency of these groups, which differ little in content and belief from other Spiritual churches, to disassociate themselves from the larger Spiritual movement seems to be a result of the negative stereotypes associated with it in the Black community.

In order to distinguish Spiritual churches from other religious groups in the Black community, a colleague and I (Baer and Singer 1981) have developed a typology in which we recognize that the content, structure, and variability of Black religion derives primarily from three sources: (1) African cultures; (2) religious patterns in Euro-American culture; and (3) religious responses on the part of Blacks to their minority status in American society. Our typology focuses upon the third source, largely because it appears to be the factor shared by all Black religious groups in the United States. Yinger (1970:324) appears to concur with this assessment when he states that "Negro sectarianism is a product of the same fundamental causes

1. St. Philip's Spiritual Cathedral is actually housed in a modest storefront building in Detroit. Although I did not have the opportunity to attend a religious service at this church, the sign posted outside its entrance, listing its founder as Prophet M. T. Asaka and the congregation as Mosque No. 1 of the United Nubian Tribe of America, strongly suggests that the group has a Black nationalistic orientation, as is true of some other Spiritual churches.

as sectarianism in general, but there are some special factors that have affected it. It can be understood only in the total context of the Negro's place in American society."

Much of the literature on religious organizations is devoted to making fine distinctions among various types, such as the "church," the "denomination," the "sect," and the "cult." While these distinctions may be useful in many cases, we dispensed with them for purposes of our typology, and I will do so in this book. Instead, we emphasized the sectarian nature of Black religious groups, even the Baptist and Methodist churches that constitute the mainstream of religious life in the Black community, in that *they all exist in a state of tension with the larger society*. While religious sects generally find themselves in conflict with some aspect of the larger society, racial status contributes an additional element to this tension that distinguishes Black from White sectarian groups. On the basis of two variables — strategies of social action and attitudinal orientation — four types of Black sects are delineated in our typology: (1) mainstream or established sects, (2) messianic-nationalist sects, (3) conversionist sects, and (4) thaumaturgical/manipulationist sects.

The established or mainstream denominations within the Black community, particularly those with large middle-class congregations (such as the larger Baptist, Methodist, and Presbyterian associations) have adopted a reformist strategy that attempts to create improvements for Blacks by working within the capitalist framework of American society. Lower-class Blacks, on the other hand, perhaps because of their greater sense of powerlessness, have been particularly creative in developing other strategies that attempt to instill dignity and meaning in their often seemingly hopeless lives in a racist and stratified society. The messianic-nationalist sects — such as Black Muslim, Black Jewish, and Black Hebrew groups, the African Orthodox Church, and the Shrines of the Black Madonna — have tended to glorify the roots of Black people in Africa, to place their trust in the hands of messianic leaders, and to construct countercultures that reject many of the values and goals of the larger culture in their efforts to develop utopian communities. Perhaps the majority of lower-class Blacks with a religious orientation have turned to the conversionist sects, such as the smaller Baptist congregations and a wide variety of Holiness and Pentecostal churches; these emphasize a strongly puritanical life-style, often seek their salvation in some ill-defined afterlife, and express their dissatisfaction in various forms of ecstatic behavior, including "shouting," trances, and glossolalia. Our fourth type, the thaumaturgical/manipulationist sects, has been the most neglected by scholars. These sects maintain that the most direct way of achieving socially desired ends — such as financial prosperity, prestige, love, and health — is by engaging in various magico-religious rituals or by acquiring esoteric knowledge in order to gain spiritual power over oneself and others. These sects tend to hold the individual responsible for his or her present condition, and stress the need to develop a positive frame of mind and overcome negative attitudes. Thaumaturgical/manipulationist groups generally accept the cultural patterns, values, and beliefs of the larger society but attempt to change the means of obtaining the "good life." Because of their individualistic orientation, such groups are largely apolitical and express little interest in social reform activities. Members of thaumaturgical/manipulationist groups view themselves as open-minded and are very amenable to religious syncretism. While this type includes groups such as Rev. Ike's United Church and Science of Living Institute, the Antioch Association of Metaphysical Science, and the Embassy of the Gheez-Americans, the largest representative of thaumaturgical/manipulationist sects in the Black community forms the focus of this book: namely, the Spiritual movement.

Although Spiritual churches exhibit many of the features found in other Black religious groups, their emphasis on the manipulation of one's present condition through magico-religious rituals and esoteric knowledge tends to differentiate them. As will be demonstrated in greater detail in the remainder of this book, the Spiritual religion concerns itself with concrete problems by attempting to provide its adherents with the spiritual means to acquire finances, employment, love, or the improvement of a strained relationship. In contrast to the common but probably exaggerated view that Black religion is "other-worldly," Spiritual people are concerned primarily with discovering solutions to their difficulties in the here and now.

Another characteristic that distinguishes the Spiritual movement from many other religious groups in the Black community is its highly syncretistic nature. While there is a considerable degree of heterogeneity in the Spiritual movement itself, essentially it combines elements from Spiritualism, Black Protestantism, Roman Catholicism, and Voodooism (or at least its diluted form, known as "hoodoo"). Furthermore, specific congregations or associations in the Spiritual movement add to this basic core elements from other esoteric systems, such as New Thought,[2] Islam, Judaism, Ethiopianism, and astrology.

Among Blacks who have some familiarity with Spiritual churches, one often finds the view that these groups are involved in "witchcraft," "fortunetelling," and "numbers." I have had Blacks tell me that they are afraid to go inside a Spiritual church. In fact, when I attempted to locate Black Spiritual churches in Lansing, Michigan, a Black Holiness pastor said that even if he knew of any, he would not tell me about them because of the spiritual danger for me that contact with them would bring. On the other hand, many of the people who seek certain services provided by the Spiritual movement are members of the more respectable Baptist and Methodist churches that constitute the mainstream of Black religion in America.

Unfortunately, negative stereotypes of Spiritual churches have been perpetuated by various scholars. Joseph Washington, Jr. (1973: 115), a renowned student of the Black religious experience, makes the following comments:

> Fundamentally, then, a Spiritualist cult is a house of religious prostitution, where religion is only the means for the end of commercialization. It is a business venture, a pleasure-seeking enterprise. It is tailored for those who are too superstitious to cut themselves off completely from religion, but who seek only its good luck. Spiritualism is syncretism pure and simple. It is opportunistic. Neither the black *cult* nor the black ethos finds expression at its center, though on its periphery the music sounds the same. Spiritualists hold out no program for black people, nor do they bother to spend their energies in search of salvation. It is a religion of form without substance which seeks through fears of bad luck a profit in selling good luck.

2. The New Thought movement has been traced back to the teaching of nineteenth-century mesmerist, Phineas P. Quimby, that the mind is the central agency in healing and well-being (Melton 1978, II:51–56). New Thought groups, which include the Unity School of Christianity, the United Church of Religious Science, Divine Science International, and the School of Esoteric Christianity, claim that humans may reach their divine potential and achieve heaven within themselves through positive thinking and the eradication of negative ideas.

In somewhat similar vein, H. Mitchell (1975:27–29), a Black pastor and theologian, argues that "Black American spiritualist churches or sects and many West African cult groups" exhibit what he terms a "low religious approach," the hallmark of which is a concern for "evil magic."

Stereotypes often have an element of truth, but basically they make exaggerated and distorted statements about social reality. Instances of dubious and fraudulent behavior do occur in Spiritual churches, but so do they in more respectable groups, not to speak of the highest echelons of the larger society's political, economic, and social institutions. Even the more questionable happenings in the Spiritual movement cannot be understood unless we consider the structural position of Blacks in American society. If indeed some Blacks have found that the Spiritual religion serves as one of a variety of "hustles" to make it in "the Man's" world, this is in large part because the poor have always been forced to live by mother wit in order to survive in a ruthless world that exploits them.

CHAPTER 1

The Spiritual Movement and
the Black Religious Experience

T HERE IS A TENDENCY on the part of scholars writing about Black religion in the United States to speak of the "Black church." While such a concept may have a certain heuristic value, it is misleading in its implication that the religious experience among Blacks has been a uniform or monolithic one. On the contrary, Black religion in this country, not unlike that in other parts of the New World, is characterized by considerable variability. Yet regardless of the specific form it takes, Black religion exhibits a common theme—namely, the element of protest against the racist and socially stratified structure of America society. This theme is quite explicit among groups like the Black Muslims and the Black Jews. In others, including the Spiritual and Holiness churches, it may be cloaked in religious rhetoric and therefore less obvious; nevertheless, it is bound to be discovered if one scratches below the surface.

Although there were elements of protest in slave religion, the first sustained religious protest among Blacks occurred with the development of independent formal Black churches. Despite some efforts by the Anglicans, Presbyterians, and Quakers, probably the majority of Blacks remained unconverted to Christianity during the colonial period. During the Second Great Awakening, however, the Methodists and Baptists won over both free Blacks and slaves in great numbers (Washington 1973:42). Initially, free Blacks in the North enjoyed a relatively intimate fellowship with Whites for a short period after the Revolutionary War, but eventually they were assigned sections on the main floors and balconies of churches. As a protest against such discriminatory practices, free Blacks began to establish their own congregations and, later, associations. According to Litwack (1961:195), "By 1830, the Negro church movement reflected much of the chaos and multiplicity of sects that prevailed among the whites." Emancipation resulted in a fusion of the institutional religion that had developed among free Blacks of both the North and the South with the "invisible institution" of slave religion (Frazier 1974:35).

Despite the fact that following the Civil War a slow but steady migration of Blacks to the cities of the South and the North occurred, by the turn of the century about nine out of ten Blacks still resided in the South, with the bulk of them located in rural areas. Emancipation did not mean that Blacks were immediately free to leave the South in order to seek economic opportunities in other parts of the country. The ever-expanding demands of capitalism for a cheap labor force in the industrial centers of the North were largely filled by immigrants from Europe; in the western states, much of the need for cheap labor was satisfied by various ethnic groups from the Orient. It was not until European and Asian immigration had virtually stopped in the twentieth century that Blacks in substantial numbers moved out of the South. According to Broom and Glenn (1965: 159), "during the decade following 1910, the great migration of Negroes from the rural South began with the push of a depression in Southern agriculture and the pull of new opportunities for industrial employment in the North."

Changes in the political economy of the country coupled with the onset of World War I resulted in the Great Migration of Blacks from the rural South to the urban North. According to Cox (1976: 58), "on the whole, the 'push' of the Negro population from the rural South has been greater than the inducements or 'pull' of the cities." Push factors in the South included the relative severity of labor exploitation, the boll weevil invasion that reached disastrous levels about 1910, soil erosion and depletion, the relocation of many agricultural endeavors in the West, and continued lynching and intimidation. Pull factors were primarily economic: the hope of better wages, improved working conditions, and steady employment.

Prior to World War I, the industrial North had relied primarily on European immigrants for a cheap labor supply. An annual average of more than 900,000 immigrants entered the United States from Europe during the period of 1910–14, but the onset of the war reduced the annual flow to about 100,000 (Geschwender 1978:172). At the same time, World War I stimulated the economy and in-

creased the demand for labor, a demand in large part fulfilled by
the migration of southern Blacks. Furthermore, the availability of
Blacks as a labor reserve allowed industrialists to undercut the demands of an increasingly militant White working class for higher
wages and better conditions.

> Migration out of the countryside started in 1915 and swept up to
> a human tide by 1917. The major movement was to Northern cities,
> so that between 1910 and 1920 the black population increased in Chi-
> cago from 44,000 to 109,000; in New York from 92,000 to 152,000;
> in Detroit from 6,000 to 41,000; and in Philadelphia from 84,000 to
> 134,000. That decade there was a net increase of 322,000 in the num-
> ber of Southern born blacks living in North, exceeding the aggregate
> increase of the preceding 40 years. A secondary movement took place
> to Southern cities, especially those with shipbuilding and heavy in-
> dustry. . . . (Baron 1976:195)

Although it fluctuated throughout the succeeding decades, falling during the Depression and rising again during World War II,
the migration pattern that started among Blacks in the 1910s continued well into the 1970s. By 1970 only 52 percent of Black Americans were located in the South, and the majority of Blacks in the
North *and* the South were situated in urban areas (Baron 1976). In
the process, Blacks were transformed from an agrarian peasantry
into a diversified proletariat.

While the North may have been presented by labor recruiters as
the Promised Land, what most Blacks found in Detroit, Chicago,
Gary, Pittsburgh, Newark, Harlem, and other cities was considerably less. In the South they had occupied the lowest rungs of the
rigid caste system; in the North — although theoretically possessing
more legal rights — Blacks (as well as southern whites) became a type
of subproletariat or underclass, which was manipulated by the capitalist class in dealing with the growing demands of White workers.
There were instances of cooperation between White workers and
Black workers during the early decades of the century, but competition for scarce jobs more often than not resulted in hostile relations
between the two. At times this conflict was translated into racial
riots in which angry Whites invaded Black neighborhoods. As Smith
(1981:343) notes, ". . . it should be clear, however, that the riots did
not grow out of the inherent racial prejudice of their participants,

but rather developed directly from the friction caused by the ways in which black labor was put to use in the North." In effect, employers were able to divide the working class into two antagonistic factions that were forced to compete for available jobs. Faced by a choice between a tolerable existence and starvation, Blacks were unwittingly used as strikebreakers, or "scabs," often at wages below those won by White workers in their struggles with industrialists. Eventually an accommodation between Black and White workers in the North, not much different from that of the Old South's caste system, developed: for the most part, Whites came to occupy the professions and the skilled technical and craft positions, while Blacks were relegated to semiskilled and unskilled occupations (or perpetual unemployment) at the bottom of the labor hierarchy. In more recent decades some Blacks have been able to make occupational advances, yet the dual labor market essentially still exists.

The process of urbanization that accompanies capitalist expansion has repeatedly been demonstrated to have unsettling effects on rural migrants, not only in industrial nations but also in the Third World today. Invariably, rural migrants attempt to adjust to their new environment by creating a wide array of voluntary associations, including religious ones. Next to the family, the church — despite its accommodative dimensions — had been the most important institution among Blacks of the rural South (Frazier 1968). In addition to providing emotional release from the oppressive conditions of the caste system, the rural churches of the Baptists and the Methodists served as social and recreational centers, maintaining strong ties with various benevolent, mutual aid, burial, and fraternal societies.

As Williams (1974:9) notes, "The migration to cities created a social crisis, for it separated masses of Blacks from their rural life style and destroyed the social organization which gave meaning to their segregated rural Southern society." While many migrants apparently did find comfortable niches in the larger churches of the old-time denominations, others who had enjoyed leadership positions in the rural South found themselves relegated to the sidelines of the large urban congregations. In addition to seeming more bureaucratic, impersonal, formal, and sedate than their counterparts in the South, the Baptist and Methodist congregations increasingly adapted themselves to the more secular concerns of a new Black middle class (Frazier 1974). Besides being threatened by that sophistication, lower-class migrants often found that they were viewed with disdain by more affluent communicants. Moreover, the mainstream churches in the Black community simply did not have the resources necessary to meet the material needs of overwhelming numbers of poor migrants.

In the midst of the social crisis faced by the migrants from the rural South, Black religion became even more diversified than it had been before. As Nelson and Nelson (1975:43) note, "The story of the urban church in the postwar years is largely an epic of established black Protestantism trying to meet a major crisis with limited material resources and, all too often, with limited imagination as well – and of a restless population first searching for renewal at the old familiar altars, then turning to the storefronts, the Father Divines, the Black Muslims in their quest for a religion which could make the new and strange burdens of urban life somehow tolerable." This process of diversification would later be accelerated by the Depression, which affected Blacks even more drastically than it did Whites. According to Wilmore (1972:222), "the Black community, by the end of the decade of the 1930s, was literally glutted with churches of every variety and description." Although storefront versions of the large Baptist congregations were established, many Black migrants were attracted to the Holiness, Pentecostal, Spiritual, Judaic, Islamic, and other sects such as the Father Divine Peace Mission and the African Orthodox Church, which emerged in tremendous profusion not only in the industrial North but also in many cities of the South. In their survey of Black churches in twelve cities, Mays and Nicholson (1933:313) found that 777 of a total of 2,104 church buildings that they surveyed were storefronts or converted residences. About half of the 777 storefront congregations were Baptist; many others were of the Holiness and Spiritual varieties.

Following Wallace's (1956) concept of the revitalization movement, Harrison (1971:244) describes storefront churches as "deliberate, conscious, organized efforts of migrants to create a more satisfying mode of existence by refurbishing rural religious behavior to an urban environment." While storefront churches in the Black community today attract many individuals who have lived in urban areas for long periods of time, if not their entire lives, they originally emerged primarily as a response to the needs of rural migrants and still serve this function. Frazier (1974:58–59) succinctly sum-

marizes the appeal that the storefront congregations have had for
certain segments of the Black community:

> The "storefront" church represents an attempt on the part of the
> migrants, especially from the rural areas of the South, to reestablish
> a type of church in the urban environment to which they are accus-
> tomed. They want a church, first of all, in which they are known
> as people. In the large city church they lose their identity completely
> and, as many of the migrants from the rural South have said, neither
> the church members nor the pastor know them personally. Sometimes
> they complain with bitterness that the pastor of the large city church
> knows them only as a number on the envelope in which they place
> their dues. In wanting to be treated as human beings, they want sta-
> tus in the church which was the main or only organization in the
> South in which they had status. Some of the statements concerning
> their reason for leaving the big denominational churches was that
> "back home in the South" they had a seat in the church that every-
> one recognized as theirs and if the seat were empty on Sunday the
> pastor came to their homes to find out the cause of their absence.
> The desire for the warm and intimate association of fellow wor-
> shippers in church services was not the only reason why the "store-
> front" church was more congenial to the recently urbanized Negro
> than the cold and impersonal atmosphere of the large denominational
> city church. In these small "storefront" churches the Negro migrant
> could worship in a manner to which he had been accustomed. . . . The
> preacher leads the singing of the Spirituals and other hymns with
> which the Negroes with a folk background are acquainted. The sing-
> ing is accompanied by "shouting" or holy dancing which permits the
> maximum of free religious expression on the part of the participants.

The Spiritual movement, like other new sectarian developments
in the Black community, took place within the context of a chang-
ing American political economy that forced increasing numbers of
Blacks from the rural South to seek employment in urban areas. It
was one of the many ways that churchgoing Blacks responded to
the racist and stratified structure of capitalist America.

The Historical Development
of Black Spiritual Churches

The origins of the Black Spiritual movement remain obscure, but
it appears to have emerged in various large cities of both the North

and the South—particularly Chicago, New Orleans, New York, Detroit, and Kansas City—during the first quarter of this century. Apparently during this period the movement began to combine elements of Spiritualism, Roman Catholicism, and Voodooism or hoodoo, as well as other esoteric belief systems. Furthermore, elements from these diverse traditions seemed to have been grafted onto or merged with a Black version of Protestantism that began in antebellum times and came to maturity in a wide array of Baptist, Methodist, Holiness, and Pentecostal denominations and sects.

According to Spear (1967:96), several "Holiness and Spiritualist churches" were established in the Black community of Chicago during the first decade of the twentieth century. While many of the storefront churches that appeared in Chicago during the early migration years called themselves Baptists, they often closely resembled Holiness and Pentecostal groups in their exuberant and demonstrative form of worship. Others called themselves "Spiritualist," a "vague term used to identify those religious groups that believed in 'communication of the spirit' and that attempted to relay messages and spirits through mediums" (Spear 1967:177). While indeed there may have been several Black Spiritualist groups, particularly of the storefront variety, at this time in Chicago and possibly elsewhere, the earliest specific congregation that Spear mentions is the Church of the Redemption. The *Chicago Defender*, a well-known Black newspaper, carried an advertisement on August 28, 1915, noting that the Church of the Redemption held regular services on State Street. Elsewhere, Kaslow (1981:61) fleetingly notes that Mother Leafy Anderson, a Black Spiritualist who was destined to play an instrumental role in the development of the Spiritual religion in New Orleans, established the Eternal Life Christian Spiritualist Church in Chicago in 1913. At any rate, according to Spear (1967:177) several "true" Black Spiritualist churches were organized between 1915 and 1920, adding elements of the Baptist, Holiness, and Pentecostal storefronts to those of Spiritualism.

NEW ORLEANS AND THE BEGINNINGS OF THE SPIRITUAL MOVEMENT

If indeed the Black Spiritual movement started in Chicago, its development in New Orleans appears to have been of vital importance in determining its present content. Although there was much opposition in the South to American Spiritualism, which began in 1848 in upstate New York with the mysterious rappings from the spirit world that the Fox sisters claimed to have heard in their home, it nevertheless spread to cities such as Memphis, Macon, Charleston, and New Orleans (G. Nelson 1969). Perhaps in part because its doctrines were favorable to equality and liberalism, as well as compatible with African religions, Spiritualism found adherents among the Black population of the South. According to G. Nelson (1969:16–17):

> A stronghold of Spiritualism in the south seems to have been New Orleans, where many circles were held not only by the white but also by the coloured population, and many coloured persons were found among the mediums. Dr. Barthet who became a leading spiritualist in the city was known to have experimented with animal magnetism in the early eighteen-forties, and Dr. Valmour, a free creole, attained great celebrity as a healing medium.

Although there seems to be a consensus that Mother Leafy Anderson, a woman of Black and Indian ancestry, started the first Black Spiritualist or Spiritual church in New Orleans, there are conflicting reports as to when she actually founded the Eternal Life Spiritualist Church in the Crescent City. Zora Hurston (1931:319), a well-known Black anthropologist, folklorist, and novelist who studied under Franz Boas for several years, reported that this congregation was established in 1918. Tallant (1946:173), however, placed Mother Anderson's arrival in New Orleans in 1921 and adds that she had previously operated several Spiritualist churches in Chicago. More recently, Kaslow (1981:61) has stated that the Black Spiritual churches of New Orleans" were officially established in 1920, under the leadership of Leafy Anderson." Because Hurston was intimately involved in various cultic circles in New Orleans and was also the apprentice of a Voodoo practitioner there, I suspect — though without means of confirmation — that her date is the most reliable one.

Mother Anderson was popular not only among Blacks but also some poor Whites. She trained several other women, who established congregations of their own in New Orleans, and eventually she became the head of an association that included the New Orleans congregations plus others in Chicago, Little Rock, Memphis, Pensacola, Biloxi, Houston, and some smaller cities (Kaslow and Jacobs 1981). Although Leafy Anderson herself detested Voodoo, other Spiritualist churches that were established in New Orleans—some of which were outgrowths of her own—did incorporate elements of the Voodooism, as well as the Catholicism that was indigenous to southern Louisiana; according to Hurston (1931:319), the "strong aroma of hoodoo" clung to a number of these. Mother Anderson passed away in 1927, but "she still appears to the women who carry on her work and gives instructions as to her wishes" (Tallant 1946:174).

Another of the earliest and best-known Spiritual churches in New Orleans was the Temple of the Innocent Blood, established in 1922 by Mother Catherine Seals (*New Orleans City Guide* 1938:199). Like the Eternal Life Spiritualist Church, this congregation was the forerunner of several other Spiritual groups in the city. The church incorporated many aspects of Catholicism, including the ritualistic use of the sign of the cross, votive candles, holy pictures, elaborate altars, and statues. The Catholic religious articles found in the church were in large part gifts from those Mother Catherine had healed; she used castor oil to cure people and gave spiritual advice to Whites as well as Blacks (Tinker 1930). Before she died on August 9, 1930, Mother Catherine, who claimed to be inspired by the Holy Spirit, prophesied that she would rise from the dead (Saxon, Dreyer, and Tallant 1945:21). She was succeeded by Mother Rita, who renamed the renowned temple on the outskirts of New Orleans the Church of the True Light. Shortly before her death, however, Mother Catherine had completed a "Manger" near the church building proper, which reportedly could seat up to three hundred people (*New Orleans City Guide* 1938:200). The Manger, used for banquets and musical festivals, was adorned not only by an altar and Stations of the Cross but also in later years with several small clay figurines and a five-foot statue of the revered prophetess herself.

Several other Spiritual temples were established in New Orleans during the early 1920s (see Table 1). Upon the "instructions" of the Blessed Virgin Mary, Mother L. Crosier started the Church of the Helping Hand and Spiritual Faith in 1923 (*New Orleans City Guide* 1928:204–07). Even earlier that year, Mother C. J. Hyde organized the St. James Temple of Christian Faith (*New Orleans City Guide* 1938:206–07). Several of her followers received subcharters under her city charter and went forth to found congregations of their own, among them Mother E. Keller, who established the St. James Temple of Christian Faith No. 2. Prior to turning to the Spiritual reli-

Table 1. A Partial Listing of
Early Black Spiritual Churches in New Orleans

CHURCH	FOUNDER	FOUNDING DATE	MOTHER CHURCH
Eternal Life Spiritualist Church	Mother Leafy Anderson	c. 1918 –21	Eternal Life Christian Spiritualist Church (Chicago)
Temple of the Innocent Blood	Mother Catherine Seals	1922	NA*
St. James Temple of Christian Faith	Mother C. J. Hyde	1923	NA
Church of the Helping Hand and Spiritual Faith	Mother L. Crosier	1923	NA
St. James Temple of Christian Faith No. 2	Mother E. Keller	NA	St. James Temple of Christian Faith
Spiritualist Church of the Southwest	Bishop Thomas B. Watson	1920s	NA
St. Michael's Church No. 1	Mother Katherine Francis	late 1920s	Spiritualist Church of the Southwest
St. Anthony's Daniel Helping Hand Divine Chapel	Mother Shannon	late 1920s	Spiritualist Church of the Southwest
St. Michael's Church No. 9	Father Daniel Dupont	1932	St. Michael's Church No. 1

*Information not available.

gion and becoming a disciple of Mother Hyde, Mother Keller
claimed that she "received training in Voodooism from a Moham-
medan prince in New York, met some of the greatest Voodoo doctors in the country, and became well versed in this mysterious art"
(*New Orleans City Guide* 1938:208).

While it appears that many of the leaders of the early Spiritual
groups in New Orleans were women, Bishop Thomas B. Watson,
a schoolteacher and a graduate of Xavier University, was the head
of a small association called the Spiritualist Church of the Southwest (Saxon, Dreyer, and Tallant 1945:407). Another male leader was
Father Daniel Dupont, who established St. Michael's Church No. 9
in 1932 (*New Orleans City Guide* 1938:210–11). He was inspired to
do so by his sister, Mother Kate Francis, who sometime earlier had
started St. Michael's Church No. 1 (*New Orleans City Guide* 1938:
208–209).

Mother Shannon, a former resident of Chicago, was the pastor of
St. Anthony's Daniel Helping Hand Divine Chapel (Saxon, Dreyer,
and Tallant 1945:397–412). Her congregation, which was reportedly
established in the late 1920s, was a branch of Bishop Watson's Spiritualist Church of the Southwest. Weighing perhaps as much as three
hundred pounds, Mother Shannon dressed in a robe with a veil and
sat on a throne during religious services. In addition to prophesying
and healing, she performed charitable work among the poor and
gave away toys, money, and baskets of food at Christmastime.

Kaslow's recent work (1979, 1981) on Spiritual churches in New
Orleans indicates that the movement continues to thrive in the locale where it received much of its early impetus. While the number
of Spiritual congregations in Chicago, Detroit, and possibly some
other cities surpasses the number of those in New Orleans, in a very
real sense the Crescent City continues to be the Mecca of the Spiritual movement. Most of the congregations listed in Table 1 appear
to exist today, and probably many other current Spiritual churches
in New Orleans derived directly or indirectly from them.[1]

THE GROWTH OF THE SPIRITUAL MOVEMENT IN THE URBAN NORTH

Like many other sectarian groups in the Black community, the
Spiritual movement apparently underwent a tremendous growth

1. St. Daniel's Spiritual Church in New Orleans, which the author visited in

during the 1920s and 1930s in various northern cities. Drake and Cayton (1945) note that the Spiritual movement flourished in Bronzeville, the Black section of Chicago, during this period. Although there was a wide variety of esoteric religions in Bronzeville at the time — Black Jewish groups, the Nation of Islam, the Moorish Science Temple, the African Orthodox Church, the Liberal Catholics — most of these sects were small compared to the Spiritual groups. "In 1928 there were seventeen Spiritualist storefronts in Bronzeville; by 1938 there were 51 Spiritualist churches, including one congregation of over 2,000 members. In 1928 one church in twenty was Spiritualist; in 1938, one in ten" (Drake and Cayton 1945:642). A perusal of the telephone directories of the metropolitan areas with large concentrations of Blacks and my conversations with members of Spiritual churches indicate that Chicago is today the largest center of the movement.

The Spiritual movement diffused to many other cities in both the North and the South during the 1920s and 1930s. Ira A. Reid, a well-known early Black sociologist, notes its presence in the Black section of Harlem by the 1920s. Among the various "esoteric cults," he notes the activities of "a large number of exploiters and charlatans," including those "who dabble in spiritualism, exhibiting their many charms and wares in the form of Grand Imperial incense, prayer incense, aluminum trumpets, luminous bands and other accessories" (Reid 1926:107). Although it is not clear which of the various congregations listed by Reid were part of the early Spiritual movement, names that he mentions — such as the Metaphysical Church of the Divine Investigation, and St. Matthew's Church of the Divine Silence and Truth — bear a striking resemblance to the names of churches that I have come across in my own fieldwork.[2]

December 1981, was started by Father Daniel Dupont as St. Michael's Church No. 9. A picture of Father Dupont's sister, Mother Katherine Francis hangs on a wall of the sanctuary of the present church building. St. Daniel's is affiliated with an association called the Israelite Spiritual Church, headquartered in New Orleans and headed by "Archbishop" E. J. Johnson. At the present time, there are reportedly at least fifty regular Spiritual congregations in the New Orleans area (Kaslow and Jacobs 1981:20–21).

2. Dillard (1973) argues that while the individual words in the names of Black storefront churches may be standard English ones, the combinations of these words appear to be distinctly Afro-American. For example, as opposed to the names of

Another Black writer, Claude McKay (1940:74), remarks upon the "innumerable cults, mystic chapels and occult shops" that existed in Harlem during the Depression. Although he does not specifically refer to any of these as "Spiritual" or "Spiritualist," his narrative strongly suggests that at least some of them fit into this category. Many distraught persons resorted to the services of these institutions in seeking comfort and solace, employment, love, friendship, and marriage. McKay (1940:77) notes that "heavy aromas of burning oils and incense" filled the atmosphere of a chapel that he visited. On the white altar in the front, he found a cross, a star, a crescent, a bouquet of roses, colored candles, and a painting of the Tree of Life and Hope. The audience, consisting primarily of women, was led by a "priestess," who wore a black and white robe and a headdress. In addition to giving public prophecies from the spirits, for a nominal donation the pastor offered private revelations and "consecrated numbers."

Brief sketches of three Spiritual associations of varying size will serve to illustrate the diversity of development within the Spiritual movement in the urban North. The first, the Metropolitan Spiritual Churches of Christ, is significant because it is probably the largest of the Spiritual associations and includes several congregations in West Africa. The second, Spiritual Israel Church and Its Army, is of medium size but adds elements from Black Judaism and Ethiopianism to the general core found in most Spiritual groups. Finally, although a relatively small association, Mt. Zion Spiritual Temple is, with its colorful founder and leader, an excellent example of the type of Spiritual church that is organized as a "kingdom."

1. Metropolitan Spiritual Churches of Christ, Incorporated

THE MOTHER CONGREGATION of the Metropolitan Spiritual Churches of Christ was established on September 22, 1925, in Kansas City, Missouri; its founders were Bishop William F. Taylor, a former

---

most White religious groups, many Black storefront churches are characterized by long titles with three to five premodifiers (St. Anthony's Daniel Helping Hand Divine Chapel) and/or postmodifiers consisting of one or prepositional phrases (the United House of Prayer for All People or the Church on the Rock of the Apostolic Faith).

Methodist minister, and Elder Leviticus L. Boswell, a former Church
of God in Christ (Pentecostal) preacher. According to Tyms (1938:
112–14), by 1937 the group had grown to encompass thirteen congregations and some seven thousand members: in addition to its
national headquarters, the association had two congregations in
Chicago, one in Gary, two in St. Louis, one in East St. Louis (Illinois), one in Detroit, one in Tulsa, one in Oklahoma City, one in
Omaha, and two in Los Angeles.

In 1942 a new organization, called the United Metropolitan Spiritual Churches of Christ, was established as the result of a merger
between the Metropolitan Spiritual Churches of Christ and the Divine Spiritual Churches of the Southwest, based in New Orleans
under the leadership of Bishop Thomas B. Watson.

> The Southwest organization had saved the considerable assets of
> Metropolitan (estimated at between one and two million dollars) from
> reverting to the family of the late Bishop Taylor, who founded the
> association in 1925. Metropolitan had no bona fide state charter, un-
> like Southwest, and thus entered the merger for somewhat opportu-
> nistic reasons. Bishop Watson quickly assumed a somewhat autocratic
> rule of the United organization, leading to a split only three years
> later, after he unilaterally called a conference in New Orleans with-
> out consulting with the national executive board. Two groups emerged
> as a result: the United Metropolitan, under Watson, and the Metro-
> politan under Cobbs and the Kansas City people. (Kaslow and Jacobs
> 1981:100)

The United Metropolitan group experienced yet another schism in
1951, resulting in the establishment of the Israel Universal Spiritual
Churches of Christ with Bishop E. J. Johnson as its head.

Under the leadership of Rev. Clarence Cobbs (who moved the
headquarters of the association to Chicago), the original Metropolitan organization prospered and grew. Cobbs, who had been ordained
by Bishop Taylor, had started the First Church of Deliverance with
four members in a storefront on Chicago's South Side in 1929 (*Ebony*
1960). From these humble beginnings, the First Church of Deliverance grew into a large religious center with a community hall and
a convalescent facility. By 1968, the Metropolitan Spiritual Churches
of Christ had 125 churches and some ten thousand members (Melton 1978, II:106). My data on the association indicate that the group's

congregations today are heavily concentrated in Illinois and Michigan, but it also has churches in many other parts of the country, as well as several in Liberia and Ghana.[3]

According to Melton, the Metropolitan Spiritual Churches of Christ draw elements from Christian Science and Pentecostalism and emphasize a "foursquare gospel" consisting of preaching, teaching, healing, and prophecy. My own visits to three congregations affiliated with the association indicate that it is a reflection *par excellence* of the Spiritual movement, adding elements of Spiritualism, Catholicism, Black Protestantism, Voodooism or hoodoo, astrology, and probably others to those mentioned by Melton.

Cobbs's appeal to lower-class Blacks was manifested by several events, such as one "candlelight service" at Comiskey Park (the baseball stadium of the Chicago White Sox), to which he drew nearly three thousand spectators on a cold, rainy night; and a service attempting to vindicate him of alleged wrongdoings, which packed an audience of nearly 10,000 people into a downtown auditorium (Drake and Cayton 1945:646). Cobbs was a classical example of the "prophet" found in the Black community who assures the hopeful that they will receive a blessing if they engage in certain magico-religious rituals. One account (Carter 1976:87) describes a service in Baltimore at the end of which he gave those in attendance an opportunity to be the beneficiaries of his spiritual powers: after each believer came forward to confide to Cobbs his innermost desires, he or she received a candle from the prophet; as compensation for this favor, each one was expected to place a monetary offering on the altar. Cobbs, who resided in a mansion until his death a few years ago, was in a sense the informal leader of the diffuse Spiritual movement.

2. Spiritual Israel Church and Its Army

As is true of the Spiritual movement in general, the roots of Spiritual Israel Church and Its Army are obscure. My interviews with several leaders of the group — including its present "King," Bishop

3. Another concentration of congregations affiliated with the Metropolitan Spiritual Churches of Christ is located in the New York–New Jersey megalopolis, where it has eight congregations in New York City proper and another three on the New Jersey side of the Hudson River.

Robert Haywood, and its "Overseer," Bishop George Coachman[4] — provided me with only fragmentary data on its origin. It is not clear whether the group emerged as early as the mid-1920s or as late as the late 1930s. The forerunner of the Spiritual Israel Church and Its Army was the Church of God in David, which was established by Bishop Derks Field in Alabama. At some point, either in Alabama or in Michigan, Derks Field met W. D. Dickson, who had arrived at similar ideas about Israel from studying the Bible. According to one informant, Field was forced to leave Alabama by Whites who became agitated by his doctrines on Israel. Another informant, however, stated that W. D. Dickson moved the Church of God in David to Detroit after being instructed to do so by the Spirit of God. Regardless of who moved the group to Michigan, after the death of Field, Dickson emerged as the leader of the Church of God in David. Bishop Dickson, who became known as "the King of All Israel" (a title also carried by his successors), pulled Spiritual Israel "out of David" upon instructions from the Spirit. His leadership had been unsuccessfully opposed by the two surviving Field brothers, Doc and Candy. Both were pastors of congregations affiliated with Spiritual Israel in Detroit, and both established their own organizations, but they did not survive. One informant claimed that several other groups, all retaining the word "Israel" in their titles, also broke away from Spiritual Israel Church and Its Army.

Because of the severe winters in Michigan, Dickson moved the church to Virginia for a while, but returned it to Detroit upon further instructions from the Spirit. Since the death of Bishop Dickson, the line of succession in Spiritual Israel has included Bishop Martin Tompkin and Bishop Robert Haywood, the current King. The leader of Spiritual Israel is also reverently referred to by members as the "Holy Father." The largest concentration of the about thirty churches and several missions of Spiritual Israel Church is located in southeastern Michigan: the Detroit metropolitan area, Ann Arbor, Flint, and Saginaw. There are other congregations in New York City, Chicago, Milwaukee, New Orleans, Florida, Alabama, Mississippi, Georgia, and three cities in Indiana (Gary, Fort Wayne, and Muncie).

---

4. The main duties of the Overseer appear to be to visit and provide guidance to the various congregations in the association.

While like other Spiritual groups, Spiritual Israel Church and Its Army has incorporated various elements of Spiritualism, Black Protestantism, Catholicism, and possibly Voodooism and/or hoodoo, its inclusion of certain dimensions of Judaism gives it, at least in theory, a strong nationalist tone. In this regard, Spiritual Israel shares certain traits not only with various Black Muslim and Black Jewish sects, but also with the Universal Hagar's Spiritual Church, which will be the focus of discussion in Chapter 3.

Members of Spiritual Israel Church view themselves as the spiritual descendants of the ancient Israelites or "spiritual Jews," and their organization as a restoration of the religion of the ancient Israelites. In their belief, "Ethiopian" is the "nationality" name of Black people whereas "Israel" is their "spiritual" name. The original Ethiopians were "pure" Blacks, they say, but the Ethiopians of today are in large measure of mixed racial ancestry. Furthermore, the first human beings were Black people, starting with Adam, who was created from the "black soil of Africa." All of the great Israelite patriarchs and prophets, including Noah, Abraham, Isaac, Solomon, David, and Jesus, were Black men. In time, however, with the sons of Isaac, a division in humanity arose. Jacob became the progenitor of the Ethiopian nation and Esau of the White nation. Although these two nations have been in constant struggle with one another since their creation, they must learn to live in harmony and peace because they are "close kin."

According to the doctrine of the church, being an "Israelite" is more a matter of spirituality than of race and nationality. A Gentile, or "unbeliever," may be White or Black; and although most members of Spiritual Israel Church are Black, the group reportedly has some White members as well. Spiritual Israelites maintain that most Whites who identify themselves as "Jews" are actually the descendants of Gentiles who intermarried with the original Jews or Israelites. Unlike traditional Jews, however, members of Spiritual Israel Church do not observe any particular dietary prohibitions.

Spiritual Israel Church and Its Army, often simply referred to by members as "Israel," is regarded to be the "one true Spiritual church." Spiritual Israelites believe that God is not "something in the sky" but the Spirit that dwells in all people. When one's body dies, one's spirit or soul does not go to heaven or hell, both of which are merely projections of the human mind, but simply rejoins the all-pervasive Spirit of God. Spiritual Israelites also believe in reincarnation, or the return of one's spirit to earth in a new body. The Christ Spirit, which is simply the "anointed power" of God, has occupied the bodies of the many kings of Israel, including Bishops Field, Dickson, Tompkin, and Haywood, as well as Jesus. As a consequence, the present head of Spiritual Israel is on occasion referred to as "Christ Haywood."

3. Mt. Zion Spiritual Temple

ONE OF THE MOST COLORFUL Spiritual associations is the Mt. Zion Spiritual Temple, Inc., which was founded in 1943 (and incorporated in 1945) by King Louis H. Narcisse, D.D. The "International Headquarters" of the group is in Oakland, California, where King Narcisse maintains one of his two residences; the "East Coast Headquarters" of the association is the King Narcisse Michigan State Memorial Temple in Detroit. In addition to these two temples, the association has seven other congregations, including a second temple in Detroit and temples in Sacramento, Richmond (California), Houston, Orlando, New York City, and Washington, D.C.

On the occasion of one of my visits to his eastern headquarters, I had the opportunity to meet King Narcisse, a tall stately man who appeared to be in his late sixties. He was dressed in a most regal manner, wearing a golden toga and cape with a white surplice, a white crown with glitter and a golden tassel, eight rings on his fingers, and a ring in his left ear. In a style befitting a potentate, King Narcisse was chauffeured to the temple in a shiny black Cadillac limousine with his title and name inscribed upon the door. As he proceeded down the center aisle of the sanctuary, the congregation stood to welcome its majestic leader. During the remainder of the service, except when he was preaching and conducting various rituals, King Narcisse sat on a throne in the front, occasionally sipping a beverage from a golden goblet.

For those occasions when King Narcisse cannot be with his flock in Detroit, a large picture of "His Grace" faces the congregation, reminding its members of their spiritual leader. Below the picture is a sign which reads as follows:

GOD IS GREAT AND GREATLY TO BE PRAISED IN THE SOVEREIGN STATE OF MICHIGAN IN THE KINGDOM OF "HIS GRACE KING" LOUIS H. NARCISSE,

DD WHERE "ITS'S [sic] NICE TO BE NICE, AND REAL NICE TO LET OTHERS
KNOW THAT WE ARE NICE."

Ironically, in contrast to the massive sanctuary with its elaborate
altar and chandeliers, the presence of only thirty or so individuals
at the service suggested that perhaps the Kingdom of Louis H. Narcisse has seen better days.

The Development of Spiritual Churches in Nashville

A brief historical account of Spiritual churches in Nashville will
provide a better understanding of their development in a specific
locality, as well as illustrate the processes of fusion and fission characteristic of the Spiritual movement.

It appears that Redeeming Christian Spiritualist Church was the
first Black Spiritualist or Spiritual congregation established in Nashville. This church, which may have been indirectly linked for a while
with the National Spiritualist Association of the United States, was
established sometime during the 1920s by Sister Moore, a tall Black
woman (Lockley 1936:13). After losing her husband at the age of
nineteen, Sister Moore received training from a Spiritualist medium
in St. Louis (Lockley 1936:26–27). She decided to return to the South
in order to serve her people and began holding séances in her private
room in Nashville. After several months she opened her church in
a building with a seating capacity of about 300, affiliating her group
with an association headquartered in St. Louis. Although the church
at first had an interracial membership, the White members, probably as a result of external pressure placed upon them for violating
the caste etiquette of the South, established their own Spiritualist
church and affiliated themselves with the Independent Spiritualist
Association of the U.S.A. (Lockley: 29).

Services at Redeeming Christian Spiritualist Church were conducted on Sunday, Monday, and Wednesday nights. Sister Moore,
who claimed to be inspired by the Holy Spirit, was assisted by two
aspiring ministers and a coterie of mediums, male deacons, mothers,
and ushers. The major portion of the typical service was devoted
to the séance, which generally lasted over two hours (Lockley 1936:
46). Messages came primarily from the deceased friends and rela-

tives of those in attendance. The most common questions directed by the participants to the spirits concerned the search for employment and strained marital relationships. At any given service, only about one-fourth to one-third of the congregation consisted of actual members of the church. These were primarily unskilled, semiskilled, or unemployed Black people; others who sought messages from the spirit, either during the service or in private consultations, represented a more diversified cross section of the city's population, including a fairly large number of Whites.

Despite the fact that the séance constituted the central focus of the service, its ritual content "may be characterized as a conglomeration of the forms of service of many churches" (Lockley 1936:37–38). Unfortunately, Lockley is not explicit about either the nature or the source of these other religious elements. She notes, however, that the interior of the church was rather elaborate, containing large pictures of Jesus Christ at various stages of his life, as well as some of the Blessed Virgin. Seven candles representing the "seven churches of Asia" and the "seven friendly spirits" stood upon the altar. Members of the church wore white robes and crucifixes, and the mothers of the church each wore a purple and white satin ribbon as well. As is the case in many Black Spiritual churches today, members drank holy water — blessed by some religious functionary — for a variety of reasons, such as good health, prosperity, or harmony in their homes.

Redeeming Christian Spiritualist Church was the forerunner of all the other Spiritualist or Spiritual churches that existed in Nashville during the early 1930s. A male informant in his late seventies, who was a member, reports that Sister Moore broke away from the St. Louis organization with which it was affiliated and renamed the church the House of Redemption Spiritual Church. As the result of a power struggle between the pastor and her assistant ministers, the congregation disbanded sometime in the late 1930s.

While some Spiritual people trace the origin of their religion to the time of Jesus Christ or even Moses, most lack a strong interest in the history of the movement or of their specific congregations. Consequently, it was somewhat difficult for me to learn much about other early Spiritual churches in Nashville. However, many of my informants were members of or are familiar with St. Joseph's Spiritual Church. This church was established by Bishop Wilma Stewart sometime in the 1940s and was affiliated with an association head-quartered in Cincinnati, Ohio. St. Joseph's appears to have been the largest Spiritual congregation in Nashville during the 1940s and 1950s, with a membership of over 300. When Bishop Stewart died sometime in the 1960s, her husband became the pastor of the church and changed its name to St. Michael's Spiritual Church. Apparently he lacked his wife's charisma, because the congregation rapidly de-clined, resulting in his decision to close the church and move to Michigan.

The older Spiritual churches in Nashville that are still in existence were organized during the 1930s and 1940s. Newer congregations include two that were established as recently as 1976. Most found-ers of Spiritual churches appear to have been affiliated with other Spiritual congregations at one time or another. An ambitious indi-vidual who wishes to assume the role of pastor may decide the best way to achieve this is to establish his or her own church. At first, the new Spiritual pastor will conduct services at home or rent a por-tion of a commercial building. If successful in attracting a follow-ing, the pastor will seek more permanent quarters, perhaps a for-mer residence or a small building being vacated by another church. It is not uncommon for Spiritual churches to change their location several times for a variety of reasons, including an increase in mem-bership, the desire for better quarters, and displacement by urban renewal.

Table 2 lists the eleven Spiritual congregations that existed in Nash-ville during the period of my fieldwork there. (Note: I have chosen to use pseudonyms for all eleven churches, as well as for their lead-ers and members who are mentioned by name.) Of these, the oldest is Zion's People Spiritual Church. Sometime in the mid-1930s Mother Benson, from Tuscaloosa, Alabama, was sent by a small Spiritual association headquartered in her state to establish a branch in Nash-ville. After the death of Mother Benson in 1958, Reverend Robinson became the pastor of the congregation. Upon his death in 1976, he in turn was succeeded by the present pastor, Rev. Edna Williams, who had at one time been the assistant pastor of St. Paul's Spiritual Church.

Zion's People Spiritual Church is located in a house in a transi-tional neighborhood that has attracted working-class Blacks in re-cent years. Although like most Spiritual churches, Zion's is not a

Table 2. *Local and Regional Affiliations of*
*Spiritual Churches in Nashville, Tennessee**

CHURCH	LOCAL MOTHER CHURCH	ASSOCIATIONAL HEADQUARTERS*
Zion's People Spiritual Church	none	Gaston, Ala.
Unity Fellowship	Zion's People	Nashville, Tenn.
Sacred Heart Spiritual Temple	none	independent
Temple of Spiritual Truth	Sacred Heart	St. Louis, Mo.
House of Almighty God	Sacred Heart	independent
St. Paul's Spiritual Church	none	St. Louis, Mo.
All Souls Christian Church No. 2	St. Paul's	Indianapolis, Ind.
St. Matthew's Spiritual Temple	none	Nashville, Tenn.
Resurrection Temple	none	Atlanta, Ga.
St. Cecilia's Divine Healing Church No. 2	none	Cleveland, Ohio
St. Jude's Spiritual Church	Zion's People	Indianapolis, Ind.

*Reproduced by permission from Hans A. Baer, "An Anthropological View of Black Spiritual Churches in Nashville, Tennessee," *Central Issues in Anthropology* 2 (2): 53–68. All church names are pseudonyms.

*Unity Fellowship belongs to an association which was established by the pastor of St. Matthew's Spiritual Temple and which also includes a congregation in South Carolina. All Souls and St. Jude's are members of different associations in Indianapolis.

neighborhood congregation and attracts members from many parts of the city, it seems to be emulating the modest upward social mobility of its immediate neighbors. Despite the fact that it retains the term "Spiritual" in its formal name, one Spiritual pastor commented that it is very similar to the typical Baptist church, adding, "They do not prophesize or heal, at least when I have been there." Another informant noted that "at one time" it was like a "typical Spiritual church," but today—in contrast to most of the other Spiritual churches in Nashville—there are no votive candles, statues, incense, or altar. Even the two crucifixes that I saw hanging on the front wall of the sanctuary on my first visit disappeared later, during my fieldwork in the city. And while some members occasionally visit other Spiritual churches in the community, a trustee admitted that Zion's has more contact with various Baptist and Methodist churches. In addition, he expressed disapproval of some of the practices in certain Spiritual churches in Nashville and lamented the "superstitious" proclivities of some Spiritual people. Zion's People Spiritual Church has about thirty individuals present at its regular Sunday morning services, including a small choir consisting primarily of young people.

Bishop Jackson, a tall, lanky man in his early sixties, established St. Paul's Spiritual Church in 1947 after he was ordained as a Spiritual minister in St. Louis. St. Paul's is currently situated on the ground floor of a small apartment house in a lower-class neighborhood. Its interior is probably the most elaborate of all of the Spiritual churches in Nashville. In addition to the typical Spiritual altar, one finds a cross with colored lights, two crucifixes, and a picture of the Last Supper on the front wall. Pictures of the Good Shepherd, the Sacred Heart of Jesus, the Sacred Heart of Mary, and John F. Kennedy hang on the side walls. In addition, two large red globular lamps representing the sun and the moon hang from the ceiling in the front of the sanctuary.

Unlike other Spiritual churches in the city, St. Paul's does not hold its main Sunday worship service in the morning; Bishop Jackson has scheduled it for the evening instead. Perhaps partly thanks to his cantankerous and brusque demeanor, there are generally fewer than ten individuals at his services. Despite his idiosyncratic personality, however, he is regarded as a gifted prophet.

St. Matthew's Spiritual Temple was established in the late 1940s by Elder Marcus, who had previously organized several Spiritual churches in the Memphis vicinity. St. Matthew's is located in a residential area in the largest Black section of the city. Inside there is an elaborate altar with a large statue of the Blessed Virgin and tiered shelves supporting many votive candles. Although at one time Elder Marcus's congregation was considerably larger, she claims that it now has eight "regular members." Occasionally, however, when she conducts her "love feast"— a communion ritual involving the blessing of crackers and water — members of the other congregations appear in her little church.

For a while, Elder Marcus was the Overseer of another Spiritual church in a small city about thirty-five miles southeast of Nashville. Her congregation was also formerly affiliated with a Chicago-based association, but at the present time she is the Overseer of her own association, which includes another Spiritual church in Nash ville as well as St. Matthew's Spiritual Temple No. 2 in a small city in South Carolina. Elder Marcus is not as active in religious affairs as she once was, but she is a respected and well-liked prophetess who maintains loose ties with several Spiritual churches in the community.

Although I was unable to determine the exact date when Sacred Heart Spiritual Temple was established, it appears to be one of the older Spiritual churches in the city, perhaps dating back to the 1940s. After having been situated in various locations, it moved in 1971 to its present site, a small church building that has housed several other Spiritual groups. Over the course of its history, Sacred Heart has undergone several changes in associational affiliations. It has been part of associations headquartered in Chicago, St. Louis, and Louisville and is currently considering establishing formal ties, with a Spiritual church in Jackson, Tennessee. Its leader, Bishop Ladner, also established her own association at one time, called Sacred Heart International Churches, which included several now defunct congregations in Nashville and in another Tennessee city.

When Bishop Ladner's health deteriorated and she began to show signs of senility, the congregation elected Reverend Smith, a middle-aged handyman for a construction company, to be its pastor. He annoys the women of the church by citing scriptural passages which, he maintains, prove that a female may not occupy the office of "bishop"— a very unusual view in Spiritual circles. Furthermore, Reverend Smith believes that the Spirit has designated him to be appointed a bishop sometime in the near future. In addition to serving as master of ceremonies each Sunday, he conducts a special anointing ritual in the early part of the morning service. Late-comers who arrive after the ritual has been completed nevertheless go to the front to receive this special blessing from the pastor.

Two other members appear to be the informal leaders of the congregation. The first is Evangelist Anderson, the middle-aged daughter of Bishop Ladner. When, for instance, in her booming and authoritative voice she shouts, "Let's have church!" from her seat at the organ, it becomes quite apparent that she is the real leader. Second in command is Reverend Wilson, a self-possessed middle-aged man who conducts the regularly scheduled Wednesday night services. Generally, twenty or more individuals attend the Sunday morning service at Sacred Heart Spiritual Temple.

Resurrection Temple, which is located in a small church building in a working-class Black neighborhood, was established in 1958. Its pastor, Bishop Rogers, was born in 1911 in Athens, Georgia, where he went to school through the fourth grade. In his early twenties he moved to Atlanta, where he eventually joined one of the larger Spiritual congregations in the South. Later he joined the church that serves as the headquarters of the small Spiritual association his present congregation is affiliated with. Subsequently, the Spirit directed him to take a certain northbound bus, and upon reaching Nashville he received further instructions that this was to be the location of his own church.

On a typical Sunday, one will find fifteen to twenty individuals in attendance at Resurrection Temple. A large Star of David, several votive candles, a kerosene lantern, and a small statue of the Blessed Virgin holding the infant Jesus rest upon the altar. Bishop Rogers wears a purple robe and cape, a red fez, and a talisman on a chain around his neck. His wife, who is referred to as the "Queen Mother," often wears a green robe and green turban; many of the other women in the congregation wear white robes and white turbans. On Tuesday evenings Bishop Rogers conducts a "Development Class," which involves Bible study and instructions in techniques for acquiring blessings. The high point of the annual ritual cycle at Resurrection is the Harvest Feast, which is conducted on the third Sunday in November by Elder Davis, a medium in the church.

The House of Almighty God, like Bishop Rogers's church, was also established in 1958. Its founder and pastor, Elder Moore, is a slender woman in her early sixties. Although she was at one time a member of Sacred Heart Spiritual Temple, she was instructed by the Spirit to start her own church after being ordained a minister by Bishop Ladner. Elder Moore presides in a small building behind her house, not far from the downtown area of Nashville. In addition to the Sunday morning services, she conducts a "preaching and healing service" on Tuesday nights. Elder Moore said that although formerly she had a much larger following, now about sixty of those listed on her church roster can be expected to show up for her services at some time or other; generally, however, only a fraction of this number will be in actual attendance at any particular service. Although Elder Moore maintains informal ties with several Spiritual churches in the city, she stresses the "interdenominational" orientation of her own church and has never affiliated it with any particular association.

All Souls Christian Church No. 2 was established in 1963 by Bishop Gilmore, who resides with her husband in a working-class neighborhood. After serving as a medium in St. Paul's Spiritual Church, she decided to start her own congregation, which at first was affiliated with the same large St. Louis-based association as its parent church. Several years later, Bishop Gilmore attached her congregation to a splinter group, a new association started in 1966 by the female pastor of a church in Indianapolis. Although the new organization retained many of the basic elements of the Spiritual movement, its leaders felt that many Spiritual people had, in the words of Bishop Gilmore, made the term "Spiritual" a "dirty" one, and they substituted the more respectable term "Christian." After the founder of the new association died in 1970, her daughter, Bishop Anderson, was elected its Supreme Bishop. Despite the fact that she was at the time wearing garb very similar in appearance to the vestments worn by a Catholic priest while saying Mass, Bishop Anderson told me that her organization is more similar to the churches in the Holiness movement than to those in the Spiritual movement. This same notion was expressed by several members of the Nashville branch of the association. Nevertheless, it should be noted that All Souls Christian Church No. 2 continues to maintain informal ties with several other Spiritual churches in the city.

The Temple of Spiritual Truth is the second church to have emerged from Sacred Heart Spiritual Temple. Its founders are Bishops Frank and Glenda Jones, both of whom were Elders at Sacred Heart. Bishop Frank Jones, a hard-working man in his early fifties, attended college in Nashville for a couple of years. Like so many college-educated Blacks, he was unable to find work commensurate with his education; he has been employed for many years as a plumber and general workman for a small construction firm. His wife, the assistant pastor of the church, is a few years older than he. She too attended college for a time, but although she has occasionally served as a substitute teacher in the Nashville schools, most of her work experience has involved semiskilled and unskilled jobs.

It was Bishop Glenda Jones who first joined Sacred Heart Spiritual Temple. Shortly after her husband joined, the two of them decided to establish a church of their own, and in 1965 they received "papers of authority" from the St. Louis-based association that Sacred Heart was affiliated with at the time. The Temple of Spiritual Truth conducted its first service in September 1965 in a funeral home's chapel. Since then, the church has held its services in several locations, including the home of its leaders. In April 1973 the temple moved to its present location in a former commercial building on the northern periphery of the central business district of Nashville.

On a typical Sunday morning between twenty and thirty individuals will be in attendance. While his wife starts the service, Bishop F. Jones chauffeurs certain members of his flock in his well-used automobile, returning in time for the second half of the service. With a home-prepared meal, an afternoon program, and an evening service, Sundays are extremely busy days at the Temple of Spiritual Truth. The church also frequently holds Friday night services as well as occasional classes in Bible study and instruction in the performance of various rituals that the Joneses refer to as "mysteries." Bishops Frank and Glenda also broadcast a Saturday morning program, from a local radio station.

Considering the variable longevity of Spiritual churches, it should come as no surprise that one of the eleven congregations in Nashville closed its doors during the period of my fieldwork there. Although I visited St. Jude's Spiritual Church only twice, the fact that so few people were present on those occasions suggested that it had probably seen better days. The first time I attended, Rev. Thelma Gibson, the pastor, was assisted by Bishop George Tompkins; a middle-aged man and I constituted the remainder of the congregation. The second time, those in attendance included the same people, with the addition of my young son.

Just before it closed down, St. Jude's was housed in a modest storefront building. Reverend Gibson, who was born in 1915, was raised a Catholic, attended Catholic school, married her first husband in a Catholic church, and still considered herself to be a Catholic. She noted that this was the reason for the abundance of Catholic articles in her church. Before residing in Detroit from the early 1940s to the late 1950s, she had joined Zion's People Spiritual Church in Nashville in 1940. After Mother Benson, the founder of Zion's People, died in 1958, Reverend Gibson decided that it was time to establish her own congregation; this was sometime in the 1960s. During that decade she also lived in Tyler, Texas, for about four years and pastored a Spiritual church there. After she returned to Nashville a second time, she reestablished St. Jude's in 1970.

The congregation was affiliated with a small Spiritual association headquartered in Indianapolis. Bishop Douglas, the Overseer of the association, visits Nashville for several days each month in order to do spiritual advising. During her visit she conducts a service in a friend's home, generally on the fourth Saturday night of the month, and sometimes prophesies in various Spiritual churches in the city as well. Because she is a popular prophetess, her monthly services often attract fifty or more people, not only from Spiritual churches but also from other religious groups.

Unfortunately, the seeds that Bishop Douglas sowed did not flower in her subordinate's garden. Not even Bishop Tompkins, who is regarded as somewhat eccentric by many Spiritual people but is nevertheless respected in his own right, was a regular member of St. Jude's. He is a free spirit who travels wherever the greater Spirit of God directs him. A man in his sixties, of medium build and height, wearing a gray beard and mustache, he looks every bit his self-acclaimed role of prophet when he dons his yellow robe, blue jacket, blue cape with a design of birds, and elaborately ornamented blue turban. It is rumored by some that Bishop Tompkins is an expert in the writings of the notorious Books of Moses — well known in Voodoo circles for their many "mysteries" and "secrets"— and he is feared by some people, yet he is generally welcome in the various Spiritual churches in the community. On the occasion of our first encounter, he was acting as the master of ceremonies for the week-long anniversary of a Spiritual pastor. When I last attended a service at St. Jude's Spiritual Church, both Reverend Gibson and Bishop Tompkins anticipated that the Spirit would direct them to further their work in other parts of the world. Apparently it did so, for when I tried to visit St. Jude's several months later, the premises had been vacated.

Unity Fellowship was established in January 1976 by Reverend Cardwell and his mother, Elder Bates. Mrs. Bates joined Zion's People Spiritual Church in 1939, only a few years after it was founded. But as the congregation began to shift away from the kind of religion that Mother Benson had practiced, she and her son found themselves increasingly dissatisfied. Whereas they were interested in studying such books as *Pray and Grow Rich* and *The Science of the Mind*, most members of Zion's had come to depend almost exclusively upon the Bible for their source of religious inspiration. Consequently, Reverend Cardwell and Mother Bates began in 1975 to attend services at St. Jude's Spiritual Church, Resurrection Temple, and St. Matthew's Spiritual Temple, where Reverend Cardwell was ordained a minister by Elder Marcus. When Unity was established, it became a branch of Reverend Marcus's new association.

At the present time, the principal Sunday worship service at Unity Fellowship occurs in the middle of the afternoon rather than earlier in the day as is the case in most Spiritual churches. The rationale is that those who wish to attend a morning service elsewhere may also be full participants in Reverend Cardwell's church. One generally finds fifteen to twenty individuals in attendance at this service, including Elder Marcus. Although Elder Bates functions as a "divine healer," Reverend Cardwell is still in the process of developing his gift of prophecy and consequently does not often give messages in church, which means that this task is generally carried out by Elder Marcus. Reverend Cardwell instead spends much of his time developing various "demonstrations"— rituals that will enable his members and others to develop "physically, mentally, spiritually, and financially."

A direct contrast to the other Spiritual churches in the community is St. Cecilia's Divine Healing Church No. 2, the newest and by far the largest Spiritual church in Nashville. St. Cecilia's was established in 1976 by Rev. Mary Arnold, who is also the pastor of St. Cecilia's Divine Healing Church No. 1 in Cleveland and the Overseer of an association that includes churches in Indianapolis and Philadelphia. Reverend Arnold, an outgoing and dynamic woman in her fifties, was born in Mississippi. Later she lived in Pittsburgh, where she belonged to the African Orthodox Church for a while. In 1949 she moved to Cleveland in order to start a church of her own. Although she arrived there with only $55, she founded what has become one of the largest Spiritual churches in that city.

Reverend Arnold claims she was told by the Spirit many years ago that she would one day establish a church in Nashville. For about two years, St. Cecilia's No. 2 conducted its services in a small community auditorium, which was almost always filled to its capacity of 250 to 300 whenever Reverend Arnold was in town for the Sunday morning service. In 1979 her Nashville congregation purchased a building that adequately seats about 300 people, but plans to erect an elaborate temple sometime in the future. Reverend Arnold claims that the Nashville church has about 500 members, including some "associate members" who continue to maintain ties with other congregations. Unlike the Spiritual churches in the community that cater primarily to lower-class people, St. Cecilia's cuts across socioeconomic lines and has attracted some upwardly mobile working-class and professional Blacks, as well as a few Whites.

In spite of the Spirit's instructions to Reverend Arnold that the first Sunday service should begin at 7:45 A.M., it is not unusual to see the church filled to capacity at this early hour. For those who find it too difficult to rise in time or who wish to attend other churches, she offers the alternative of an evening service and frequently a midafternoon one as well. Her husband, Rev. George Arnold, serves as the assistant pastor of both the Nashville and Cleveland churches. Rev. Mary Arnold generally conducts services in Nashville on the first, third, and fifth Sundays of the month, with her husband taking responsibility for services in Cleveland on those days; when she stays in Cleveland for services at the mother church, he travels to Nashville. One member's comment that Rev. Mary Arnold is the "main drawing card" of St. Cecilia's No. 2 is demonstrated by the fact that church attendance drops 50 percent or more when her husband conducts the Sunday morning service.

Rev. Mary Arnold has received a considerable amount of publicity, both favorable and unfavorable, since she established her congregation in Nashville. According to one prominent member of St. Cecilia's No. 2, some pastors have spoken out against her in their pulpits and oppose her activities because she is a female preacher and has allegedly stolen members from their congregations. On the other hand, Reverend Arnold has received coverage from the three major network (commercial) television channels in the city and was a guest on a popular local talk show on one of them. In 1977 an article discussing her congregation appeared in one of the city's newspapers. A half-hour prerecorded program of a portion of the services at St. Cecilia's also appears weekly on Sundays on a UHF channel.

Unlike the leaders of other Spiritual churches in the city, whose congregations frequently visit one another for such special events as revivals and pastors' anniversaries, Reverend Arnold chooses to isolate her congregation from these events. On one occasion when I asked whether hers is a Spiritual church, she answered "Sort of." The same query made to her husband caused him to balk, then reply that St. Cecilia's is a "Holiness" church and comment that many of the Spiritual churches in Cleveland believe in "black arts." These responses were made in spite of the fact that many of the practices and beliefs of Reverend Arnold's association bear a strong resemblance to those of typical Spiritual groups. In the Cleveland church, one finds an elaborate altar with votive candles, crucifixes, incense burners, and statues of various figures — including Jesus Christ, the Blessed Virgin, the patron saint of the church, St. Martin de Porres, St. Leo, and St. Anthony. Although such articles were not originally present in the Nashville church, there are plans to introduce them.

CHAPTER 2

Social Organization and Religious Activities

T HUS FAR, I have rather loosely referred to the Spiritual churches in the Black community as constituting a movement. While members of various Spiritual churches or associations do not generally view themselves as being part of a larger movement (as might, for example, members of many feminist, environmental, or political groups), in many ways the Spiritual churches do conform to the model of movement organization proposed by Gerlach and Hine (1970:34). They describe movements as being characterized by three primary organizational principles:

> Decentralization has to do with the decision-making, regulatory functions of the movement.
> Segmentation has to do with the social structure — the composition of parts that make up the movement as a whole.
> Reticulation has to do with the way these parts are tied together into a network.

The decentralized aspect of the organizational structure of a movement is exhibited by its acephalous (headless) or polycephalous (many-headed) pattern of leadership. The Black Spiritual movement has no central organization to coordinate or define its structural content, beliefs, activities, and membership requirements. In this regard, it very closely resembles Spiritualism in the United States, which it has in part drawn upon (Nelson 1969). Many Spiritual churches are affiliated with one of many national associations, but others are essentially independent from such ties. Although certain individuals, such as Rev. Clarence Cobbs (the former president of the Metropolitan Spiritual Churches of Christ), have been well-known and respected by many Spiritual people, no single individual can be identified as the dominant leader of the movement either today or in the past. Instead, the Spiritual movement involves many leaders, each of whom exerts some degree of influence over an association, an informal assemblage of congregations, or an independent congregation. Sometimes, the formal leader of a Spiritual group exhibits a clear pattern of dominance over its local segments, as in the case of King Louis Narcisse, the "Archbishop" of the Mt. Zion Spiritual Temple association. Alternatively, the formal head of an association may be closer to a "first among equals" relationship with the various pastors or leaders of the affiliated congregations. This appears to be the case in the Greater Universal Spiritual Unity Union, an association consisting— according to one of my informants— of about sixty congregations. Despite the fact that I observed activities and interviewed individual members of two congregations, I never heard any specific reference to a "Supreme Bishop," by either name or title. I learned who the formal leader of the association was only by reading a copy of its manual, which had been given to me by a pastor of one of its churches.

Segmentation in a movement means that it is "composed of a great variety of localized groups or cells which are essentially independent, but which can ccmbine to form larger configurations or divide to form smaller ones" (Gerlach and Hine 1970:41). This dimension of movement organization is exemplified in the loose, amorphous structure of most Spiritual associations. The primary function of the association for the local segments appears to be providing its congregations with a certain sense of legitimacy and a supportive social network. The association charters its churches, sets minimum requirements of competence, and issues "papers of authority" for the occupants of various politico-religious positions. For example, the small association to which All Souls Christian Church No. 2 in Nashville belongs annually charges $25 for "bishop's papers," $20 for "prophet's papers," and $10 or $15 dollars for "missionary's papers."

Membership in an association may provide a specific congregation with a number of advantages, such as financial aid, access to traveling preachers and mediums, and contacts with Spiritual groups in other locales. A new Spiritual church may be particularly in need of financial assistance in attempting to establish itself. Traveling preachers and mediums help bring people in the community out for a special service: a revival, a prophecy session, or a demonstration. Such events often serve as vehicles for recruiting new members to the local congregation, or clients for mediums affiliated with it. For a variety of reasons, Spiritual people thrive upon maintaining a pattern of social interaction with their religious counterparts in other geographical areas. In addition to the sociability that such contacts provide, they allow members to travel to areas that they could not afford to visit otherwise. By chartering buses and staying in the homes of their hosts, Spiritual people are able to minimize many of the normal costs of recreational travel. The annual convention of most Spiritual associations provides their members with one such opportunity. While these events are rather modest affairs among the smaller groups, for the larger associations they tend to be considerably more elaborate, typically involving a banquet at a large hotel and a variety of other festivities.

Nevertheless, despite the fact that associations sometimes attempt to impose certain uniform policies, regulations, and even beliefs upon their constituent parts, for the most part they fail to exert effective supervision or control. Instead, each local congregation has a considerable amount of autonomy, in large measure dictated by the whims of its pastor and prominent members. In fact, *The Doctrine and Manual of the Greater Universal Spiritual Unity Union, Inc.*, which was compiled by its bishops' council in 1969, explicitly states that "all Churches, Units, and Missions are local bodies and because they are local bodies they ought to have, and keep, local Autonomy." Like many other movements, the Spiritual religion is characterized by an "ideology of personal access of power" (Gerlach and Hine 1970: 42–43). Theoretically, anyone who is touched by the Spirit has direct personal access to knowledge, truth, and power. Although associations may attempt to place constraints on such claims by requiring individuals exhibiting a "gift" to undergo some process of legitimization, the latter may easily thwart such efforts, either by establishing their own congregations or associations or by realigning themselves with some other Spiritual group. Since the Spirit is believed to be the ultimate arbiter of the authenticity of any person's claims, the control of the association over those under its organizational umbrella tends to be minimal.

The final organizational principle of movements, reticulation, refers to the process in which the "cells, or nodes, are tied together, not through any central point, but rather through intersecting sets of personal relationships and other intergroup linkages" (Gerlach and Hine 1970:55). The linkages between cells operate at both the personal and organizational levels. Leaders of Spiritual churches are often acquainted with leaders of other local congregations. These connections may emanate from friendship or kinship ties or from mutual membership in an association. The first of these linkages can be illustrated by the friendship between Bishop F. Jones and the pastor of an Indianapolis church that I will call the United House of the Redeemer. After the two pastors became acquainted, Bishop Jones invited Reverend Brown (also a pseudonym) to preach at a revival being conducted at the Temple of Spiritual Truth. At the revival, Reverend Brown reciprocated by inviting Bishop Jones and his congregation to visit in Indianapolis. The exchange of visits between the two churches occurred despite their affiliation with different associations. Reverend Brown has urged Bishop Jones to shift the Temple of Spiritual Truth to the association that the United House of the Redeemer belongs to. Although such a realignment has not yet occurred, the invitation suggests the potential for such a process. Reticulation on the organizational level was exhibited in the series of events leading up to the establishment of the All Souls Christian Association. Prior to its formation, both its founder in Indianapolis and Bishop Gilmore of Nashville had been members of the same St. Louis-based association. Apparently, that membership provided them with an opportunity to compare notes and recognize their mutual dissatisfaction with the parent organization.

In effect, the decentralized, segmentary, and reticulate dimensions of the Spiritual movement allow for continual patterns of fusion, fission, and recombination. There seems to be a constant jockeying for position among constituent parts. As the development of Spiritual churches in Nashville indicates, these patterns occur not only at the associational level, but also at the congregational level. The pastor of one Spiritual church in that city noted that one of his elders has discussed the possibility of "jumping out" and starting her own congregation for years, but felt that she did not have the "stuff" for such an undertaking. Ironically, although he seemed to resent her desire to leave, he himself had established a congregation as the result of a schism in another Spiritual church in the community.

Organization of the Local Spiritual Congregation

Although the Black Spiritual movement has drawn its rituals and beliefs from a variety of religious traditions, the organization of individual churches in large part resembles that of many Black Protestant congregations (R. Simpson 1970; Williams 1974; Moore 1975; Burns and Smith 1978). Both tend to have a politico-religious structure comprising ministers, elders, deacons, missionaries, mothers, healers, nurses, and ushers. In addition, some Spiritual groups have created such elaborate titles for church officers as King, Queen, Prince, Princess, Royal Elect Ruler, Reverend Doctor, and Reverend Madam.

Recruitment into Spiritual churches follows various patterns. In cases where an individual establishes a new Spiritual church, there exists a common pattern of recruiting members from among relatives, friends, and the members of the former church. Since most Spiritual pastors function as mediums or healers, providing private consultations, it is not uncommon for them to attract new members from among their clients, who often belong to other churches originally. Special church events also attract visitors, some of whom may eventually decide to join.

Regardless of the path of recruitment, the opportunity for a potential member to join a congregation occurs at the end of the sermon during the Sunday morning service when the pastor "opens the doors of the church." If an individual decides to join at this time, he or she comes forward to the front of the sanctuary, indicating acceptance of the pastor's invitation. A secretary will write down information about the prospective member in a notebook, generally a roster of members. In some instances the pastor may ask the congregation to vote on whether or not to accept the individual, but since it appears that a recruit is almost always acceptable to the congregation, this procedure is essentially *pro forma*. Next, the new member may be briefed on his or her duties. In some cases these may include being baptized, but this may not be required, particularly if he or she has already been baptized in another church. In theory, a new member is expected to make regular contributions to the church and to abide by its normative proscriptions. In reality, violation of these regulations or failure to attend services regularly

rarely results in excommunication. Much more common than ex-
pulsion is the voluntary decision of the member to withdraw from
participation in church activities. Consequently, there is a tendency
for the rolls of Spiritual churches to be highly inflated.

As in any religious organization, there are various levels of involvement. Thompson (1944) recognizes this in his study of the All National Spiritualist Church of God in Atlanta. In contrast to the more
than six hundred individuals on the membership roster, he notes that
there were about seventy-five "bona fide devotees" who were officers
or were actively involved in the programs of the church in some capacity (Thompson 1944:47). In addition, an undetermined number
of "special interest devotees" regularly attended services but did not
claim membership in the group; in fact, some of these individuals
retained a formal affiliation with other religious bodies. Finally,
"casual devotees" attended the services occasionally for a variety of
reasons, such as curiosity, a healing, or the hope of obtaining a financial blessing.

My own observations suggest four basic levels of involvement in
Spiritual churches: there are (1) core members, (2) peripheral members, (3) occasional visitors, and (4) clients. Core members are those
who attend church activities on a regular basis, at least once or twice
a month. While many of these individuals (perhaps most, in the
smaller congregations) hold some sort of religious office, others may
be merely rank-and-file adherents who prefer to play a more passive
role in church activities. Peripheral members, while regarding themselves as part of the congregation, attend services on an irregular
basis. They are likely to appear at church only on special occasions,
such as Christmas or the pastor's anniversary. Occasional visitors,
although sometimes attending services on a more regular basis than
peripheral members, have not made a formal commitment to the
church by joining it. Some are actually members of other religious
bodies and may even attend services at two different churches. Clients, the final category, do not become involved in the public activities of the Spiritual congregation. Instead, each one engages in
a dyadic relationship with one of the several mediums or healers
who are commonly found in Spiritual churches.

Spiritual churches, regardless of their size, characteristically pos-
sess a rather elaborate politico-religious organization. The pastor,
at the apex of the hierarchy, is generally the most influential mem-

ber of the congregation. He or she often has received special training in Spiritual rituals and beliefs, and dictates in large part the religious orientation of the church. (It is common for the pastor to have been the founder of the church, as well. Of the eleven Spiritual churches that I studied in Nashville, nine were still pastored by their founders. The retirement, declining health, or death of the founder appears to be a major factor in the eventual demise of specific congrega- tions.) Some Spiritual churches also have one or more assistant pastors. In addition, a number of "boards" or "auxiliaries"— consisting of ministers, trustees, deacons and deaconesses, missionaries, moth- ers, mediums, choir members, nurses, and ushers — coordinate the activities of the church. Categories in the politico-religious hierar- chy of the church are not mutually exclusive, however, since any one individual may in actual practice occupy two or more positions. Such a pattern is particularly common in the smaller Spiritual congrega- tions, which often have difficulty filling all their offices on a regu- lar basis.

Pastors and other ministers constitute the elite members of the congregation. They tend to be designated by such titles as Bishop, Reverend, Elder, or even more illustrious terms. For example, the Mt. Zion Spiritual Temple association refers to its ministers as "Rev- erend Queen," "Reverend Princess," "Reverend Prince," "Reverend Father," "Reverend Mother," and "Reverend Lady." Ministers, who are particularly known for their preaching abilities and knowledge of spiritual affairs, are usually seated within or around the "sacred inner space," which often is an elevated area of the sanctuary. They either directly face the rank-and-file members of the congregation or are positioned sideways to them. While the ministers are gener- ally the closest confidants of the pastor, some of them constitute his or her most intense rivals. Any conflict that develops within the con- gregation is most likely to begin within this august circle.

The trustee board in theory supervises the business transactions of the church. Since the pastor, certain ministers, and deacons are frequently also trustees, it is difficult to separate their duties. Dea- cons and deaconesses assist the ministers in the conduct of the ser- vice: one may serve as the master of ceremonies; others supervise the collections and testimony sessions, set up the chairs in the front of the sanctuary for prospective members when the pastor "opens the doors of the church," and maintain the physical condition of the premises. Although deacons tend to be relatively young, usually in early adulthood or even late adolescence, it is not unusual to find a middle-aged or elderly deacon. However, if an individual is found in the status of deacon after the age of forty years or so, it is unlikely that he will be promoted to a higher position in the hierarchy of the congregation.

Missionaries are women who theoretically are engaged in teaching the gospel. During the course of the service, they may be called upon to say a prayer, give a sermonette, or monitor the testimony session. According to one Spiritual pastor, missionaries are to look in on the sick and the needy of the church. Some Spiritual churches have one or more evangelists whose function is also to teach. The status of evangelist is higher than that of missionary; he or she is considered a dynamic preacher who may be expected to visit other churches to spread the gospel.

Mothers are middle-aged or elderly women who occupy in large part a position of honor within the congregation. Although, like missionaries, they generally do not sit in the inner circle, they may be called upon to assist in the conduct of the service. If a congregation has as many as five or more mothers, they may be given a reserved section of the regular pews. Mothers can often be identified by their long white gowns and distinctive headdresses, perhaps a veil or a turban.

Mediums in Spiritual churches are believed to have the gift of prophecy—that is, the ability to "read" people or tell them things about their past, present, and future. The terms "spiritual advisor," "prophet," and "messenger" are commonly used in referring to mediums, but they are very sensitive about being called "fortune-tellers" or "Spiritualists" and often complain that there are many "false prophets" who exploit people. Pastors of Spiritual churches are almost always mediums, but one or more of the prominent members of the congregation may also be mediums. Although some Spiritual groups have established auxiliaries for mediums, in most congregations they are not organized. Mediums work in both public settings (special prophecy services during which they give messages to a number of individuals present) and private settings, in which they give messages to clients on a strictly individual basis. Mediums also generally claim to have the ability to heal. On the other hand, some "divine healers," make no claim to the gift of prophecy. The medium essentially focuses upon a wide variety of socioeconomic and psychosocial problems that individuals may encounter in everyday life. Although some members of Spiritual churches do seek the services of a medium for private consultation, it appears that a large percentage, perhaps the majority, of the Spiritual mediums' individual clients are not members of Spiritual churches; they include Baptists, Methodists, Pentecostalists, the unchurched, the affluent as well as the poor, and some Whites.

Many Spiritual churches have choirs, the size of which depends upon the size of the congregation. Some choirs, such as the one at the Temple of Spiritual Truth, consist of only a few individuals (in fact, it is not uncommon there for one or two young deacons to become part of the choir during portions of the service), whereas choirs in the larger Spiritual churches often have thirty or more members. While choir members in the smaller congregations may or may not wear colorful robes, special clothing seems to be the rule in the larger churches. Choirs in some Spiritual churches are age-graded. St. Cecilia's Divine Healing Church No. 2 in Nashville, for example, has an adult choir, a young adult choir, and a "peanut choir" for children between three and twelve years of age.

A category found in both Spiritual churches and many other Black churches is that of the nurses. Although they are not necessarily nurses in the conventional sense, they wear similar clothing and cater to the physical needs of the congregation. The number of nurses also varies with the size of the congregation, from one or two in small churches to ten or more in larger ones. Nurses are generally women, but some Spiritual churches, such as the United House of the Redeemer in Indianapolis, have male nurses as well. The primary functions of nurses are to look after individuals who go into trance and to protect other members of the congregation from being accidentally hurt by the violent movements of someone who is in ecstasy. When an individual begins to "shout," several nurses may quickly surround him, ready to catch the shouter if he should fall or to contain him within a small area. If a shouter collapses, the nurses will look after him until he has regained consciousness. Nurses are stationed at various strategic locations in the sanctuary. In the Temple of Spiritual Truth, which generally has only one nurse (if any) present, she sits in the back pew near the door, acting also as an usher. Pastors in some of the larger Spiritual churches may even have personal nurses: two sit beside Reverend Arnold, the pastor of St. Cecilia's No. 2 and see to it that she is comfortable at all times; help her remove, put on, or adjust parts of her attire; and fetch water or some other beverage when she is thirsty.

Other support personnel complete the hierarchy. Musicians may include an organist, a pianist, and one or more drummers. In the larger churches, the organist may receive a salary or the proceeds of a special offering once a month. Ushers, their number, again, depending upon the size of the congregation, not only direct people to the appropriate seating places but coordinate the movement of participants during special portions of the service, such as offerings and anointings. Most Spiritual churches also have one or more secretaries, whose main function is to record the amount of money that has been collected for the building fund, the pastor's salary, the maintenance fund, and other purposes. In at least the smaller Spiritual churches, a secretary or deacon will announce, toward the end of the service, the amount of the morning's offerings.

Sunday Services

As in most churches in the Black community, Sundays are extremely busy days for Spiritual churches, particularly the larger ones. Many begin with Sunday School, which may be scheduled for 9:30 A.M. but often gets started a half-hour or more later. Perhaps because of the early hour, Sunday School is not generally well attended, often involving only a few women and children. At the end of the Sunday School period, a collection (usually only a few dollars) is taken up. An intermission of varying length will follow before the main service begins.

The Sunday morning service, the most important and usually the best attended event of the day, is generally scheduled for 11:00 or 11:30 A.M. but again tends to start thirty minutes or more after the announced time. In a sense, Spiritual services do not *start* so much as *evolve*. With perhaps only a handful of people present, one of the elders may lead a hymn or two. People then sit quietly or speak in hushed tones to one another. As the service proceeds, more people trickle in, and those sitting in their regular pews (at least in smaller congregations) turn their heads to see who has just entered. The pastor will often not be present during the early portion of the service; it will be monitored by an assistant. Eventually, with a few more hymns and some prayers, the service will be well underway. It will typically include sermonettes, testifying, an altar call, and two or more collections. Depending on the church, there may be a considerable amount of ecstatic behavior, and if the congregation is subdued, someone will probably encourage them to "get the Spirit." The focal point of the service is the sermon or "message." It is delivered by the pastor, a prominent member of the congregation, or a visiting preacher; is usually from half an hour to over an hour in length; and in almost all cases is essentially extemporaneous, with the person who delivers it relying upon the Spirit for guidance.

At the end of the morning service, which generally takes about two and a half hours, people visit with one another. Some go home for the midday meal, but many eat at the church. At the Temple of Spiritual Truth, members bring dishes for a potluck dinner; in some of the larger churches, dinner or a snack may be purchased for a modest price. The remainder of the afternoon may be spent in a variety of ways; sometimes a musical program or a prayer service is scheduled. Some members may leave to visit similar events in other churches, Spiritual or otherwise, or do so in the evening. An evening service in a Spiritual church essentially resembles the morning service except that the sermon may be eliminated or abbreviated. While many of the members will not attend all the events of the day, the more prominent ones will generally do so. Finally, around 10:00 or 10:30 P.M., the long day ends as members and visitors go home to rest for work or the other activities of Monday morning.

To convey the flavor of Sunday services in Spiritual churches, I have put together two composite pictures from my observations in the Temple of Spiritual Truth and in the United House of the Redeemer. These descriptions are intended to portray two types of Spiritual congregations: the small "storefront" church and the large church with a more heterogeneous membership.

A SUNDAY MORNING SERVICE AT THE TEMPLE OF SPIRITUAL TRUTH[1]

As noted in the previous chapter, the Temple of Spiritual Truth in Nashville was established by Bishops Frank and Glenda Jones. Since 1973 the temple has been housed in a flat-roofed concrete block building. A sign outside gives the name of the church and some related information but does not state the hours of religious services. Although the sanctuary can seat 150 or so people, generally there are some 20 to 40 individuals present for the Sunday morning service. Directly below the pulpit, which is situated on a stage elevated about a foot above the main floor, is a small folding table, covered with a white cloth, which serves as an altar; it holds several statues of Catholic saints (including a large one of St. Francis of Assisi), a large "seven-day" candle with a short prayer to St. Joseph inscribed on it, several small votive candles, a picture of Jesus, a large crucifix, a bowl of fruit, a plant, a small Bible, and several other items. A large statue of the Sacred Heart of Jesus stands near the entrance, and on one of the walls hang various pictures, including a painting of the Blessed Virgin. Beyond the sanctuary, toward the rear of the building, are the offices of the pastor and the assistant pastor, a compact dining/meeting room, and a small lavatory. During the course of religious services, members frequently go to an office or meeting room to consult with the pastor concerning church affairs or to seek spiritual advice.

Although Bishop F. Jones ordinarily gives the sermon, his wife acts as the master of ceremonies for at least the first half of the Sunday morning service, since Bishop Frank usually makes several trips in his automobile to bring in various members who lack other transportation. Often he does not complete his rounds until after the service is well under way. In addition to her role as assistant pastor, Bishop Glenda serves as the president of a small choir, and the treasurer of the temple. She also conducts the Friday night "bless services," which she schedules when the Spirit guides her to do so rather than every week. Both bishops hold occasional study classes on week nights for those members interested in acquiring spiritual knowledge or learning how to conduct certain magico-religious rituals or "mysteries."

1. The following section is adapted, by permission, from Hans. A. Baer, "Black Spiritual Churches: A Neglected Socio-Religious Institution,"*Phylon* 42: 207–23.

Pre-Service Activities. Although the Sunday morning service is scheduled for 11:30, it does not start until about forty minutes later. Several people stand around the oil heater to warm themselves and catch up on news about one another's lives and those of other members. Shortly before the service begins, one of the deacons burns incense on the altar and places a large lighted candle in front of the statue of the Sacred Heart. The choir members file into the choir section, and the elders of the church take their respective places on the stage and sit facing the congregation. The elders include Bishop G. Jones; Bishop Jackson, an elderly woman who ordained both the pastor and the assistant pastor as "bishops" several years ago; Elder Potts, a middle-aged woman; and Elder James, a man in his late thirties. Bishop G. Jones is wearing a long red robe; Bishop Jackson, a black cassock and a biretta. (When he returns from picking up church members, Bishop F. Jones will change into a black clerical suit.) Although at this stage there are only fifteen people in the church, eventually there will be thirty-six individuals, including several small children, in attendance.

The Beginning of the Service. The assistant pastor comes to the pulpit and prays: "First, we give honor to God, and Jesus Christ, and the Holy Spirit, and the dear and blessed Mother Mary." Like several other elders, she is wearing a crucifix on a chain around her neck. The choir starts to sing a hymn, and the congregation joins in the singing of several more hymns. Although the church has a piano, tambourines are more often used to accompany the singing.

Petitions to "Our Heavenly Father". One of the three deacons sitting in a front pew kneels down and petitions blessings from God. He ends his prayer by making the sign of the cross.

The Offering. The assistant pastor tells the deacons that it is time to take up the offering. They bring a folding table and two chairs to the front of the church. Elder Potts and a female choir member bring out the books and assume their places at the table. This particular choir member is responsible for collecting the general offering, tithes, and pledges; Elder Potts collects money to pay the fuel, light, and telephone bills. As the choir sings hymns, members of the congregation carry their offerings to the table one by one, but some do not give. Although a young deacon contributes five dollars, most people give a dollar bill or some loose change. The deacons spend several minutes counting the money. The head deacon announces,

"We need 75¢." He gathers change from several people. The deacons and several elders stand around the table while one of the deacons delivers the offering prayer. The money is placed in an envelope, sealed, and given to the assistant pastor. The congregation is thanked for the $33.57.

The Testimony Session. Brother Hall, the head deacon, asks Sister Alexander to conduct the testimony session. Three young girls stand up in quick succession and state that they are "glad to be in the House of the Lord." A middle-aged woman delivers a more fervent and intense testimony, thanking God for his blessings, and suddenly bursts into tears. Members of the congregation encourage her to continue with responses such as "that's all right" or "tell it." She asks that a certain hymn be sung, and the choir leads the congregation in singing the requested hymn and others. While the congregation sings, Elder Potts, a frequent "shouter," goes into trance and comes down from the stage to the open space at the front of the sanctuary. She begins to dance violently and shouts, "Thank you, Jesus," over and over again. She runs into Brother Hall, a young man, and he holds her until the nurse comes from the rear of the sanctuary. Elder Potts dances again for about a minute and then regains full consciousness. She is led to one of the rooms behind the stage, where she is attended by the nurse. Several more testimonies are given. Sister Alexander turns the service "back into the hands of Brother Hall."

Scripture Reading. Deacon Hall asks Bishop Jackson to read from the Bible. She does so and delivers a short but spirited sermonette, based partly on but not restricted to the topic of her reading.

The Altar Call and Anointing. After the congregation has sung more hymns, Bishop Jackson is designated to anoint people in the congregation. Everyone in the church forms a line. As they approach the altar and before they reach Bishop Jackson, they place a few coins in a bowl of water and rub some of the water into the palms of their hands. Bishop Jackson uses olive oil from a small bottle to make the sign of the cross on the forehead and the palms of each person. Bishop F. Jones, who has just come out of his office, is also anointed by Jackson and in turn anoints her. Afterward, the participants hold hands to form two circles around the small altar. The inner circle includes the pastor, the assistant pastor, the elders, and the deacons; other members of the congregation, including small children, make up the outer circle. Elder Potts kneels down before the altar, squeezes her eyes shut, and prays intensely for several minutes. Others support her with a variety of verbal responses. After the altar prayer, members of the congregation return to their seats singing a hymn.

The Sermon. Bishop F. Jones comes to the pulpit and says, "Let's say amen." The congregation responds, and he says, "Let's say amen again." After this second response, the choir starts another hymn. Although Jones or his wife ordinarily gives the sermon, sometimes one of the elders or a visiting minister will do so. Today Elder James delivers the message. He is proud of his preaching abilities and welcomes opportunities to preach in his own and other churches. Elder James reads several passages from the Bible and announces that the topic of his sermon will be "Death Shall Have No Dominion." He starts by saying, "We believe in the Trinity. We believe that there is a visible world beyond this world — a place where good and evil are in balance together. While one is asleep, the spirit wanders about. All people are spiritual and have spirits. The trees have spirits as do the mountains, the rivers, and the valleys. . . . God is talking through me."

Elder James now comes down to the main floor and directs his preaching specifically at three women sitting together in the second pew. He says, "God has been better to us than we have been to ourselves. My two pastors express God's love and concern. I'm not going to hold you long this morning." One of the women suddenly collapses, slides across the pew, and bumps into the other two women. The nurse and several other people gather around her, and someone takes her eyeglasses. After Elder James returns to the platform, a woman begins to dance ecstatically but is guarded by several others.

The Invitation to Join the Church. Elder James ends his message, which has lasted about thirty minutes, by stating that the "doors of the church are now open." Two of the deacons bring two folding chairs to the front while the choir sings two hymns. At this particular service no one comes forward to join the church, and the deacons remove the chairs.

Pastor's Commentary. Bishop J. Jones compliments Elder James on his fine remarks and urges that the congregation show its appreciation by contributing generously to him during the special collection that will be taken up in a few minutes. He announces that he intends to resume study classes again soon: "God has given me mysteries to give you. The pulpit is for preaching and the class is for teaching. I want you to know how to live. With God's help, you make the money you have to go further and have fun. You are in a new world, and you have got to catch up. . . . I see our professor friend is with us again. I can tell that he is having a good time. If you are not careful, he will soon know more about the Spiritual work than you do. He has come to my home and learned about many mysteries and secrets."

The Offering for the Speaker. About five dollars is collected and given to Elder James.

The Benediction. The pastor directs the congregation to recite the "Pledge to the Bible," which is written in large letters on a poster at the front of the church. He then tells everyone to shake hands with one another.

Aftermath. Most of the members and visitors remain in the church in order to visit. Eventually, some go home for a midday meal; others stay to eat in the church building's dining room. Many members will return for a short musical program later in the afternoon and/or the evening service.

A SUNDAY NIGHT SERVICE AT THE UNITED HOUSE OF THE REDEEMER

The United House of the Redeemer, which was established in the mid-1950s by Mother Swanson, is a large Spiritual church located in a working-class neighborhood in Indianapolis. After Mother Swanson (again, I am using fictitious names) died in 1971, the church went without a pastor for about two years. In 1973 Reverend Brown, who has been a member of the church for over 25 years, became its pastor after being ordained by the large association with which the church is affiliated. A tall, handsome man in his early forties, he has increased the membership of the congregation to several hundred, including many young people who are attracted by his dynamic, affable, and "hip" demeanor. Like many of the larger Spiritual congregations, his church crosscuts socioeconomic lines and, he says, includes many members who are "blessed." There are also some Whites and Hispanics.

The income from his job as an outreach worker for a social service agency plus the "love offerings"and "donations" that Reverend Brown receives from his members permit him to live in a modest colonial-style house in a predominantly Black middle-class neighborhood and to drive a new automobile. On Sundays his home is a hub of activity as members of the church drop in to socialize or discuss church business. On one occasion, Reverend Brown told me that this sometimes creates a problem for him; he confessed that he locked himself in and did not answer the door the previous Sunday. He noted that he has little time for Spiritual churches other than those in his association, because it is "too messy," and so many of them "charge outlandish fees." Further, he admitted that some of the churches in his own association engage in exploitative activities and are into the "black arts."

Although many people refer to Reverend Brown as a "bishop," "doctor," "prophet," or "medium," he views himself primarily as a "minister" and criticizes some Spiritual leaders who dress like "clowns," are "into kingdoms," and confer regal titles upon themselves. Despite the fact that the mainstream denominations in the Black community have tended to avoid the Spiritual churches, Reverend Brown is a member of a local interdenominational ministerial association and was elected its "Minister of the Year" several years ago. However, he said that other members have questioned him in detail about the Spiritual religion and that he has to "watch my p's and q's in there." Reverend Brown emphasizes that his church is one with a "positive attitude" and that his religion is directed at personal growth. He regards himself as a student of religion; he attends classes at a theological seminary and studies astrology as well, in order to develop his spiritual abilities. In addition to the church's present weekly lunch program and work with needy families, he plans to build a new church, a community and educational center, and a nursing home.

The congregation's present building is much more elaborate than that of the Temple of Spiritual Truth. In fact, Bishop F. Jones confided to me that he hoped to have a church very much like the United House of the Redeemer some day. Although the exterior of the church is rather nondescript, the interior is fairly ornate and in many ways resembles a Catholic church. In addition to the sanctuary, there is a large room in the basement that serves both as a meeting room and a dining hall. The sanctuary has a seating capacity of about 250 and is highlighted in red, which in the Spiritual movement symbolizes power. The tiles on the floor, the carpeting on the stage, ver-

tical wooden panels on the walls, and a curtain behind the altar
are all red. Reverend Brown emphasizes the importance of color
schemes, both in decor and in the dress of the officers and choir of
the church. White and red are worn on the first Sunday of the month,
symbolizing purity and power respectively. According to Reverend
Brown, although black is usually associated with darkness and evil,
it is actually the basic color for "breaking up conditions" and is worn
on the second and fourth Sundays of the month. White is generally
worn on the third Sunday of the month.

Several steps lead to the stage where dignitaries sit and where the
pulpit and altar are situated. On the altar are a cross, several long
slender candles, and two large vases containing fresh flowers. Directly in front of the altar there is a small kneeling pew and a golden
trellis, apparently symbolizing the entrance to a sacred area. The Stations of the Cross — fourteen scenes depicting the events at the cruci-
fixion of Jesus Christ — hang on the side and rear walls of the sanctuary. However, there are no statues, although many of the churches
in the same association have them.

Pre-Service Activities. As people enter the sanctuary, an altar boy
dressed in a black robe, white surplice, white vest, and white skull-
cap lights the candles on the altar. Another altar boy places a con-
tainer of burning incense upon the altar. Reverend Thomas, one of
the "inspired ministers" of the church, pronounces the altar call and
says: "We ask that everyone elevate their minds. We serve a true and
living God over here at the United House of the Redeemer." Some
people come to the front and kneel at the steps leading to the raised
platform. After saying a short prayer, most of them make the sign
of the cross and return to their pews. The mothers and the missionaries, wearing long white dresses, enter one by one and take their
assigned places in the front pews on the left side of the sanctuary.

The Beginning of the Service. Although the service was scheduled to start at 7:30 P.M., it is about 7:40 when Reverend Thomas
and other devotional leaders begin to lead the congregation in singing. At this point there are about 100 people in the sanctuary, but
in an hour or so there will be well over 200. After a few hymns, Reverend Jordan, the assistant pastor, comes to the pulpit and announces,
"The Lord is in his holy temple." The congregation immediately responds by singing a hymn that also announces the divine presence.
Several altar boys and a single altar girl, varying in age from about

eight years to the early twenties, kneel at the steps of the altar as the head altar boy periodically rings a set of bells. Reverend Brown, dressed in a purple cassock and a biretta, and several officers of the church and visiting dignitaries observe the proceedings from their places upon the stage. Reverend Brown eventually comes to the pulpit and leads the congregation in several more hymns, accompanied by the organist and two drummers.

Congregational Prayer. A female devotional leader comes to the pulpit and leads the congregation in prayer. The head altar boy rings the bells while kneeling before the altar.

The Testimony Session. Several members testify to the importance of the Spirit and the church in their lives. As Deacon Montgomery gives a particularly spirited testimony, several people go into trance, and some begin dancing in their pews. One young woman runs out of her pew to the front, falls backward, and is caught by several others. She finally gets up and walks around, still in trance. This brief outburst of ecstatic behavior is followed by several more testimonies.

The Processional. Around 8:20 P.M. the choir marches up the center aisle with their right hands raised. Except for the director, a woman in her early thirties, all of the thirty or so singers are in their teens or early twenties. Most of them wear black robes and white surplices; a few female members, however, wear white dresses, and some of the males wear white shirts, black pants and ties, and white shoes. Before proceeding to the choir loft, they genuflect in unison and make the sign of the cross.

The Pastor's Prayer. As Reverend Brown comes to the pulpit, his personal altar boy (also the head altar boy) genuflects quickly in front of the altar and runs over to take his pastor's biretta. Reverend Brown then tells the members to hold the hands of those sitting beside them as he leads them in prayer. As the pastor returns to his seat, the head altar boy places the biretta on a small stand behind him.

An Ecstatic Interlude. While the choir sings several hymns, an inspired minister dances at the front of the sanctuary. Whether or not he is in a state of trance, several others — including a young White woman — do go into trance and begin to dance. Some mysterious contagion seems to spread throughout much of the congregation. The choir continues to sing, with even greater exuberance than before, as the organist and the drummers intensify their beat. It is impossible to keep up with the excitement that has infected the congregation. The White woman screams, turns several times, and sits down briefly, then starts dancing again. The head altar boy and several choir members also begin to dance in ecstasy. A girl of about ten goes into trance and is brought from her pew to the front. A middle-aged woman runs back and forth, stops to catch her breath, and continues her running. At the peak of activity about thirty individuals are simultaneously in trance and dancing in the front, center, and side aisles. Reverend Brown, followed by his personal altar boy carrying a bowl of holy water, walks quickly down the center aisle to the rear of the church and turns back. Taking water from the bowl, the pastor blesses people and also lays his hands on certain individuals. A young man in trance falls to the floor, is permitted to lie there unconscious for a minute or two, and then is picked up by several people. Deacon Montgomery goes into violent convulsions. Reverend Brown also dances briefly but does not go into a trance. One woman, pointing at her pastor, shouts over and over again the words "bless him." Eventually the choir, the organist, and the drummers reduce the intensity of their music. As people recompose themselves, the period of ecstasy, which lasted close to thirty minutes, draws to a close.

The Pastor's Message. Reverend Brown comes to the pulpit and states that he will be brief because of the late hour. He instructs the congregation in how to deal with adversity in their lives and how to obtain prosperity and success:

> Take a light and when your enemy tries you, turn it on. When you open your billfold or your purse and there is not much there, turn on your light. . . . Watch your colors, especially red. Spiritual people are not really spiritual. You carry the title and that is all. We got the worse hang-up that someone is burning a black candle. No one can do anything to me unless I let them. I like this experience called life. I am going to take care of myself. What we have are hang-ups. We are so confused that we need to hook up with the Redeemer. . . .
>
> They say that I'm crazy. I call a spade a spade. If you are Black, you are Black. If you are White, you are White. You can't change that. If you knew who you are, you wouldn't have so many hang-ups. . . . That which lives inside of you is spiritual. I knew a woman who when she was dying said, "Since the spirit was never born, it

can never die." Indianapolis is not a spiritual town. There are people who are into denominationalism. My denomination is not a church but a way of life. I am not a preacher, but I can prophesy for you. Most folks don't prophesy. They probably lie. . . .

We have one of the most blessed churches. What is in your mind, you can get. Some people give up too soon. If you want a suit, ask for a three-piece suit. Otherwise you may get a $49 suit. If you want a car, ask for a brand-new Monte Carlo. If you want a house, you have to get up and do something about it. Get a job. When we want power, we want red. When we want prosperity, we wear orange. When we want to clean up dirty thoughts, we burn a pink candle. Jesus is a spirit. He was delivered in the flesh. Jesus is a heart-fixer and mind-regulator. I don't care what your title is. If you don't have Jesus it doesn't mean anything.

The Invitation to Join the Church. At the end of his sermonette, Reverend Brown "opens the doors of the church." Two young women come forward to join. As the pastor and several officers of the congregation welcome them, the choir sings a hymn.

The Offering. Reverend Brown announces that it is time for the offering and that those making their tithing contribution should bring up the money in their envelopes. He also asks for a "love offering" for a visiting pastor. The ushers, dressed in short white jackets (very similar to those worn by waiters in exclusive restaurants), and the usherettes, who wear dark blue dresses, direct people down the side aisles to the rear and up the center aisle to the front. There, an altar boy is holding a large open Bible and an altar girl a plate. Contributors are to place bills in the Bible and coins in the plate. Those individuals who want change from the bills they placed in the Bible hold up the appropriate number of fingers, indicating to a deacon standing in the front how much should be returned to them. The contributors return to their pews by way of the side aisles. The sequence of contribution reflects the hierarchy of the church: first the rank-and-file members and visitors in the congregation, then the choir members, followed by the male and female nurses, the ushers, the deacons, and finally the officers of the church and visiting dignitaries. Afterward, the altar boy closes the Bible, and the assistant pastor prays over the offering.

The Closing of the Service. A deaconess makes a short announcement concerning upcoming events in the church. Reverend Brown asks the congregation for money to help a woman buy her children something for Easter. He also complains about the "loungers" who hung out in the vestibule in the rear of the church and those who took a "smoke break" during the course of the service. A visiting minister is asked to give the benediction. The service ends at 10:15 P.M. As people begin to file out, Reverend Brown takes the flowers from the vases on the altar and distributes them among certain individuals.

Bless Services

Although Spiritual churches engage in a variety of practices— such as testifying, shouting, and anointing with holy oil—which they share with many Black Protestant groups, their emphasis on public prophecy is one of the characteristics that distinguish them from the others. Prophesying generally takes place within the context of a special service called a "bless service" or a "prophecy service." In some Spiritual churches it occurs toward the end of a regular Sunday service; prophecy sessions are particularly common on occasions when prophets from other cities visit a Spiritual congregation.

In some churches, separate prophecy sessions are held regularly on a particular night of the week; in others they are scheduled only when the Spirit directs the pastor or prophet to hold them. In most cases a bless service is much like the regular Sunday morning service except that prophecy session will be substituted for the sermon. During the session, the prophet relates various aspects of the "present, past, and future" of selected individuals in the congregation. As few as three or four individuals or more than ten may be chosen by the prophet to receive messages. In most small Spiritual churches, the prophet will deliver the messages from the pulpit or the front portion of the sanctuary; in a larger church, he or she may move up and down the aisles, selecting recipients for messages.

Prophets sometimes approach and give certain individuals private messages or tell them that they will receive a private message after the service. Ordinarily, the recipient is not expected to make a financial donation to a prophet for this particular service. On certain occasions, however—for example, when a traveling prophet is in town—there may be such an expectation.

Bless services conducted by prophets from distant cities often attract large numbers of people. According to one informant, a prophet is generally not appreciated in his or her own locale; he or she is more likely to be successful in drawing crowds for bless services and clients for private consultations in another community. A pastor of a particular Spiritual congregation who wants a good turnout for special events, such as a series of revival meetings, often invites a traveling prophet to give messages or readings. For example, a personable prophetess of West Indian ancestry who lives in New York City, whom I will call Reverend Dixon, conducted several bless services at St. Stephen's Spiritual Church (also a pseudonym) in Indianapolis during the early spring of 1980; because she had attracted many people to services at St. Stephen's on a previous visit, its pastor paid her airfare. Reverend Dixon told me that on one night of this second visit, she "read" seventy-four individuals during the course of the bless service. At least one person felt that the prophet had been overworked that night and complained that the regular pastor merely stood in the front of the sanctuary collecting five dollars each from the "blessed ones." After the Sunday night bless service to which two women and I accompanied Reverend Dixon, she said that most of those who filled St. Stephen's to standing room that night were not members of Spiritual churches but people who had been unable to receive "deliverance" in Baptist and other churches.

A BLESS SERVICE AT THE SACRED HEART SPIRITUAL TEMPLE

At the Sacred Heart Spiritual Temple in Nashville, the bless service is regularly conducted on Wednesday nights by Reverend Wilson, at least during the warmer months of the year. During the winter the bless service is held only sporadically because of the expense of heating the church building. Reverend Wilson, a man in his early sixties, was born in Mississippi but lived for many years in various parts of the Midwest and also in a medium-sized Massachusetts city. Although he was raised a Baptist, he converted to Catholicism during his youth and, while on a Catholic retreat, discovered that he possessed the "gift of prophecy." Unfortunately, he felt that there was little opportunity for him to develop and use his gift in the Catholic Church, so he drifted into Spiritualism. For a while dur-

ing his residence in Massachusetts, Reverend Wilson was a member
of a predominantly White congregation affiliated with the National
Spiritualist Association. After he moved to Nashville in 1965, he
"worked" in many of the community's Spiritual churches and was
a "friend" of Sacred Heart Spiritual Temple, conducting weekday
services there for several years before actually joining. He was attracted to Sacred Heart because it gave him the freedom to "prophesize" and "teach" and had a pattern of regularly visiting other
Spiritual churches.

Reverend Wilson is an intelligent, articulate, and well-read individual who attended several colleges and graduated from a church-
related Black college in Nashville. He has read a great deal on Spiritualism and is also interested in sociology, particularly that of the
Black religious experience. (Needless to say, he has been keenly interested in and supportive of my own research on Spiritual churches.)
Although he enjoys teaching and prophesying, he feels that he would
be an ineffective preacher in the Spiritual circuit because his sermons would be "too academic" and would lack a strong emotional
appeal.

There are only two men and four women present when the bless
service starts at 7:45 P.M. After several hymns, Reverend Wilson comes
to the pulpit and states, "Each Wednesday night I turn to the master and ask him what I can talk about. I know that God will provide. He has stepped into my life on many occasions." He reads a
number of scriptural passages and comments on each one.

As the service proceeds, others enter the church until a total of
fifteen people are in attendance. Following several more hymns, Reverend Wilson asks a deacon to turn off some of the lights, then re-
quests the ministers to come forward to assist him in conducting the
healing prayer. Sister Jackson steps forward to be prayed for by the
small group in the front. Evangelist Anderson makes the sign of
the cross after the prayer.

Reverend Wilson asks that the lights be turned on again, and he
lights a candle that stands on the pulpit, explaining that the "light
is a symbol which holds our attention." He also acknowledges my
presence, noting, "We hope some day to read about ourselves. His
work is a form of publicity for us. He is still on the job, checking
and rechecking." Reverend Wilson then asked Reverend Marcus and

Reverend Odum of St. Matthew's Spiritual Temple to make some remarks to the congregation.

After a short testifying session, Reverend Wilson begins the prophecy portion of the service. He directs his attention to me: "I see a trip coming up — a trip that you have been planning for some time." He mentions a "sister" who will meet with me and asks whether I understand. When I reply that I do not have a sister, he seems annoyed and states that he is referring to "something like a Catholic sister."

Reverend Wilson has a message for everyone in the congregation except Reverend Marcus and Evangelist Anderson. He orders a young woman who is slouching in her seat to sit up and tells her, "If you continue in your present thoughts, you will stay in a rut." He next turns to a middle-aged woman: "I get some beautiful plans and thoughts for you. You must continue to fight for what you want. The only thing holding you back is a negative attitude. You have the capacity to make a lot of dreams come true." To a missionary of the church he says, "I get an old-fashioned person planting sweet potatoes." Wilson instructs her to bake a sweet potato and use it to obtain a blessing. Finally, he tells the wife of Reverend Odum, "I pick up a house with you. When we get messages, we talk about things that we don't know. We see you stepping up a little higher — in a material sort of way. I see green grass — a symbol of prosperity. The Lord is healing you. Don't think negatively about your condition. Think positively."

After the prophecy session, at about 10:20 P.M., an offering is taken up and the service is ended with a hymn. Afterward, Reverend Wilson takes certain individuals aside and attempts to clarify for them the meaning of the messages that they received from the Spirit.

A BLESS SERVICE CONDUCTED BY A TRAVELING PROPHETESS

Bishop Douglas, a Spiritual pastor from Indianapolis who visits Nashville once a month, is an excellent example of the popular traveling prophet. The following is a composite account of two bless services that she conducted in Nashville.

The service starts at 7:45 P.M. on a Saturday night. In addition to two pastors of other Spiritual churches in the city, a White Holiness preacher who occasionally visits some of the Spiritual groups is seated up front, facing the congregation. Following the preliminaries of hymn singing, praying, sporadic preaching by various ministers, and several outbursts of shouting, Bishop Douglas comes to the pulpit. She first cautions the congregation to forget about "hoodooism and witchcraft," for these nefarious practices are of no concern to her: "Some of you have come to see what I am going to do. I am a preacher. I have been born again." She briefly "speaks in tongues" and then resumes: "I am trying to get people interested in going to church again. You can't be Spiritual without belonging to a church. You need to be born again." She comments on the presence of two Whites in the congregation—the visiting preacher and me. First referring to Brother Matthews, she says, "Someone might say that you got a White man there today. He is my brother, too." In calling attention to my presence, she remarks, "Some people say you can't love a White man. Yes, you can! The trouble with Spiritual churches is that they do not cater to all colors and classes."

One of the assistants announces, "If you want to see Bishop for a reading, it is three dollars," and asks that those who wish to receive a message raise their hands. Bishop Douglas quickly reprimands her assistant: "You cannot charge in church. Someone will say we are charging something. You have got to watch your words." (While two assistants collect money from about twenty people out of the fifty or sixty present in the crowded house, Bishop Douglas teasingly asks Brother Matthews if he is a policeman. She states that the day before, a man told her he had won $1300 on the numbers; she jokes that she wanted a share of his blessing. While her intentions in relating this story are not clear, the effect is to suggest that perhaps she was the source of the winning number.) After the donations are collected, Bishop Douglas's brother blesses them.

When it is time for Bishop Douglas to give messages from the Spirit, one of the assistants asks the congregation, "Who paid for a reading?" Again Bishop Douglas corrects the slip of the tongue, noting that the funds collected for messages are "donations." Because the congregation sings hymns to the loud accompaniment of a piano and several tambourines, it is extremely difficult to hear what she prophesies to various individuals in the congregation. She instructs several recipients of messages to see her after the service. Bishop Douglas reminds them that sometimes it takes a while for a prophecy to be fulfilled and that they must be patient in the meantime. When I left the service shortly after midnight, she had a few more readings to do. While some individuals had left before I did, others chose to stay, perhaps hoping that they would receive one of the several messages that Bishop Douglas gave gratuitously that night.

Offerings

Although, as H. Lewis (1955:148) notes, "a large portion of the time, energy, and inventiveness invested in religious or church matters is devoted to money raising," this topic has received little attention in the literature on Black American religion. In addition to Lewis's general discussion of financial collections in Black Baptist and Methodist churches in Kent (his pseudonym for a small mill town in the South) and the surrounding vicinity, several other social scientists have written brief descriptions of the manner in which offerings are made in Black Protestant congregations (R. Simpson 1970; Holt 1972:199–200; Williams 1974:102–03, 106; Moore 1975; Dougherty 1978:36–37). My own observations indicate that the manner of taking up offerings in Spiritual churches is very similar to that in Black Protestant churches, particularly those with small memberships. In light of the paucity of data on this practice, I will discuss its general patterns in Spiritual churches.

One of the major reasons that the offering is the object of considerable focus in many Black congregations is the poverty of many of their members. In addition, the small size of many of these congregations makes it extremely difficult to accumulate the monetary resources necessary to maintain the premises and to compensate the pastor for his or her services. In addition to mortgage payments or rent on the church building, the congregation must be able to pay a number of other recurring expenses, including those for church furnishing, utilities, telephone, and general repairs and upkeep. Indeed, failure to meet these expenses is an important reason for the considerable turnover in small religious congregations in the Black community.

A universal function of religious rituals is to impress upon the participants the significance of a particular occasion or an expected behavioral pattern. Since financial solvency is an absolute requirement for the continued existence of a congregation, it follows logically that a mundane affair such as the gathering of funds would be transformed into an elaborate sacred event. Those individuals who contribute the largest amounts of money inevitably gain status and prestige within the encapsulated world of the religious group. While there are other avenues available in Black religious congregations for obtaining a high rank, apparently the ability to contribute handsomely is a particularly important route for achieving such a position (H. Lewis 1955; Williams 1974).

There are generally two collections during the Sunday morning service in a Spiritual church. The lesser of these, often referred to as the "silver offering," "consecrated offering," or "penny collection," tends to occur during the earlier portion of the service, although as we have seen in the case of the Temple of Spiritual Truth, it may follow the regular offering. In either case, it involves the contribution of loose change—quarters, dimes, nickels, and even pennies (although sometimes it is explicitly stated that pennies are not desired) and often revolves around some kind of ritual. At the Cathedral of Spiritual Science (pseudonym), a large Spiritual church in Memphis, the silver offering actually starts before the service begins: as members of the congregation enter the sanctuary, they proceed to the front, drop one or more coins on the marble steps leading to the sacred inner area where an elaborate altar is situated, pray briefly, make the sign of the cross, and then take a seat. Even after the service gets started, latecomers go to the steps to make their silver offering. Periodically, the deacons collect the many coins that have been placed on the steps. At the King Narcisse Michigan State Memorial Temple in Detroit, members and visitors are invited to come to the front during the early portion of the service in order to light a white candle; participants in this ritual are expected to make a donation of one dollar. As each person comes before the votive candle stand, he or she silently says a short prayer petitioning the Spirit for a blessing.

The more important of the two offerings at the Sunday morning service is the "regular offering," which may also be referred to as the "general offering," the "tithes and pledges collection," or some other term. In many instances, it occurs sometime after the sermon and shortly before the end of the service. The collection of the regular offering tends to be an elaborate procedure which, particularly in the larger Spiritual churches, may last as long as thirty minutes. Either the members of the congregation come to the front of the sanctuary and place their contributions in some receptacle (a basket, a plate, an open Bible, a miniature model of a church building) or the deacons pass a basket or plate. According to Puckett (1931:27), the practice of having members carry their offerings individually to the front of the sanctuary is widespread and uniform among religious Blacks. On the other hand, Holt (1972:200) maintains that this practice is "fast-disappearing" in Black churches. My own observations indicate that it is more common in Spiritual churches than simply passing the plate.

The pastor will often start off the regular offering by placing his or her own contribution in the collection receptacle first; in smaller Spiritual congregations particularly, the church officers follow suit, sometimes giving $10 or more. Finally, the rank-and-file members and the visitors come to the front to make their offerings. (In some instances, however, as we have seen in the United House of the Redeemer in Indianapolis, the higher-ranking members of the congregation follow the others.) While the procedure of coming to the front tends to be very casual in the smaller churches, it is more organized in the larger ones. It is not uncommon for people to march up the center aisle and return to their seats down one of the side aisles. Two or more deacons and perhaps the pastor may stand near the collection area, subtly but carefully observing the amount that each person gives; the pastor may even call special attention to an individual who makes an especially large contribution. For example, at one Sunday morning service, Reverend Arnold asked one particular man about the $2,000 that he had pledged to contribute. When he came forward with two $1,000 bills, she embraced him tightly, kissed him several times, and excitedly proclaimed to the congregation, "God is working it out." Apparently such exhibitions are intended not only to give the large contributor public recognition but also to motivate others to be generous.

As each person comes to the collection area, he or she may make an offering at two or more stations. At one Sunday morning service at St. Cecilia's Divine Healing Church No. 2, several recording secretaries were seated at a long table with separate collection points for those fulfilling their three- and five-dollar pledges, making a $50 contribution toward the down payment on Reverend Arnold's house in Nashville, meeting a portion of their "tithes," and making a "general offering." The pastor's personal nurses collected "love offerings" for their religious leader. In order to motivate people to make love offerings, Reverend Arnold reminded them that the round-trip fare for her airplane ticket was $132. While the regular offering is not quite such a complex affair at the Temple of Spiritual Truth, even there the potential contributor may give to one or more of several collections, including the "general offering and pledge," the "utility collection," and the "broadcast collection" (which is used to finance the congregation's weekly religious radio program). In addition, members are urged to contribute "pastor's dues" of three dollars on the fourth Sunday of the month.

Special offerings are sometimes conducted in conjunction with the regular offering or at another point during the service. They include collections to assure the organist a token salary, to assist a needy person or family, and to provide a love offering for a visiting preacher or perhaps a member of the congregation who has delivered a moving sermon. Or a special offering may follow an ecstatic interlude — a time at which members of the congregation are perhaps most willing to make a financial contribution.

For those individuals with denominations of currency exceeding what they wish to contribute, change is available. In some instances, as the contributor comes to the collection table, he holds up as many fingers as he wants dollars returned to him. If there is not enough change available at the moment, one of the deacons will bring it later to the contributor's pew.

During the course of the offering, hymns are sung, music is played, or the pastor or an elder makes impromptu remarks to the congregation. After everyone making a contribution has come forward, the deacons carefully count and even recount the money. Once this task is completed, especially in the smaller Spiritual churches, one of the deacons may announce that an additional amount is needed to meet their goal. For example, if it was hoped that at least $50 would be collected but the total is only $47.35, it will be announced that $2.65 is still needed. Furthermore, an effort is made to end up with "even money"— that is, to have the total amount come out to a whole number of dollars. While some individuals may volunteer additional contributions, one or more deacons may circulate through the congregation in order to encourage the reluctant to give more. In many cases, the extra money goes beyond the requested sum. Again the contributions are counted; then one of the deacons announces the final tally and thanks the congregation for its generosity. The offering ritual is concluded with a short prayer by one of the deacons or some other respected individual.

Sometimes the process of collecting additional money becomes extremely involved and prolonged, particularly in the storefront type of Spiritual church. Following the offering one Sunday morning at the Temple of Spiritual Truth, Deacon Hall asked for an additional $1.70 and then increased his request to $3.00 He collected at least $2.00, but noted that he still needed $1.84 and he managed to garner a little more. After another counting, his wife, a recording secretary, reported that they were still 64¢ short. Deacon Hall rounded up some more loose change but said he was still 36¢ short. After still more collecting and counting, it was announced that the "general offering" came to $25 and the "utility offering" to $15. Upon hearing this, the pastor stated that the temple needed more than $15 for the utility offering in order to pay the telephone bill. Following a futile attempt to obtain additional funds from the congregation, one of the deacons added one dollar to the collection.

As H. Lewis (1955:150) notes, many of the techniques used for raising money in Black churches are standardized; "frequently, however, some ingenious person or group will develop or import a novel method that is soon imitated." An example of this pattern is illustrated by the offering called for by a visiting preacher at a service of the Cosmic Kingdom of the Spiritual Mind (pseudonym) in Flint, Michigan. She first asked those who were willing to give five dollars to recite a "blessing prayer" with her, promising a hundredfold increase for such an offering. The visiting preacher then requested those who were "not blessed to give five dollars" to give what they could, urging that "you are blessed according to what you give."

Special Events

DEMONSTRATIONS

Special services called "demonstrations" are conducted in many Spiritual churches. While highly variable in ritual content, their principal goal is to obtain a blessing. Some demonstrations will draw more people to church than do Sunday services. The distinction between the demonstration and the bless service is not entirely clear, since both have essentially the same aim. The bless service, however, tends to focus on the giving of messages from the Spirit, whereas the demonstration involves some idiosyncratic ritual which has been developed by a prominent member of the congregation. This is not to say that prophecies may not be made during a demonstration or that a demonstration may not be conducted during a bless service.

Reverend Cardwell, the pastor of Unity Fellowship in Nashville, conducts demonstrations on the evening of the first Saturday of the month. In addition, he holds a number of special demonstrations at various times of the year, the most unusual of which is the "Devil's Funeral." When I attended this demonstration, it was held in a school auditorium because it was believed that the church would not be large enough to accommodate the crowd. However, to the dismay of Reverend Cardwell, fewer than fifty people turned out. Various officers of Unity Fellowship as well as distinguished guests, including three Whites, from other churches were seated on the stage. Reverend Cardwell announced that "the Devil died last night and he is going to be buried." Below the stage was a coffin surrounded by several floral bouquets. Between hymns and prayers, various speakers made short remarks concerning the iniquities of the Devil and the confusion that he has created in the world. Eventually, Reverend Cardwell instructed the congregation to list on paper "twelve things that you want burned out of your life." He noted that these were to be burned the following day in the "fire of truth" and invited everyone to witness the Devil's final burial. Reverend Cardwell then read the Devil's obituary, focusing on the trials and tribulations that he created for various Biblical characters. Symbolically burying the Devil is intended to eliminate all negative forces, allowing the positive thoughts that remain to ensure prosperity, happiness, and health.

One of the best attended demonstrations among the Spiritual churches in Nashville is the Harvest Feast conducted at Resurrection Temple by Elder Davis, who received this demonstration from the Spirit during a "time of despair" following the death of the husband. In addition to the congregation of Resurrection Temple, members of other churches in the city attend. People are requested to bring cans of food, which will be donated to the needy. Toward the middle of the service, those in attendance come forward to be anointed with holy oil. Finally, the congregation is invited to receive one of many fruits that Elder Davis consecrated the previous night. The eating of the fruit will result in a blessing for its consumer. At the end of the service, Elder Davis gives messages to several people in the congregation.

DEVELOPMENT CLASSES

In many Spiritual churches classes are held to provide esoteric knowledge and techniques to acquire blessings or "power." In some groups, an aura of secrecy surrounds these "development" classes, and only selected members are entitled to attend. In the Black sections of some large cities, schools of the occult and of the esoteric sciences offer similar instruction. For example, on the South Side of Chicago the Unity Temple of Scriptural Sermons and Academy of Theological Writers, a storefront school, advertises as follows on its door:

BE A PRACTITIONER, EARN WHILE YOU LEARN TO BE A CONSULTANT IN BIBLICAL AND TRANSCENDENTAL MEDITATION. CHRISTIAN AND DIVINE SCIENCE, METAPHYSICS, ROSICRUSIONISM [*sic*] AND SUPER MIND SCIENCE — ALCHEMICAL TELEPATHY AND THEOSOPHICAL LIGHT.

It is important to note that such schools are not necessarily affiliated with a Spiritual group, but several Spiritual pastors and members have told me that they learned many of their "secrets" at schools of the occult.

Bishop F. Jones permitted me to attend one of his development classes, but he noted that there are others he could not permit me to attend. The main purpose of this class was instruction in the "dressing" of candles. Bishop Jones placed a small dish and a small candle in front of each person seated at a table. He then passed around a tiny bottle labeled "Dr. Japo Oil" and told us to anoint ourselves with it. Next, he passed around a vial of oil with the words "love luck" printed on it, instructing us to use this for dressing the candles. The proper technique for doing so was to apply the oil by twisting the candle up and down in one's fingers. We were then instructed to present the candle to Jesus by burning it in the dish, allowing the melted wax to keep it upright. Afterward, we were told to close our eyes and meditate upon our deepest desires. At the end of the class,

Mrs. Jones demonstrated to us the manner in which she fingers the contours of the wax drippings on the dish in order to receive a prophecy.

SÉANCES

Séances, similar in form to those in predominantly White Spiritualist circles, are common in Black Spiritual groups. As noted earlier, the séance constituted the central focus of services at Redeeming Christian Spiritualist Church, the forerunner of the later Spiritual churches in Nashville. An elderly man, who had been a member of both congregations at earlier times in his life, told me that while séances were common at Redeeming Christian Spiritualist Church, he never witnessed any at St. Joseph's. The secretary of a congregation affiliated with the Ancient Ethiopian Spiritual Church of Christ, an organization that believes in "communication with the spirits of departed ones," told me that séances have not been conducted in her temple since the mid-1950's. Despite this decline, séances are still held sporadically. Bishop F. Jones stated that they have occurred at the annual conferences of his association. He once even attempted one himself but quickly discarded the idea because some "hanky-panky" went on. Reverend Brown admitted that he occasionally conducts séances but restricts them to individuals who are at "higher levels of consciousness." Bishop Rogers said that occasionally the Spirit directs him to have a séance.

PASTORS' ANNIVERSARIES

Like many other churches in the Black community, Spiritual churches celebrate the pastor's anniversary with a series of services and events that often last seven or eight days. The celebration generally starts at a Sunday service and culminates with a banquet the following Saturday night. The auxiliary organizations of the church alternate in sponsoring the events. Programs are distributed to other people in the community. During the services the pastor is seated in a place of honor in his or her finest religious garb or secular clothes, often surrounded by elaborate bouquets of flowers. When I attended one of Elder Moore's anniversaries, a procession marked her entrance into the sanctuary each night. Two male escorts (including the author on one occasion) marched with her and sat beside her during the service. The pastor generally does not preach on his or her anniversary but confers this privilege on prominent members of his church or dignified visitors. They in turn give talks of varying length which, in addition to being inspirational, extol the virtues of the pastor. Great emphasis is given to the trials and tribulations that the pastor has had to face through the years of his or her ministry and the good fortune of the church in having such a dedicated and generous leader. Collections for the paster are taken up at each service, and various auxiliaries of the church and sometimes visiting congregations present money and a gift as tokens of appreciation. Spiritual people take pride in the amount of money that their pastor receives at an anniversary celebration and often talk about this for several weeks afterward.

TRIPS TO OTHER CHURCHES

Many Spiritual people visit congregations other than their own, particularly for such events as pastors' anniversaries, revival meetings, demonstrations, and musical performances. In many, if not most, instances they visit other Spiritual congregations, but they also visit Baptist, Methodist, Holiness, and Pentecostal churches. Generally only a few members of any particular congregation will be on hand for a special event at another church in the community. Pastors and elders are frequently invited to be guest speakers at other churches. On some occasions, representatives of a particular Spiritual temple will visit a Spiritual group in another city. This is especially common in the case of the annual convention that many Spiritual associations conduct. Spiritual people may also visit a Spiritual congregation in a distant city even if it is affiliated with some association other than their own. Special preparations are made for all intercity visits, and members are urged to save their money so that they may go on such a trip. If a relatively large number plan to go, it is quite common for them to charter buses. In the event that the visitors will be staying overnight or for several days, members of the host congregation may provide housing for them, although sometimes travelers will stay in a hotel.

In October of 1978, I had the opportunity to accompany twenty-six members of the Temple of Spiritual Truth on a trip to visit two Spiritual churches in Indianapolis. About half an hour before the charter bus departed, Rev. F. Jones lit a large blue votive candle and placed it before the statue of the Sacred Heart of Jesus in the rear of the sanctuary in order to ensure a safe journey. After everyone had boarded the bus (around 3:30 A.M.), Rev. F. Jones said a long prayer. In part because a large proportion of the travelers were adolescents and young adults, a festive mood filled the bus for the first hour or so of travel. After this initial period of excitement, most people settled down and went to sleep so that they would be well rested for the events of the day. Others conversed quietly with one another. After our arrival at St. Stephen's Spiritual Temple in Indianapolis, a number of the members of the Temple of Spiritual Truth went to the nearby home of the pastor to change into their church-going clothes — for many, their best suits or dresses, since this was a special occasion. Another charter bus from Nashville with members of Sacred Heart Spiritual Temple, as well as several people from a Baptist church, also made the trip to St. Stephen's for "Tennessee Day."

After the morning service at St. Stephen's, which was packed to its capacity of about 150 persons, the bus carrying those visitors from the Temple of Spiritual Truth transported them to the United House of the Redeemer, a larger Spiritual church in another section of the city. The other visitors from Nashville remained behind to spend the remainder of the day at St. Stephen's. At the second church, Reverend Brown, its pastor, invited the guests to his home for a midday meal; later they returned to the United House of the Redeemer for the afteroon and evening services. Since there was only a brief intermission between the two, several of us — including Rev. F. Jones — walked to a small grocery store nearby to purchase some snacks to tide us over.

Although the evening service ended shortly after 10 P.M., it was almost another hour before our bus began its return trip to Nashville. One woman on the bus expressed the sentiments of others when she exclaimed, "I never had that kind of good time in my life!" Around 2:30 A.M., someone decided to take up a collection as a token of appreciation to our bus driver, a reserved but amiable White man who seemed to have enjoyed the trip in his own quiet manner. The bus arrived in Nashville at 4:30 A.M. giving many of us only a short time to rest before returning to work on Monday morning.

Numbers, Prophets, and Charlatans

In their classic study of the Black community, Drake and Cayton (1945:470–94) describe the variety of ways by which some of its residents obtain a "number" in order to play the "policy"—an illegal lottery game. These include using a dream interpretation book, translating personal experiences and public occurrences into numerical expressions, and visiting independent "spiritual advisors" and numerologists. They also add that "some few Spiritualist pastors do actually give out numbers." Elsewhere, McCall (1963:366) notes that "some widely-known readers have specialized exclusively in number divination and operate largely by telephone and telegraph, advertising in the Negro press. By telegraphing 'donations' of $10 and $20 to these big-time readers, one can obtain by return telegram the 'blessing' of a certain Psalm — of the three digits, of course." The validity of the notion that prophets and advisors within the Spiritual movement are an important source of betting numbers is difficult to ascertain, but it is nevertheless held by many Black Americans, including those who belong to Spiritual churches.

Many prophets and advisors in Spiritual churches are sensitive about this belief and vehemently deny that they engage in such activities, but it is not uncommon for them to admit that people in other Spiritual churches give out numbers. Bishop Gilmore, who feels that this practice gives the Spiritual movement a tainted image, stated that many Spiritual prophets and advisors do give out numbers, but also noted that the same thing occasionally occurs in Baptist and Holiness churches. Spiritual people are aware that some nonmembers frequent their services specifically to obtain a number. Elder Davis, for example, lamented that this is one of the main reasons many visitors attend Resurrection Temple's Harvest Feast each fall: some people will use a "dream book" to look up the number associated with the consecrated fruit that they receive and place a bet on it. Bishop Gilmore added that if she repeats a particular Biblical passage in church several times, the number associated with it becomes "hot."

Although the majority of individuals who visit spiritual advisors apparently do so in order to be treated for a condition or ailment, the mediums I interviewed acknowledged that some people ask them for a number. Most mediums stated that they do not oblige, because they disapprove of gambling or because numbers are "of the Devil." Yet Bishop F. Jones stated that while he himself does not give numbers, his wife has done so on a few occasions.

While most spiritual advisors are emphatic in denying any involvement with numbers, one whom I interviewed openly admitted to regularly playing numbers herself and boasted that she had been of assistance to some of her clients who "hit it big." To justify playing the numbers, she noted that "God said that he would make a way." On one occasion this advisor, whom I will call Mrs. Collins, asked me to help her to obtain a "blessing" for a client. Teasing that my wife would regard me as crazy for cooperating with her, she requested that I place a glass of water under our bed before retiring for the night and call her the following morning to tell her the content of my dream. When I warned her that I generally do not have vivid recollections of my dreams, she assured me that in this instance I would. After following her instructions, I dreamed that my wife had long flowing hair — perhaps a subconscious reaction on my part to her new haircut. When I related the content of my dream to Mrs. Collins, she seemed pleased, remarked that the key word was "hair," and suggested that I call her again in the late afternoon. When I did so, she told me that one of her clients had called her earlier, saying that she was in need of a blessing. Mrs. Collins told her to play "hair"; the woman reportedly looked up the associated number in the dream book and won $60 on a dollar bet.

Perhaps one of the most sensitive topics for mediums is the issue of compensation for private consultations. Most mediums vehemently deny that they "charge" for their services but admit that they will accept a "donation" or a "freewill offering." It is often maintained that since the ability to prophesy is a gift from God, it is not proper to charge people for its use; however, clients are usually aware that a "donation" of a certain amount is expected by a spiritual advisor. For example, it is generally known that the standard donation when seeking the help of Reverend Arnold is $10. While she admits that this is the usual amount, she adds that she often receives less or even no money — but that occasionally someone donates as much as $50 or $60. On the other hand, both Bishop Jones and his wife admitted independently that they "charge" standard "consultation fees" of $10 and $15, but noted that they also have a divine duty to help a person who cannot afford to pay the fee. While advisors generally receive a donation for each client visit, Mrs. Collins told me that since she does much of her counseling on the telephone, her clients often give her donations in relatively large lump sums (perhaps $50) from time to time. She estimated that she takes in $200 to $250, sometimes as much as $300, a month for her counseling service. Although the more popular mediums may receive $10 or more for a session, they are apparently given only a few dollars by some clients, or perhaps merely an expression of gratitude. For the majority of mediums, counseling activities are at best a supplement to other sources of income.

A common stereotype in the Black community is that of the medium as a charlatan or phony. Spiritual people are able to recall seemingly countless numbers of incidents in which a medium swindled a congregation or an individual out of large sums of money. One informant spoke of a prophet who sold rocks, which he claimed were from the Holy Land, and another prophet who sold an imprint of a "blessed hand" for $50. She also spoke of a Spiritual prophet from Cincinnati who placed a snake underneath one woman's doorstep; then he told her someone had hoodooed her, but for $500 he could kill the snake that had been sent after her. One pastor noted that a lot of "quacks have gotten into the Spiritual work in the last twenty years" and added that they hurt Spiritual people. A second pastor complained that some Spiritual mediums "sell numbers, give people private consultations for $50 or $60, and tell them a big lie." Another informant told of a Spiritual prophetess who erected a "fortune tree" in her church. She told the congregation that she had placed 150 "fortunes" on the tree and that for a seven dollar donation the Spirit would direct people to the fortunes intended for them. According to my informant, at the appointed time there was a mad rush to the tree.

Nevertheless, despite the fact that I have myself observed certain questionable practices in Spiritual churches, the majority of pastors, prophets, and advisors I interviewed live in modest surroundings, have a salaried occupation or other legitimate source of income, and seem to be sincere in their beliefs. Any financial benefits that they may reap from their church positions are not generally commensurate with the time and energy that they invest in them.

CHAPTER 3

The Father Hurley Sect:
The Untold Story of
a Black God's Kingdom

W HILE FATHER DIVINE and his Peace Mission have received fairly extensive treatment, the Universal Hagar's Spiritual Church[1] established in 1923 by Father Hurley, a contemporary of Father Divine and also a self-proclaimed god, has been almost entirely overlooked in the literature on the Black American experience (Hoshor 1936; Parker 1937; Braden 1949; S. Harris 1971; Burnham 1979). In fact the only reference to this group that I have been able to find in the literature is a brief comment by Parker (1937: 105), which claims that Father Hurley was vehemently opposed to the establishment of a Father Divine mission in Detroit.

Father Hurley was the founder of one of the earliest Black Spiritual associations in the United States. His movement is interesting not only in this regard, but also because (as will be discussed in greater detail in Chapter 4), it exhibits linkages with various other socioreligious developments among Black Americans during the early part of this century, including Garveyism and the messianic-nationalist sects, as well as the Peace Mission. This chapter will focus in large part on the history, social organization, and beliefs of the Father Hurley sect and present an ethnographic overview of ritual events in several congregations affiliated with the Universal Hagar's Spiritual Church.

History and Social Organization

George Willie Hurley was born on February 17, 1884, in Reynolds, Georgia, a small village located about thirty miles southwest of Ma-

---

1. "Hagar" in the name of this association refers to Ishmael's mother in the Old Testament.

con. After completing high school, he received ministerial training at the famous Tuskegee Institute in Alabama and also taught in public schools in the South. In 1908, he met Cassie Bell Martin—his future wife, who would bear them six children—at a Baptist convention (*Aquarian Age*, Oct. 1974). Although he was raised a Baptist and trained as a Baptist minister, he later became a Methodist. After moving to Detroit with his wife in 1919, he joined a small Black Holiness sect called Triumph the Church and Kingdom of God in Christ. Triumph the Church was founded in Georgia in 1906 by Elder (or Father) Edward D. Smith and teaches the "cleansing from sin in all 'justified' believers through the shed blood of Christ; entire sanctification as an instantaneous, definite work of second grace obtained through the faith of the consecrated believer; the second coming of Christ; and baptism by fire as a scriptural experience also obtained by faith" (Mead 1975:252). Hurley was quickly elevated to the position of "Elder" in the church and became its "Presiding Prince of Michigan."

Sometime during the early 1920s, Elder Hurley was invited by a White man to a service of the International Spiritual Church. This individual preached the "doctrine that life is intended to be a place of peace and happiness" and said that "God was spirit and not baptist or methodist" (*Aquarian Age*, July 1947). Hurley joined the International Spiritual Church and was sent out by it as a "spiritualistic preacher." Shortly thereafter, Prophet Hurley[2] had a vision in which a "brown-skinned damsel," who turned into an eagle representing the church that he was to establish, appeared to him. He started his church on Columbia Street in Detroit on September 23, 1923, but later moved it to Gratiot Street, and still later to 944 Napoleon Street (*Aquarian Age*, Feb. 1967). In 1924 Hurley established the School of Mediumship and Psychology, which eventually became a part of each congregation in the Universal Hagar's Spiritual association. In later years, when his church had expanded to include additional congregations, he maintained a migrating "eastern headquarters" of sorts in various locations in New York and New Jersey. During the early 1940s Father Hurley signed his articles and letters in the *Aquarian Age*, the newspaper of his association, as the

---

2. Father Hurley was also called Prophet Hurley and, at least as a Holiness minister, Elder Hurley.

"founder of the largest Spiritual Association in the world." In one issue, it was claimed that the Universal Hagar's Spiritual Church had "about 185,000 members and about 95 churches" (*Aquarian Age,* June 1941), yet the directory of churches that the association published (and still publishes today) in its newspaper during the early 1940s indicates a considerably smaller number of congregations. At any rate, the association that Father Hurley had established twenty years earlier had grown from one temple to at least thirty-seven (eight in Michigan, eight in Ohio, six in Pennsylvania, seven in New Jersey, five in New York City, and single congregations in West Virginia, Delaware, and Illinois) on the eve of his death.

On June 23, 1943, Father Hurley "passed on to the spirit plane" as a result of a throat ailment following months of illness (*Aquarian Age,* Aug. 1943). His body lay in state for two days and nights at the "Supreme Temple" on Napoleon Street in Detroit as his followers and admirers came to wish him farewell. A procession of almost ninety automobiles, including three flower cars, accompanied his body to its final interment in the Detroit Memorial Cemetery.

Father Hurley had created an intricate cosmology and an elaborate politico-religious organization. While the founder served as the spiritual head of the Universal Hagar's Spiritual Church, Rev. Thomas Surbadger functioned for many years in the capacity of Supreme Prince. The Supreme Prince also serves as the business manager of the church and the president of the Wiseman Board, the executive body of the association. (Since many women have served on the board, sometimes constituting the majority of its members, a standard joke in the Hagar's Church is the proposal that it should be called the "Wisewoman Board.") The Wiseman Board consists of seven regular members and two alternate members drawn from among the state or district Princesses and Princes of the association. At the death or retirement of the president, the board members elect a new chief executive officer. Other officers include the vice-president, the chairman of the finance committee, the president of devotional services, and the chief secretary. A Junior Wiseman Board, consisting of several younger aspiring members of the association, functions under the auspices of the senior board.

Sometime before his death, Father Hurley designated Prince Surbadger of Chicago as his "Successor." Following the death of Father Hurley, Surbadger assembled a conclave of the Wiseman Board on

June 30, 1943, announcing to the members that he had no desire to be the spiritual head of the association (*Aquarian Age*, Aug. 1943). Upon his nomination Mother C. B. Hurley, Father Hurley's widow, was elected the Successor or spiritual head of the Universal Hagar's Spiritual Church — a position that she occupied until her death on June 28, 1960. Since then no one has been elected to this office.

Prince Surbadger continued to serve as president of the Wiseman Board for the next twelve years. He had met Prophet Hurley in 1919 when they were both members of Triumph the Church (*Aquarian Age*, Aug. 1943). In addition to giving Hurley the highest office in the state of Michigan, Father Smith had designated Surbadger for the same ecclesiastical position in the state of Illinois. However, because of changes that occurred in the church after the death of Father Smith, Surbadger decided to resign from his office.

Between 1921 and 1928, Surbadger was out of touch with Prophet Hurley. He was residing in Evanston, Illinois, when he reestablished contact with Hurley and shortly thereafter joined the Universal Hagar's Spiritual Church. In addition to being a member or former member of ten Masonic organizations, including Prince Hall and Knights Templar lodges, Reverend Surbadger was the Most Royal Exalted Master of the Knights of the All Seeing Eye, an auxiliary of the church. After spending many years as the State Prince of Illinois and the Supreme Prince of the Association, Thomas Surbadger died on February 22, 1955. Rev. Ronnie Tatum, the Princess of Pennsylvania and the pastor of a Philadelphia church, was elected president by the members of the Wiseman Board and served in this capacity until her death.

Mother Mary Hatchett, known as the "Mary Magdalene of the New Age," succeeded Princess Tatum as president of the Wiseman Board in the early 1960s. Born in 1908, she completed her religious education at the Universal Hagar's Spiritual Seminary in Detroit and played an important role in the development of the church on the East Coast, becoming (*Aquarian Age*, March 1965) a member of the first Hagar's congregation in the state of New Jersey. In 1943, Reverend Hatchett was designated the pastor of the Hackensack, New Jersey, church. Under her leadership a new church building, seating about five hundred people, was completed in 1950. Mother Hatchett held a number of important offices in the politico-religious organization of the association, including those of State Princess of

New Jersey and the Royal Noble Mistress as well as Supreme Healer of the Knights of the All Seeing Eye. Despite her death in 1977, her memory lives on vividly in the minds of many Hurleyites, particularly in the New Jersey churches.

The long reign of Mother Hatchett as president of the Wiseman Board was followed by the short one of Prince Alfred Bailey, who died in 1980. Prince Bailey had previously served in other leadership positions of the association. During the late 1930s, while he was the pastor of the Atlantic City, New Jersey, church, he had been chairman of the finance committee of the Wiseman Board; and for many years, he was the pastor of the New York State Headquarters in Manhattan, the State Prince of New York, and the Most Exalted Master of the Knights of the All Seeing Eye.

The present president of the Wiseman Board is Rev. G. Latimer, a daughter of Father and Mother Hurley, who has served for many years as the pastor of the national headquarters church and as the State Princess of Michigan.

Table 3 presents a partial diagram of the politico-religious organization of the Universal Hagar's Spiritual Church. Auxiliary organizations exist at national, state or district, and local levels. Officers and auxiliaries assemble at the respective national and state/district meetings of the association.

Thanks to its esoteric orientation and emphasis on occult abilities, the Mediums' League is probably the most prestigious auxiliary in the association. Concerted study of several years in one or more branches of the School of Mediumship and Psychology is a prerequisite for advancement in the internal structure of the school as well as in the larger hierarchy of the association. The school, which is dedicated to the injunction "Man Know Thyself," attempts to develop the spiritual potential and abilities of its students. Father Hurley taught that the School of Mediumship and Psychology is a branch of the Great School of the Prophets, which Jesus attended during the eighteen years of his life that are not accounted for in the Bible.

Only Hurleyites who are invited to do so may attend one or more of the branches of the School of Mediumship and Psychology. They are taught skills in communicating with the spirit realm (including loved ones), "spiritual advising," "reading," and "counseling," and a wide array of other "secrets." Upon successful completion of the school's basic curriculum, the student becomes an "uncrowned me-

Table 3. Politico-Religious Organization of the U.H.S.A.

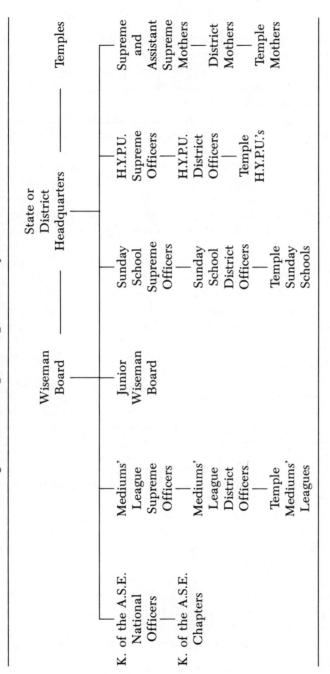

dium" and is given a "wand," bearing hieroglyphic inscriptions, which is used in certain rituals. Successful completion of the "master's" curriculum permits the graduate, now a "crowned medium" or "adept," to become a "spiritual advisor" or "reader." On special occasions, students and uncrowned mediums wear blue—caps for males and robes for females—symbolizing their "learning, prominence, spiritual power and development." Adepts, on the other hand, wear purple, indicating their level of mastery. Students and graduates are not permitted to discuss the specific content of lessons and activities occurring in the School. One Hagar's pastor told me that nothing "all that mysterious or unknown" is taught in the school. She confessed that she did not really understand the reason for its secretiveness but felt that she must abide by the policy of the association on this matter.

The Knights of the All Seeing Eye (K. of the A.S.E.) is a secret Masonlike auxiliary of the Universal Hagar's Spiritual Church. Unlike most Masonic organizations, which are sexually segregated, the K. of the A.S.E. is open to both men and women. The directory of its chapters in the *Aquarian Age* includes the following statement:

> The K. of the A.S.E. is a Mystical Benevolent Order that has been ushered in on the sands of time tracing the footprints of the Ancient Initiates and Brothers down through the ages. Each loyal member of the U.H.S.C. will become a member of this mystical society in order to promote the elevation of the race to a higher calling.
>
> Each chapter throughout the bounds of the organization meets on the 4th Tuesday night in each month.

The auxiliary currently has seventeen chapters in many of the cities where Hagar's temples are located. The Most Royal Exalted Master and the Royal Noble Mistress are the national heads of the K. of the A.S.E. Each chapter has an Exalted Knight (male or female) and an Exalted Scribe at its helm. On special occasions, members of the auxiliary wear a scarf, a fez, and an apron with a picture of the All Seeing Eye.

Many of the other auxiliaries in the association are very similar to those found in other churches in the Black community. The Hagar's Young People's Union (H.Y.P.U.) is a youth group. Each Hagar's congregation has — at least in theory— a deacons' board, a deaconesses' board, a mothers' board, a nurses' guild, an ushers' board, a choir, a Sunday School, a feast club, and a pastor's aid club. In addition, there are several organizations that appear to be unique to the Universal Hagar's Spiritual Church. One of these is the Sacred Sisters or U.H.S.A. Virgins. This sodality of girls, most of whom are between the ages of twelve and eighteen years, was established by Father Hurley "for the purpose of lifting the burdens from our race at home and abroad" (*Aquarian Age*, May 1939). Likened to Catholic nuns, the Sacred Sisters are to dedicate their lives to prayer. Consequently, they are not permitted to date boys or to have boyfriends. One pastor told me that although she remained a member of the Sacred Virgins until she was twenty-two years old, she did not find it difficult to obey the rules of the auxiliary because it kept her extremely busy with attendance at various church functions.

When Father Hurley created the office of Supreme Mother, it was occupied by his wife. Since then, other women have held this largely honorary position. The Assistant Supreme Mother serves in place of the Supreme Mother if she cannot be present at a particular event. Each district or state association also has a special Mother, as does each temple. The Temple Mother is in charge of the Altar Staff, a group of altar girls and altar boys who assist in various rituals during religious services. She, along with the deaconesses, is also responsible for the general housekeeping activities of the temple. Many Hagar's congregations also have a Temple Father, whose duties roughly parallel those of the Temple Mother.

It is difficult, if not impossible, to directly determine the changes in the membership of the Universal Hagar's Spiritual Church since it was established by Father George W. Hurley in 1923. According to several longtime members of the church, attendance at Hagar's religious activities was considerably higher during Father Hurley's lifetime. On the other hand, the death of Father Hurley did not result in a significant decline in the actual number of congregations in the association. Table 4 indicates the number and location of Hagar's congregations for selected years. Although there are fewer congregations in the association now than when Hurley died in 1943, for a period during the 1960s there were apparently a few more.

As is suggested by the data in Table 4 and as is the case for many other Spiritual groups, there has been considerable turnover in congregations in the Universal Hagar's Spiritual association. For example, whereas in 1950 there were five Hagar's congregations in

Table 4. Locations of U.H.S.C. Temples*

YEAR	STATE	CITIES
1938	Michigan	Detroit (5), River Rouge, Pontiac, Flint
	New Jersey	Jersey City, Hackensack, Passaic, Patterson, Atlantic City, Newark, Camden
	Pennsylvania	Philadelphia (2), Germantown, Pittsburgh (2), Aliquippa
(30)**	Ohio	Cleveland (3), Cincinnati, Columbus, Canton
	New York	Manhattan, Brooklyn
	Illinois	Chicago
1950	Michigan	Detroit (3), Ferndale, River Rouge, Pontiac, Flint
	New Jersey	Jersey City, Hackensack, Passaic, Patterson, Atlantic City, Newark, Montclair
	New York	Manhattan (5), Brooklyn
(34)	Pennsylvania	Philadelphia, Pittsburgh, Aliquippa, Beaver Falls
	Ohio	Cleveland (3), Cincinnati, Columbus, Canton, Massillon
	Illinois	Chicago
	Delaware	Wilmington
	W. Virginia	Charleston
1965	Michigan	Detroit (5), River Rouge, Pontiac, Flint
	New Jersey	Jersey City, Hackensack, Passaic, Patterson, Atlantic City, Newark, Montclair
	New York	Manhattan (2), Brooklyn (2), Queens (2), Bronx, Bayshore, Mt. Vernon
(41)	Pennsylvania	Philadelphia, Pittsburgh, Beaver Falls, Aliquippa
	Ohio	Cleveland (2), Cincinnati, Columbus, Massillon, Lima
	Indiana	Gary, Indianapolis
	Illinois	Chicago
	Delaware	Wilmington
	W. Virginia	Charleston
	S. Carolina	Charleston
	California	Los Angeles
1980	Michigan	Detroit (6), Pontiac, Flint
	New Jersey	Jersey City, East Orange, Hackensack, Passaic, Patterson, Atlantic City, Montclair
	New York	Manhattan, Brooklyn, Queens, Bronx
	Pennsylvania	Philadelphia (2), Aliquippa, Beaver Falls
(35)	Ohio	Cleveland (3), Columbus, Lima
	Indiana	Gary, Indianapolis
	Illinois	Chicago
	S. Carolina	Charleston
	California	Los Angeles
	Connecticut	Stamford
	Florida	Jacksonville

*Based on information derived from church directories published in *Aquarian Age*.
**Total congregations for the year.

Manhattan alone, by 1980 this number had declined to a single congregation. It may be that the Hagar's churches followed the demographic shifts of New York's Black population from Manhattan, particularly Harlem, to the other boroughs of the city and some outlying areas. Following a somewhat different pattern, the number of Hagar's congregations in Detroit proper has varied from five in 1938 to three in 1950, back up to five in 1965, and to an apparent high of six in 1980. Although some have endured for several decades, others have come and gone.

Over the years, the heaviest concentrations of Hagar's churches have been in southeastern Michigan — the location of the association's headquarters — and the New York–New Jersey megalopolis. Ohio and Pennsylvania have also had a fair number of congregations, but these have been more widely scattered over various population centers. It is interesting to note that throughout its history the Universal Hagar's Spiritual Church has had perhaps no more than two and often only one congregation in Chicago. This is particularly ironic in light of the fact that Chicago has been the center of the Black Spiritual movement at least since the 1930s. By contrast, the Metropolitan Spiritual Churches of Christ, in the bulletin of that association's 53rd annual congress in 1978, listed sixteen congregations in the metropolitan Detroit area and another eleven in other parts of southern Michigan, including several in small towns.

Since the early 1960s, the Universal Hagar's Spiritual association has experienced not only fluctuations in the number of its congregations but also a pattern of geographical diffusion, particularly to California and into the Southeast. While Father Hurley's church appears to have passed its zenith, it continues to thrive in various parts of the country. In a sense, the demographic shifts that I have been able to infer from the meager data may be a fair reflection of similar trends in the Black Spiritual movement as a whole.

Father Hurley's Message to the "Ethiopian" People

Like other Spiritual groups, the Universal Hagar's Spiritual Church contains aspects of Spiritualism, Catholicism, Protestantism, and possibly Voodooism or hoodoo. Father Hurley also incorporated concepts from the *Aquarian Gospel of Jesus Christ*, astrology, messianic nationalism, and other belief systems. The *Aquarian Gospel*, which was first published in 1907 by Eva S. Dowling and Levi Dowling, is the purported account of the life of Jesus between his early childhood and his ministry as they are related in the New Testament. It is a popular source in various Spiritualist and other occult circles in the larger society. Father Hurley frequently quoted from the *Aquarian Gospel* in his writings, and some Hurleyites still read this book and refer to it in sermons and other talks.

Evidently, sometime around 1933 if not earlier, Father Hurley began to teach his followers that his "carnal flesh" had been "transformed into the flesh of Christ" (*Aquarian Age*, Sept. 1939). Elsewhere, he identified himself as the "black God of this Age" and the "Christ, the God, the Saviour, the Protector of this seven thousand year reign of the Aquarian Age" (*Aquarian Age*, Oct. 1938; Sept. 1939). Father Hurley claimed that the Holy Spirit called upon him at the age of thirteen years to fast for forty days (just as God had asked Jesus to do), eating only one graham cracker and one glass of milk daily (*Aquarian Age*, Feb. 1975). At the end of the fast, God told him that the existing religions of the world were not congruent with His will. Instead, His doctrines as they were originally taught through Zoroaster, Brahma, Buddha, Mohammed, the major and minor prophets of the Old Testament period, and Jesus had been altered by "unbelievers" who created "segregation, hatred, jealousy, rape, robbery, murdering, and stealing." In order to reform the religions of the world, God told Father Hurley, the Spirit of God was dwelling within his body. The Spirit of God had at various times occupied the office of the Christ in the form of mortal men. Just as Adam had been the God of the Taurian Age, Abraham the God of the Arian Age, and Jesus the God of the Piscean Age, George W. Hurley, a Black man of humble birth in the deep South of racist America, was born to be the God of the Aquarian Age — a period of peace and social harmony.

Father Hurley, who claimed to have been a former member of the Mystical Brotherhood of India and a "man of Chokmah," did not deny the work of Jesus but maintained that his own work was to supersede it (*Aquarian Age*, Feb. 1975). Christ is the "wisdom and power of God love," rather than a person per se, and has been embedded in each of the gods of the various ages (*Aquarian Age*, Jan. 1948). Adam, who came into the world under the planet Venus and the sign of Taurus, was the Christ of the Taurian Age. During this time, however, the peoples of the earth became so wicked that God became displeased, placed them in the hands of the evil spirits, and allowed the world to be destroyed by a flood. Abraham became the Christ of the Arian Age, which was ushered in during the rule of Mars. It was during this period that the prophets of Israel lived. Jesus, who studied the works, teachings, and life of Buddha, was born in and became the Christ of the Piscean Age under the rule of the planet Jupiter (*Aquarian Age*, Oct. 1938). He attended school in Italy under his godfather Hillel, learned the Qabbalistic rules in Egypt, and traveled at the age of twenty-four years to visit the Three Wise Men in Persia (*Aquarian Age*, Jan. 1952). Mary was the Goddess of the Piscean Age (*Aquarian Age*, Oct. 1938).

The armistice ending World War I resulted in the passing of the Piscean Age and the ushering in of the Aquarian Age under the rule of the planet Saturn. Father Hurley claimed, "I was born to be the God of this Aquarian Age" (*Aquarian Age*, Oct. 1938), and Hurleyites are taught that Christ came into the world as "a thief and robber by night into a black body" (*Aquarian Age*, June 1941). Father Hurley was told that although minor prophets would be raised up to carry on his mission after his death, his would be the last gospel to be preached on the earth (*Aquarian Age*, Feb. 1975). The reign of Father Hurley as the God of the Aquarian Age is to last for 7,000 years, and "his name will be universal in the year 6953 A.D." (*Aquarian Age*, Feb. 1967). The Aquarian Age will mean the end of Protestantism and the "end of segregation and of big men over little men" (*Aquarian Age*, Dec. 1952).

Father Hurley taught his followers that the Spirit of God is embedded in each person. The Prophet wrote that as the "major God," he brought the "true light unto this age," and "ye believers in this true light are the minor gods and goddesses" (*Aquarian Age*, April 1939). In place of the traditional Christian concept of the afterlife, he taught that heaven and hell are "right here on earth within every man and woman"; the former is a state of "peace, joy, happiness and success which is satisfied mind on earth" (*Aquarian Age*, April 1940; Aug. 1934). In seeking salvation, Father Hurley urged his followers not to rely on the religion of the Protestant "Gentiles" but rather to develop their "innate forces, to think, to will, and to imagine" (*Aquarian Age*, April 1940).

Many of the themes in Father Hurley's teachings bear striking similarities, at least in substance, to those found in the beliefs of various Black messianic-nationalist sects, such as some of the Black Jewish groups and the Nation of Islam under the leadership of Wallace D. Fard and Elijah Muhammed. He argued that "the white race all over the world styles the name Nigger, Negress, Negritos, Negro as inferior" (*Aquarian Age*, April 1940). Therefore the term "Negro" must be eliminated from the dictionaries, eradicated by law, and replaced by "Black" or "Ethiopian." Father Hurley taught that Ethiopians were the first people in the world, the original Hebrew nation, God's chosen ones, the speakers of the original language of Arabic, the most industrious people on the earth, and the creators of civilization and hieroglyphics (*Aquarian Age*, Aug. 1934; Oct. 1938). The first religion was the Coptic Ethiopian religion. All the Old Testament patriarchs and prophets — including Adam, Abraham, Moses, Solomon, and Daniel — as well as Buddha, Jesus, and the Apostle Paul were Ethiopians. Jesus Christ, a descendant of the tribe of Judah, traveled back and forth from his motherland, Africa, to the European countries. Like Father Hurley, he taught the doctrine of "equal rights to all and special privileges to none" (*Aquarian Age*, April 1940).

Whereas Blacks were the first people, Whites are the offspring of Cain, who had been cursed with a pale color because of leprosy (*Aquarian Age*, Nov. 1938). Furthermore, according to an article that Father Hurley reportedly wrote in 1923, the "white people whom we call Jews" are an "inner mixture between the darker race and the white man" (*Aquarian Age*, June 1969). On the other hand, the "real Jew . . . is really a black man, copper colored or brown, and not the so-called white Jew of today." After the fall of the original Ethiopian race, it became the most downtrodden of all the races, while Whites received the secrets of God.

Father Hurley maintained that the White people organized their church, the Catholic Church, upon what they mistakenly believed were the principles of the "old Coptic spiritual church" (*Aquarian Age*, Dec. 1953), but actually upon the concepts written in a book entitled the *Great Work*, which discussed the findings of a Roman research society sent to discover the missing link of religion in Egypt hundreds of years ago. What the members of this society found was a "little crowd that was doing black art and witchcraft work," and they used these practices as the foundation of a new religion (*Aquarian Age*, Dec. 1953). The Catholics also derived "part of their worship and rules from Solomon's Temple handed down to King Mennlech the black King of Abyssinia" (*Aquarian Age*, July 1949). On the other hand, Jesus Christ, whom the Catholic Church claims as its founder, never organized a church per se. Instead of using the term "church," which was created by the White people, God used the term "temple" for a place of worship. (Despite this claim, Father Hurley referred to his organization as a "church.")

All the other religions of the world derived from the Catholic Church. Among those developed by the Whites were the "protestant or orthodox such as Methodist, Baptist, Presbyterian, Catholic White Horse Riders, Sanctified or Holiness, Triumph Spiritualist who believe in a downward burning hell, Christian Science and Seventh Day Adventists and other white men's religions too numerous to mention" (*Aquarian Age*, Aug. 1934). It was Father Hurley's contention that Whites forced the Ethiopian people to join their churches during "slavery times and held up before us a white God, a white Jesus, white prophets and white prophetesses" (*Aquarian Age*, April 1940). He viewed the traditional Christian concepts of the afterlife as a means of oppressing Blacks with a pie-in-the-sky philosophy, and argued that "Christianity has caused segregation, jim-crowism, hatred and jealousy, covetousness and selfishness to exist throughout the world" (*Aquarian Age*, Feb. 1936). The Protestant religions among Blacks are a "farce," a White tool of propaganda devised to divide and conquer the Ethiopian people.

In an article entitled "Is the Hamitic Canaanite or Black Race Cursed?" Father Hurley gave the following answer:

> My black brothers and sisters, the protestant religion is the cause of you and I being in the shape we are in today. How could the true God be Baptist, Methodist, Presbyterian, Catholic, so-called Holiness, Sanctified, Jesus Only, Foot Wash, Fire-Baptized and many other creed names too numerous to mention? How could he be all of these creeds and how could he be any of them? Allow me to say it is fabulous. Is the Hamitic Canaanite or Black Race cursed? I should say not, not by the true God; but they have cursed themselves by their erroneous belief and their fake religion that was given unto them by the white man. . . .
>
> But my brothers and sisters of this black race, allow me to tell

you if you will serve God in spirit and truth, if you will know yourself, if you will do away with your protestant creed religion, if you
will call upon his spirit through your Lord God today, your burdens
will be lifted, your wounds will be healed, your sorrows will be
soothed. Ask of me anything through my father and I will give it unto
you. Thou shalt decree a thing and it shall be so. If anyone interferes
with any one of my little ones they just as well be cast in the depths
of the sea with a millstone about their neck. (*Aquarian Age*, Nov. 1939)

Although Father Hurley emphasized "his people" in his work, a
prominent member of the Universal Hagar's Spiritual Church told
me that the message was not intended exclusively for the Ethiopians, but for all of the peoples of the earth. The founder lamented
that most Black Protestant preachers do not realize that they and
their followers are the "real Jews" (*Aquarian Age*, July 1949). He
urged that Ethiopians must give up Protestantism and asserted that
Whites themselves must also "give up the propaganda of Luther,
John Wesley and Roger Williams" (*Aquarian Age*, Dec. 1952).

In contrast to the seemingly apolitical posture of many Spiritual
groups, Father Hurley took unequivocal stands on a number of political issues, particularly the status of Blacks in American society.
At times his writings suggest that the Aquarian Age will eventually
be one of Black dominance. For example, in an article entitled "Ret-
ribution," he stated that the "black man at one time reigned supreme
and he is bound to reign again" (*Aquarian Age*, June 1942). A more
prevalent theme in his writings is the notion that the Aquarian Age
will be a period of social equality and tranquility. However, Father
Hurley warned of the consequences of his wrath if the demands of
the Ethiopians for justice were not met: "I, the God of this age have
all power in heaven and within earth within my hands and I shall
bring destruction on the earth all over the world until we righteous
black men and women whom are serving God in spirit and in truth
are reasoned with. We as black men and women must be called in
council by the white heads of each government and given a place
in the sun" (*Aquarian Age*, April 1939).

Although he was a virulent critic of racism, Father Hurley rejected the idea of intermarriage between Blacks and Whites (as did
Marcus Garvey). What he wanted was for Black Americans to obtain an equal share in the American Dream; he never rejected the
American political economy. Father Hurley was a strong supporter

of President Franklin D. Roosevelt, whom he regarded as a great humanitarian — one "capable of fair judgment to all mankind, regardless of nationality, creed, or color" (*Aquarian Age*, Aug. 1940). He urged that his followers vote for Roosevelt during the presidential campaign of 1940 and may have done so in earlier campaigns. Following Roosevelt's reelection Father Hurley wrote, "We know what Franklin D. Roosevelt has done in the behalf of the black race, regardless to whether the insignificant, ignorant black man will give him credit or not. He has done much for the black men of the United States. He has taken them out of the bread line, and put many of them in better houses in which to live and has saved quite a few of the black men's farms. What has Mr. Wilkie done? Not one thing. He has only talked" (*Aquarian Age*, Dec. 1940). During the first year of World War II, he pledged the political loyalty of his followers to the United States government, writing "We are with and behind Uncle Sam one hundred percent" (*Aquarian Age*, Aug. 1942). He referred to the United States as "our home" and pledged the willingness of his followers to fight in the war.

Since Father Hurley's death the strongly nationalist and critical rhetoric of his church has been not eradicated, but considerably tempered. While he often cried out against the oppression of Blacks and the racism of America, the writings and sermons of those who assumed his mantle of leadership, including Mother Hurley and Prince Surbadger, have tended to be more inspirational and less political in tone. Nevertheless, each issue of the *Aquarian Age* still generally carries one or more of the articles that Father Hurley wrote, undoubtedly serving as a reminder to Hurleyites that, as one prominent member of the Hagar's church commented to me, their God was indeed a "very radical man who felt our people were being kept under bondage."

The Ritual Remembrance of Father Hurley

Although Father George W. Hurley passed to the "spirit plane" on June 23, 1943, the presence of his spirit is still felt in the temples of the church that he established. At the present Supreme Temple of the association in Detroit, which is located in a church building vacated by a Lutheran congregation, one quickly becomes aware that this is not the typical Spiritual church. There are votive candles and incense burners, but crucifixes and images of Jesus, Mary, and the saints are nowhere to be seen. Instead, a six-foot statue of Father Hurley is situated behind the altar, representing him in a long white frock coat, white pants, and white shoes — a uniform that he often wore in real life. His left hand is raised and his right hand is placed upon his heart, a posture that Hurleyites characteristically assume in the recitation of many of their prayers. In addition, the niche high above the front portion of the sanctuary contains a large picture of Father Hurley. On the right side of the sanctuary, at the base of the raised sacred inner area, four metal posts connected with a rope guard a large picture of Mother Hurley. Although most Hagar's temples are not as elaborate as the Supreme Temple, one will always find some image of Father Hurley, and of Mother Hurley as well, generally placed upon the altar or before a stand of votive candles. Members of the Universal Hagar's Spiritual Church direct their prayers, petitions for help and guidance, and hymns to Father Hurley, their Black God, as well as to his spouse and the other "patriarchs," "prophets," and "prophetesses" of the association who are now in the spirit world.

What follows is a composite description of a religious service in each of two different Hagar's temples, which I will refer to simply as Temples A and B in order to ensure their anonymity. (Temples in a state or district of the association are generally numbered. Since some congregations have been disbanded, there are usually missing numbers in the sequence for any particular region. At the present time, for example, the temples in the state of Michigan are numbered 1, 3, 5, 6, 9, 10, 12, and 16. Although old numbers may be reassigned periodically in order to establish an unbroken sequence, years generally pass before this is done.) Temples A and B represent approximate ends on a continuum of congregations in the Universal Hagar's Spiritual association, in terms of both size and ritual orientation. Temple A is located in a modest church building capable of holding two hundred or more people comfortably. Some fifty or sixty individuals generally attend its Sunday morning services. Temple B, a "storefront" type of church, has a sanctuary which could probably seat about eighty people. Normally, fifteen to twenty-five individuals are present at its services. Temple A can be described as "high church"; Temple B as "low church." In fact, the pastor of

Temple B, Reverend Bloch (again a pseudonym, as are all the names associated with these two temples), suggested that dichotomy to me when she noted that services at Temple A are "more Catholic" than those at her church, which she described as being "more plain."

SUNDAY MORNING SERVICE AT TEMPLE A

Temple A has an elaborate altar, with a large black and white silhouette of Father Hurley and medium-sized pictures of Mother Hurley, Rev. G. Latimer, and a deceased prophet. In addition to a large red candle holder, alternating rows of white and yellow candles adorn the altar. On the right side of the sanctuary, just below the sacred inner space, there are two votive candle stands, one of which holds a picture of Father Hurley and the other a picture of Mother Hurley. A small choir section is situated on the right side of the sacred inner space.

The Beginning of the Service. Deacon Roberts (also sometimes addressed as Professor because of his position as a teacher in the School of Mediumship and Psychology) starts the service with several hymns. In one of these the congregation sings, "Hurley is on the mainline. Hurley is what you want. . . . If you want spiritual power, Hurley is what you want. . . . Call him up. Tell him what you want." The hymns are followed by prayers addressed to Father Hurley, asking him for blessings.

The U.H.S.A. Kingdom Prayer. A deaconess leads the congregation in the Kingdom Prayer. The members of the congregation face the east, raising their left hands and placing their right hands on their hearts, and pray in the following words:

> O God, my enemies are coming into thine inheritance. . . . We, thy saints, are becoming a reproach to our neighbors, a scorn and derision to them that are about us. How long, O Yod, He, Vah, and Christ Hurley, will thou be angry with us? Shalt thy jealousy burn like fire? O Yod, He, Vah, Christ Hurley, power out thy wrath upon our enemies that have not known thee, and upon their wicked kingdoms that have not called upon thy name. Destroy them, O God. . . . Give us the good things of this life and blot out our transgressions, and we will praise thee daily in spirit and in truth. . . . I am creating for each an abundance of blessings of such as they stand in the need of.

The prayer is ended by making of the sign of the cross and saying the following words three times: "In the name of the Father, Son, and the Holy Spirit, through Christ Hurley, Amen."

The Processional. Following several more hymns, the church officers and altar staff march from the rear down the center aisle. First in line are two deacons and three deaconesses, followed by four altar boys and six altar girls, then Deacon Roberts, a visiting pastor, and Reverend Caufield, the pastor of the temple. The participants in the processional take their respective places in the sacred inner area. As the congregation exuberantly sings another hymn, a middle-aged woman in the rear shouts, runs into the center aisle, dances briefly, collapses into the arms of two nurses, and is assisted back to her pew.

The Meditation and Concentration Ritual. Deacon Robert announces that it is time for "our meditation and concentration service," which is performed in order to obtain the "thought of your desire." He notes that a two-dollar donation is required to light one of the "seven-day candles" on the main altar, which are dedicated to the memory of a "patriarch" of the association who died within the past year, and a 25¢ donation to light a "novena candle" at one of the votive candle stands. All the lights except for a few in the front are turned off. Although some people go to the main altar, most form two lines leading to the votive candle stands. Two deaconesses assist people in the lighting of the seven-day candles. Several members of the altar staff stand by the votive candle stands, repeating over and over again a prayer to Father Hurley, while two of them assist people in lighting the novena candles. As each person approaches the stands, he or she places money in a little box. Some people kneel, but most stand as they pray before the picture of Father Hurley or Mother Hurley. Most individuals who participate in the ritual end their prayer by making the sign of the cross three times. The altar staff, the deacons, the deaconesses, the visiting pastor, and the pastor are the last ones to light candles. This portion of the service lasts about thirty minutes.

The Offering. An altar girl goes from pew to pew collecting loose change from the congregation, while some members go to the front to make their offering. Meanwhile, Deacon Roberts leads more hymn singing. As the congregation starts a hymn entitled "Hurley Is the Light of the World," the deacon expresses his frustration with their restrained performance and says, "Wait a minute. I believe in doing things right. Let's get in tune."

Sermon. Deacon Roberts says, "I am blessed because I am still in the land of the living. I realize what Father Hurley means for me. We don't worship a man. We worship the Spirit." He then instructs the congregation to stand as a gesture of respect for their pastor, Reverend Caufield. After leading the congregation in the singing of a hymn, Reverend Caufield preaches to the congregation as follows:

> Heaven is nothing but a state of mind. Hell, they tell me, is a deplorable condition. Hell is when you have no money in your pocket. Hurley gives us many promises. Hurley gave us everything. Hurley gave us something worth more than pearls and diamonds. When Hurley came, he freed our minds. Freedom comes from within. Freedom is not where you come from or how much money you have. . . . Keep your minds free from the yoke of bondage. As man thinketh, so he is. . . . Jesus said that a comforter would come. That comforter was Hurley. He could have gone to the rich, not us. But he came to the meek and the lonely. . . . Death is nothing but change. We die daily. We are the very expression of God. God has to have a body. We are that body.

After the sermon, Deacon Roberts comments, "We as a Black race were not ready to accept a doctrine like Spiritualism. We were taught to be afraid of the spirits. Every 2,001 years a new Savior is born. This dispensation will last seven thousand years."

The Healing Ritual. After "opening the doors of the church," Reverend Caufield asks the congregation, "Is there anyone who is sick or desires a prayer?" She instructs those in need of prayer to write down their petitions on slips of paper. A deaconess collects the petitions and gives them to the pastor. Reverend Caufield notes that Professor Layton, the organist, is in the hospital and asks the congregation to "place our thoughts on him." Referring to a deceased patriarch of the association, she adds that "Prince _____ can help all things." Several people form a line in the front in order to be healed. Only the "saints," the actual members of the Universal Hagar's Spiritual Church, are to stand during the healing ritual.

A middle-aged woman with a pronounced limp comes first. Reverend Caufield stretches out her hands and claps them several times.

She then instructs the woman to walk up and down the aisle. Since it appears that the woman's gait has improved, the pastor tells the woman to do the same thing three times. While the congregation applauds, the woman beams with joy as she takes her stroll. The pastor asks the woman how she feels now. When the woman indicates that she feels better, Reverend Caufield says to her, "You take one more walk down there fast." Again the congregation applauds in approval.

After Reverend Caufield heals several more individuals, she goes to the altar, raises her right hand with the petitions for blessings, and says a prayer, turning to each of the cardinal directions briefly. She then blesses two infants by laying her hand on them in turn.

Distribution of Candles. Following two hymns, Reverend Caufield announces that a memorial service marking the first anniversary of Prince _____'s death will begin the following Sunday night. She states that the Spirit has instructed her to give each person present a blue candle. She tells the congregation that they should meditate in silence while the candles burn and ask the Prince for a blessing. The congregation is cautioned not to blow out the candles, but rather to extinguish them with the fingers.

The Close of the Service. Deacon Robert makes several announcements, emphasizing that the Mediums' League will meet later that afternoon at 3:30. Reverend Caufield reports that a member of the temple who is residing in Texas has contributed $50 to the church. She suggests that visitors who would like to stay for dinner go upstairs, and requests that the saints remain in the sanctuary to discuss some church affairs. About half an hour later, the members join the nonmembers for dinner in the church hall.

SUNDAY MORNING SERVICE AT TEMPLE B

In contrast to Temple A, which has a busy schedule all week, the only regularly scheduled event at Temple B is the Sunday morning service. Several years ago, however, there was a regular Friday night service, and the School of Mediumship and Psychology still occasionally holds classes on Wednesday evenings. Reverend Bloch inherited the pastorship of Temple B from her older sister, who suffered a stroke several years ago and has not yet fully recovered. Saint Ansley, another sister of the pastor, functions as the healer of the temple and is in the process of developing her gift of prophecy. The three sisters were raised in South Carolina; their mother introduced them to the Universal Hagar's Spiritual Church shortly after they all moved to the North in the 1930s. Father Davis is the only adult male who regularly attends services at Temple B. He was raised in West Virginia and resided for years in Washington, D.C., and an eastern state before moving to this city in 1959. Because his apartment is almost adjacent to the temple, Father Davis is able to keep a close eye on the premises. Like him, many members of the congregation joined the temple as a result of their initial contact with Reverend Bloch, whom they had sought out for counseling.

The service begins with some hymn singing around 11:40 A.M. Reverend Bloch has made a resolution that she will start services as close to the scheduled hour as possible. Although only nine people are in the temple by this time, some dozen or so more souls will trickle in during the next hour. After a hymn, entitled "To Be like Hurley," Reverend Bloch complains, "They are late as usual. One day the Spirit will wake them to the need to be on time." She welcomes Saint Ford to the service, noting that she has returned to the city after living for several years in another community. Upon being asked to say something to the congregation, Saint Ford first reads a passage from the *Aquarian Gospel of Jesus Christ*. She briefly discusses death as a "transition" to a better life, not in a nebulous heaven but back on earth.

Father Davis asks whether anyone would like to testify. After several brief testimonies, Saint Shaw fervently makes the following remarks on the meaning of Father Hurley in her life: "Before I came into the truth, I was in a state of confusion. On my job, I am being taught what the Christ-force is. At times I call on Father Hurley. I am not afraid to admit that I belong to Universal Hagar's Spiritual Church which I tell people was founded by Prophet George W. Hurley, the Christ of the Aquarian Age."

After the testimony session, the congregation sings several hymns. Saint Shaw, who apparently is still moved by her own testimony, goes into a trance and dances in the open area at the front. Several times she exclaims, "Oh yes. Oh yes. Oh thank you, Father Hurley."

Several rituals follow: consecration and meditation before an image of Father Hurley; recitation of the Kingdom Prayer; and the healing, conducted by Saint Ansley. Eventually, Reverend Bloch comes to the pulpit to deliver her sermon, which includes the following remarks:

> The whole nation is going into mourning for one soul [John Lennon]. They will take ten minutes to pray for one soul all over the world. He has donated music to the world. Get your soul right with God before you die. No one can go to God for you. They are making a man seem like God. He does not have that much going for him in the spiritual sense. . . .
>
> Man has let his morals lower to such a degree. Soap operas are filled with fornication. There is very little respect in the family today. The man is looking for his extra woman. The woman is looking for her extra man. The churches are empty because the ministers do not know how to preach. . . . Be proud that you are living a clean life. The science of psychology teaches that every thought expresses itself in a bodily act. If you lay down with dogs, you will get up with fleas. You must fight every impure thought the instant it occurs. . . .
>
> Lots of people think Spiritualism is hoodoo, Voodoo, or you-do. Spiritualism is the highest religion. When I tell people that I am a member of the Universal Hagar's Spiritual Church, I get a double take from them. How little we get to know about true Spiritualism. Spiritualism has given freedom to slaves and has broken the bonds of mental bondage. It was instrumental in the larger emancipation of women. There are many places where a woman may not grace the pulpit. . . . It has taken the sting of death. Death is only a change. When I say you are Spiritual, stand proud. Stick out your chest.

After the sermon, Reverend Bloch asks Evangelist Abbott, the "State Evangelist" who visits temples in the state and elsewhere, to "open the doors of the church." Evangelist Abbott is a man in his early seventies and is well known for his knowledge of the "secrets" of the ancients as well as astrology. Despite his advanced age, he is a dynamic man who apparently still has a knack for bringing members into the Hurleyite faith. Abbott notes that he has been a Hurleyite for almost fifty years and adds, "The only way you can learn Spiritualism is to come in. So we extend you a hand." He warmly embraces a middle-aged woman who comes forward to join the temple. The congregation applauds. Evangelist Abbott, noting a conference between a mother and her son, remarks, "The mother and son are talking over there." The young man finally steps forward and takes a chair facing the congregation. Evangelist Abbott gives the mother some time to come forth also; her failing to do so results in a gentle reproach: "You as a mother have been stumbling a long time. What you need to do is to obtain enlightenment. You keep on coming. Don't let no one force you to come in." The two members are voted into the church. As the congregation comes forward to shake their hands, Reverend Bloch kisses and hugs the woman.

Next, the pastor asks Evangelist Abbott to speak to the congregation. In addition to his discussion of how the religion of the great teachers of history, including Socrates, originally came from Africa, his remarks include a reference to the mysterious slayings of Black children in Atlanta: "The great confusion in Atlanta is not your portion. The toe of this great body is in Atlanta. Don't worry about it. Racial hatred is as old as time. Here in _____ it is just as bad. It is just camouflaged. It is going to get worse. We are part of the great body."

The service ends with an offering, in which nearly $95 is collected, and a prayer to Father Hurley.

RITUAL EVENTS IN HONOR OF FATHER AND MOTHER HURLEY

Father Hurley taught his followers that the celebration of Christmas time in December was instituted hundreds of years ago by Whites (*Aquarian Age*, April 1940). In place of this event, the Spirit instructed him to create another Christmas for the Ethiopian people and to name it "Hurley's Feast." The first Hurley's Feast celebration occurred in 1934 and is repeated every year between February 11 and February 17 (*Aquarian Age*, Feb. 1936). During this time, Hurleyites erect "feast trees" in their homes and temples and load them with gifts for one another, send Hurley's Feast cards to friends and acquaintances, and greet each other with expressions such as "Happy Hurley's Feast" or "Merry Hurley's Feast." The climax of the week-long celebration comes on February 17, the day on which the Prophet Hurley was born. On this day, Hurleyites are to assemble at 6:00 A.M. for a "sunrise prayer session" to commemorate the birth of their God in 1884 to a humble Black family in the racist climate of the post-Civil War South. At 7:00 A.M. — the hour of Father Hurley's birth — all Hurleyites are to "go down on our knees" and meditate on the significance of this momentous event. Each member of the church should make a concerted effort to take the day off from work and remain at a Hagar's temple during the course of the day in order to celebrate Hurley's Feast with other saints. February 17 is meant to be a day of joy and relaxation, filled with banquets, the exchange of gifts, socializing, playing cards, or other forms of pleasure.

The Hurleyite New Year occurs a week after the birthday of Father Hurley and is called the Dawn of New Progression. Between 11:00 P.M. on February 23 and 1:00 A.M. on February 24, members of the Universal Hagar's Spiritual Church conduct a "watch meeting" service to see the end of the old Dawn and the beginning of the new Dawn.

The celebration of Hurley's Feast and the Dawn of New Progression varies considerably from temple to temple. Some members give Hurley's Feast breakfasts and dinners in their homes during the week of February 11–17. I had the privilege of celebrating Father Hurley's birthday on February 17 with the members of Temple B. After the morning service, we adjourned to a back room of the temple to eat a potluck breakfast of beef sausage, eggs, rolls, and herbal tea. Saint Ansley also served us pineapple juice, noting that this was Father Hurley's favorite beverage and that we should make a wish before drinking it. The saints talked about all sorts of things and even gossiped a little about other Hurleyites. Reverend Bloch indicated her disapproval of the pastor's tuxedo and the choir's pink robes at another pastor's recent anniversary that several of us had attended. She believes that such attire is too "materialistic," and distracts Hurleyites from spiritual matters. It was pointed out that there are four standard colors in the Universal Hagar's Spiritual Church: black and white for ministers, purple for the crowned mediums, blue for the uncrowned mediums, and white for the saints. If black and white were good enough for Father Hurley, why should they not be good enough for others? On the occasion of his anniversary, the pastor should have worn a white robe instead of a fancy tuxedo.

Since some members of Temple B had to leave for work immediately after the service, they were unable to enjoy the socializing of the day. However, it was hoped that they would be able to attend the Hurley's Feast dinner being held at Saint Shaw's home that evening.

In addition to Hurley's Feast and the Dawn of New Progression, a seven-day Memorial Service each year commemorates the passages of Father Hurley and Mother Hurley to the spirit plane. The first Sunday in June is Homegathering, celebrating Mother Hurley's return from her trip to Europe. Mother's Day in May is also dedicated to the honor of Mother Hurley, whom one Hurleyite referred to as the "greatest mother who ever lived."

Following the regular Sunday morning service that I attended one Mother's Day, a bless service was conducted. For a five-dollar donation, individuals could obtain a "blessing" from Mother Hurley. During the service, a large picture of Mother Hurley was placed on a "throne" covered with a white sheet that symbolized the "hem of Mother Hurley's garment." Each person receiving a blessing kneeled before the picture and held the cloth in both hands while asking Mother Hurley for a favor. The ritual was ended by making the sign of the cross three times. According to the pastor of the temple, Hurleyites feel the same way about Mother Hurley as some people feel about Mary, the mother of Jesus.

RITUAL PROSCRIPTIONS AND PRAYERS

Social scientists have frequently commented upon the tendency of various ethnic, religious, and social groups to use boundary maintenance mechanisms in order to differentiate themselves from others in the larger society. These include adherence to peculiar normative patterns and proscriptions, wearing distinctive styles of clothing, and grooming in a particular fashion. In the Father Hurley sect, some of these practices bear a strong resemblance to those found among messianic-nationalist groups in the Black community. Unlike many other Spiritual associations, which tend to be rather loose in delineating their formal beliefs, the Universal Hagar's Spiritual Church explicitly states them in a creed that lists twenty-eight specific points of doctrine. The association also has its own version of the Ten Commandments:

1. Thou shall believe in Spirit (God) within matter.
2. Thou shall ignore a sky heaven for happiness and a downward hell for human punishment.
3. Thou shall believe in heaven and hell here on earth.
4. Thou shall believe in the fatherhood of God and the brotherhood of man.

5. Thou shall believe in what you sow, you shall also reap.
6. Thou shall believe that the Ethiopians and all Nations will rule the world in righteousness.
7. Thou shall believe that the Universal Hagar's Spiritual Church was revealed to Father G. W. Hurley for the blessing of all nations that believe in him.
8. Thou shall not pray for God to bless your enemies.
9. Thou shall ask God to give you power to overcome them.
10. Thou shall believe that our relatives and friends, whose spirits have departed from the body, is within our own bodies to help us overcome all difficulties in life.

Clearly, the Hagar's Ten Commandments are a supplementary statement of dogma rather than a listing of mores.

Although Hurleyites do not wear a distinctive type of clothing in everyday life, as do certain Black Islamic and Black Judaic groups, they do — like the latter — observe certain strict dietary prohibitions. Included among these are abstinence from pork products, regular teas, coffee, and tobacco. On the other hand, the consumption of alcoholic beverages, which are sometimes served at church banquets, is permissible in moderation. Hurleyites also drink a variety of herbal teas, including a special blend called "Father Hurley tea." In a sermon to her congregation, one Hagar pastor made the following comments about the merits of fasting and proper eating habits:

Fasting is as old as humanity. Men and women found deliverance from fasting and praying together. They will heal the sick, will cause the lame to walk, the dumb to speak. If your blessings have not been fulfilled this week, go on another fast. Jesus fasted for forty days and nights. . . .
There is a lot of toxic waste in us. That poison gets through the system and causes all kinds of diseases. Fasting helps to eliminate those poisons. . . . Many foods are chemically treated. Those chemicals stay behind. I thank God for Father Hurley. He saw that it was necessary to rest our stomach and bodies. So we fast on Fridays or we are supposed to. . . . The foods that we eat have a vibratory side. Sometimes we get into a fit of depression because we are eating foods on a low level. Muhammed wrote a book, *You Are What You Eat.* . . . Fruits and sun-ripened foods are on a higher level of vibration. Leafy vegetables and nuts constitute foods on the second scale. Dairy products and fleshy foods are on the lowest scale. . . . Too many pork chops will send you into a fit of depression. The pig will eat anything. Fa-

ther Hurley took us off of pork. Chemicals, pills, tranquilizers. Hmm,
hmm. You may think that you are flying high, but you are flying low.
Take cigarettes out of your mouth. . . .

As the Muslims enjoin that a believer should pray to Allah five
times a day, Father Hurley instructed his followers to "call my name
seven times a day." Over the years, he and other Hurleyites prepared
a large number of prayers that the saints are to direct as frequently
as possible to their Savior. The following prayer, for example, was
to be recited seven times each day—four times at 7:00 A.M. and three
times at 7:00 P.M.: "Saint Hurley is my Lord and the Christ, within
him is my Savior and my helper each day in every way. I feel the
Christ within Saint Hurley's body. Through Saint Hurley the Christ
I am headed for success, financially and industrially, and I am now
happy through Christ alone. Amen. Amen. Amen" (*Aquarian Age*,
Aug. 1934).

Every three months, the association publishes a meditation leaf-
let, which may be obtained for a donation of two dollars. The leaf-
lets deal with a wide variety of topics, such as a "new life," "confidence," and "love," and they include prayers for the various weeks
of the three-month period covered. On the last page of each book-
let, the reader will always find the following reminder, composed
by Father Hurley in 1929: "Ethiopians awake and see yourself coming into the glorious light of the Sun. Prosperity is howling every
day, will you accept it, for it will be peace, joy and health to the
soul. 'Think for your self then you will Create what you think.'"

For those with an "astrological perspective," Father Hurley published monthly "dream and success charts" (*Aquarian Age*, Oct.
1938).[3] The pastor of a Hagar's temple in New Jersey is involved in
keeping an emphasis on astrology alive today by offering classes on
this subject.

3. Hurleyites often asked my zodiac sign.

CHAPTER 4

Religious Syncretism
in the Spiritual Movement

SCHOLARS have discussed at some length the process of syncretism among a number of Afro-American religions in the Caribbean and in South America, such as Haitian Voodooism and
the variety of cultic groups found in Brazil (Herskovits 1941; Metraux
1972; Leacock and Leacock 1975; G. Simpson 1978). Relatively little attention has been focused on this phenomenon among Afro-
American sects in the United States. The Black Spiritual movement,
which has incorporated elements from a diversity of religious traditions, is a superb example of syncretism. Bourguignon (1970:142) indirectly supports my contention by noting that Afro-American cults
from Louisiana were greatly influenced by both Protestantism and
Spiritualism. Although all religious systems in complex societies and
probably many in preliterate societies are to some degree syncretistic, this pattern is much easier to detect in the Spiritual movement
than in many older religious traditions because of the movement's
relative newness.

Spiritual churches probably represent the most explicit and rich-
est examples of this process among religious groups in the Black
American community. For one thing, there is a pattern of great flexibility in beliefs and practices in the movement as a whole, even
among those groups that publish manuals and formal creeds in an
attempt to make their doctrines fairly explicit. The manner in which
elements from various religious traditions are combined depends
largely on the perspective of the local pastor and some of his or her
lieutenants. A local pastor may choose to deviate from the beliefs
and practices of other congregations in the same association, or a
member of a particular congregation may interpret various theological matters in a different manner from the others in the same

church. Although these deviations may be viewed negatively, sanctions against them are seldom invoked. It is not uncommon for the leader or a member of a particular Spiritual church to criticize the beliefs or practices of other Spiritual congregations while at the same time engaging in a pattern of visiting the objects of scorn. In fact, the pastor of one Nashville Spiritual church noted that he visits other area churches whose practices are contrary to his because it provides him with an opportunity to preach the "truth." As this chapter will demonstrate, religious syncretism in the Spiritual movement is a dynamic process susceptible to a number of structural, cultural, and psychological factors, such as the social composition of the local congregation, the prevailing religious patterns of the Black churches in its geographical area, and the predilections of the founder or a prominent leader of a particular church or association.

Although I intend to present the most extensive discussion yet published of the syncretistic nature of the Spiritual movement, I am by no means the first person to comment on this subject. In her early work on "hoodoo" in New Orleans, Hurston (1931:318–19) noted that "spiritualism" often provides a protective screen for the "hoodoo doctor" and his or her congregation. On the other hand, she adds, not all "spiritualistic" congregations practice "hoodoo." Hurston also recognizes the presence of Catholic elements when she states that "hoodoo worship in New Orleans makes use of the altar, candles, incense, holy water, and bless oil of the Catholic Church." As is indicated in the following passage, folklorist Robert Tallant (1946: 174–75) viewed the Spiritual religion in New Orleans as a syncretism of Spiritualism, Catholicism, Protestantism, and Voodooism:

> Nearly all these spiritualist churches have statues of Black Hawk among the images of bona fide saints, for the churches are odd conglomerations of many sects. Most of them exhibit Roman Catholic statues and candles, and use incense and holy water. They sing Baptist and Methodist hymns, and the congregation "testifies" and suffers attacks of the "jumps" and the "jerks," such as are common to all cults of the revivalist type. The "Mothers" heal by prayer and the laying on of hands, hold spiritualist séances, and sometimes tell fortunes as a side line. And though they all deny it, they sometimes do business in *gris-gris*.[1]

1. *Gris-gris* refers to a variety of powders, oils, and other potions that are used in Voodoo and hoodoo rituals.

In their description of the "Spiritualist denomination" in Bronzeville, Drake and Cayton (1945:642) note that "it borrows its hymns
from the Baptists and Methodists and appropriates altar, candles,
and statues from the Catholics." More recently, Washington (1973:
112–13) has pointed out the elements of Spiritualism, Voodooism,
Catholicism, and Protestantism (particularly from the Baptist,
Methodist, Holiness, and Pentecostal groups) in the Black "Spiritualist cults."

According to one anthropologist, "syncretism may be characteristic of a system whether or not those who participate in it are aware
of the history of their institutions" (Edmonson 1960:192). While, as
this statement implies, syncretism is in large part an unconscious
process, many Spiritual people are cognizant, at least to a degree,
of the syncretistic nature of their religion. Reverend Brown noted
that his large Indianapolis congregation feels a common bond with
the Catholic Church (which he referred to as a "holy, universal
church") and acknowledged that it has borrowed elements from the
Pentecostalists, who "tarry," and the Methodists, who "meditate."
A prominent member of St. Cecilia's Divine Healing Church No. 2
in Nashville maintained that her church has incorporated aspects
of both Catholicism and Christian Science.

Reverend Gibson, the pastor of a now defunct Spiritual church
in Nashville, while stressing the origins of all churches from Catholicism and acknowledging the similarities between it and the Spiritual movement, stated that the Spiritual groups have incorporated
the "leftovers of the other churches." The pastor of a congregation
in the Universal Hagar's Spiritual Church noted that services in another Hagar's congregation in New York City were more "Catholic" in their content than hers, which were plainer and simpler.

Despite my informants' acknowledgement that their movement
shares certain elements with Catholicism, Protestantism, and even
Spiritualism, however, there is a uniform pattern of denying the influence of Voodooism or hoodoo. They may accuse other churches
in the Spiritual movement, but none of my informants admitted the
existence in their own congregations or associations of Voodoo and
hoodoo; they are associated with "witchcraft or evil," and the "black
arts."

To a large degree, the Spiritual religion is distinguished from other
religious groups in the Black community by its highly syncretistic

nature. While there is a considerable degree of heterogeneity within the Spiritual movement itself, essentially it combines elements from Spiritualism, Catholicism, Black Protestantism, and Voodooism and hoodoo — each of which is discussed below. Specific associations, congregations, and even individuals may also add elements from other esoteric systems, including New Thought, Christian Science, Islam, Judaism, and astrology, to this basic core. Some groups — such as the Universal Hagar's Spiritual Church, and Spiritual Israel Church and Its Army — have adopted aspects of Black messianic nationalism.

Although for comparative and analytical purposes I prefer to view Black Spiritual groups as sects rather than cults, it may be argued that they are part of what C. Campbell (1972:122–23) terms the "cultic milieu" — a cultural underground that includes various deviant belief systems, such as unorthodox science, alien and heretical religion, and fringe medicine: "Substantively, it includes the worlds of the occult and the magical, of spiritualism and psychic phenomena, of mysticism and new thought, of alien intelligences and lost civilizations, of faith healing and nature cure." The wide array of esoteric groups within the cultic milieu pride themselves on their flexibility and openness of belief and practices, and consequently feel free to borrow liberally from one another. In essence, since it seems there are a diversity of paths to "truth," or, perhaps better yet, to a multiplicity of "truths," the cultic milieu "tends to be ecumenical, super-ecclesiastical, syncretistic and tolerant in outlook." For the most part, these generalizations accurately characterize the Black Spiritual movement.

American Spiritualism and the Black Spiritual Movement

It appears that American Spiritualism served as the springboard for the present Black Spiritual movement. This is not to say that only a White version of Spiritualism is present among Black Americans today; rather, Blacks have taken Spiritualism and molded it to their own experience in America. In other words, the Spiritual movement per se cannot be viewed merely as a Black counterpart of White Spiritualism. Bearing in mind this caution, it is important to note that many similarities continue to exist between the two movements.

In arguing that the origins of modern Spiritualism can be dated with reliable accuracy to the year 1848, G. Nelson (1969:3) notes that "before that year there was no Spiritualism in the modern sense of the term. There were indeed many instances of the occurrence of the phenomena that later became distinctive of Spiritualism before 1848, for such phenomena . . . are a universal element in all human societies, and many groups and individuals throughout history have claimed the ability to communicate with the 'dead' or other spirits in civilized societies entirely based on a belief in, and the practice of, regular communication with the dead." The notion that "the dead can return to their living in spiritual visitations that are not necessarily ill-intended or dangerous" (Genovese 1974:217) is one among the Black beliefs of African origin that were prevalent in slavery times and continued to exist in both the rural South and the large cities. Thus, in the nineteenth century, there was a certain cultural readiness for Spiritualism among Black Americans.

It was not until the second decade of the twentieth century, however, that Black involvement began to take on an institutional form, particularly in the shape of organized congregations. In fact, historical data from New Orleans, Nashville, and Detroit suggest that there was a certain degree of racial integration among some of the forerunners of the present Black Spiritual movement (Hurston 1931; Lockley 1936; Melton 1978; Kaslow and Jacobs 1981), and my own observations indicate that even today some Whites are members of predominantly Black Spiritual churches. In addition, particularly in such places as New York City, Hispanics may be found as members of Spiritual churches. Even though a pattern of partial integration tends to be characteristic only of the larger congregations, it is important to note that there appears to be little, if any systematic effort to exclude Whites from Spiritual churches. On the contrary, my own experience suggests that Spiritual groups are generally quite receptive to the potential of White membership.

Perhaps the most explicit link between White Spiritualism and its development in the Black community is the National Colored Spiritualist Association. When the growing Black membership in the White-controlled National Spiritualist Association of Churches separated from its parent body and established the National Colored Spiritualist Association in 1922, the new organization made Detroit its headquarters (Melton 1978, II:98). In addition to several congregations in that area, this association has others in Chicago, Columbus, Miami, Charleston, St. Petersburg, Phoenix, and New York City. Melton states that the National Colored Spiritualist Association follows closely the doctrines and practices of its parent body, and in a study of Black churches in Chicago during the 1920s, Sutherland (1930:40) notes that worship and preaching in this group were subordinated to "readings and séances."

It appears that the term "Spiritualist" was contracted to "Spiritual" at some point in the evolution of the contemporary Black Spiritual Churches. In the case of Nashville, it is interesting to note that Redeeming Christian *Spiritualist* Church was renamed the House of Redemption *Spiritual* Church sometime in the 1930s (emphasis mine). Furthermore, the cornerstone of the building which was once occupied by St. Joseph's Spiritual Church in Nashville reads "St. Joseph's Spiritualist Church"; the newer title must have developed sometime during the actual existence of the church.

Although some Spiritual people today recognize a historical connection between their religion and mainstream Spiritualism, there is a strong tendency among them to view the latter in a cautious, even disparaging manner. Members of Spiritual churches generally reject the term "Spiritualist" in referring to themselves or their religion. They repeatedly emphasize that since God is a spirit, they worship him in "spirit and truth" and therefore are "Spiritual." Many Spiritual people—like others in both the Black and White communities—identify Spiritualism with communication with loved ones, séances, and fortune-telling. According to Bishop Rogers, the pastor of Resurrection Temple in Nashville, Spiritualism does not include an emphasis on the "Holy Spirit" and is essentially "Voodoo or hoodoo." He noted that Spiritualists "take some Spiritual work and use it for the wrong purpose" and that many of them are "money grabbers and peace breakers." Bishop Gilmore, the pastor of All Souls Christian Church No. 2, stated that "'Spiritualist' is a word that we have fought so hard." In her opinion, spiritualism deals chiefly with séances, whereas the "Spiritual way means life."

On the other hand, some Spiritual people are more receptive toward the Spiritualist movement in the larger society. The manual of the Greater Universal Spiritual Unity Union states that "Spiritualism is a science, a philosophy and a religion of continuous life." Reverend Wilson, the leading medium in the Sacred Heart Spiritual

Temple, makes no sharp distinction between the terms "Spiritual-ist" and "Spiritual." This may in part be related to his former af-filiation with a predominantly White Spiritualist congregation in Massachusetts and his continuing interest in mainstream Spiritual-ism. Folklorist Gilbert E. Cooley obtained the following interpreta-tion of the two terms in an interview with Rev. K. J., a renowned psychic in Gary, Indiana, who claims to be affiliated with the Metro-politan Spiritual Churches of Christ:

> When we talk about things which are of a divine nature, we speak of God as the spirit. When you start to approach that aspect of reli-gion, this is called "spiritual." There is a difference between "spiri-tual" and "spiritualist." The old songs of the followers are spiritual because they embody the certain movement of thought and a cer-tain belief that divine influence and help would come to those who were the persecuted, which is also alleged to in the Scripture.
>
> Now if you are a "spiritualist," it means that you believe that life does not terminate with the passing of an individual, of coming out of the body, as the expression goes. We believe that life continues after the change, which we call death and we maintain, as spiritualists, that those who are "out of the body" are able to communicate as spirits with those who are in the body. A spiritualist is one who believes in the part of his religious devotion, in the continuation of life, a com-munication with life. . . . (Cooley 1977b:209–10)

Elsewhere in the interview, Rev. K. J. speaks interchangeably of the "Spiritual Church" and the "Spiritualists Church." I also found that some members of the Universal Hagar's Spiritual Church refer to their group on occasion as "Spiritualist" and to their religion as "Spiritualism." But Hurleyites view their form of Spiritualism as the authentic one; they see other Spiritual *or* Spiritualist groups as per-versions or degenerate imitations.

Mainstream Spiritualism is characteristically associated with the séance. Although the séance seems to have been an important di-mension in at least some Spiritual or Spiritualist groups in the Black community at one time, it is only a minor aspect of the contempo-rary Black Spiritual movement. The manual of the Greater Spiri-tual Unity Union, the association with which the Temple of Spiri-tual Truth is affiliated, lists the séance as one of its "special spiritual services." My own observations of several congregations in this asso-ciation indicated that it is a rare occurrence among them. This is

not to say that Spiritual people deny the possibility of communication with loved ones in the spirit world. For example, the Universal
Ancient Ethiopian Spiritual Church of Christ, an association headquartered in Pittsburgh, teaches its members that the phenomenon
of "communication with the spirits of departed ones" is a possibility. The manual published by the small association established by
Reverend Arnold, the pastor of St. Cecilia's Divine Healing Churches
No. 1 and No. 2, states "We affirm that communication with the
so-called dead is a fact scientifically proven by the phenomena of
spiritualism." Among the various Spiritual churches that I am familiar with, it appears that the séance most frequently occurs in
certain congregations of the Universal Hagar's Spiritual Church. In
addition to believing that one may communicate through dreams
or visions with loved ones who have passed into the spiritual plane,
Hurleyites occasionally resort to a séance for making such contact.
Séances open to the general public occurred in several Hagar's temples during the course of my fieldwork with the Father Hurley sect
in New York. Although I did not attend any, one member told me
that one of the séances would be preceded by a service which was
scheduled to begin at 4:00 P.M. on a Sunday. Attendance required
the purchase of a five-dollar ticket. After the service, the congregation was to be broken up into several small groups, with a medium
assigned to each group. In addition to messages from friends and
relatives, messages from various patriarchs of the association were
anticipated.

While the séance is one form of communication with the spirit
world in mainstream Spiritualist circles, perhaps more important
in many groups is the message session that is conducted in a number of Spiritualist congregations as part of a religious service, either
on Sunday or during the week. On three occasions, when I visited
three separate White Spiritualist congregations (one in Lansing,
Michigan, and two in Jackson, Michigan), a message session occurred
during the regularly scheduled Sunday service. Each time, a medium gave messages from the spirit world to selected people in the
congregation. The manner in which the message was given resembled the approach followed during bless or prophecy services in Black
Spiritual churches. In both situations, the recipient of a message was
expected to assist the medium in the interpretation of its content.
It was the source of the messages that differed: in the White Spiri-

tualist congregations the messages purported to come from deceased relatives, friends, or acquaintances; in the Black Spiritual churches, the source was generally believed to be the Spirit.

Another resemblance between mainstream Spiritualism and the Black Spiritual movement is an emphasis on therapeutic activities (Fishman 1979; Good and Good 1980; Baer 1981a). Individual spiritual advising, counseling, and the healing of physical ailments are integral parts of both movements. (As will be noted later, however, spiritual advising and healing are also performed by various other types of folk therapists in the Black community.) Mediums in Spiritual churches often bitterly complain that they are confused with Spiritualists, both in the White and Black communities. Apparently some Spiritualist mediums and advisors overcome their tainted status by converting their practices into religious congregations. In his survey of Black churches in Chicago, Sutherland (1930:39) comments that Spiritualists "who seek to give dignity to their work change the letters on their windows to read 'Spiritualist Church.'"

According to Braden (1949:340), the concept of reincarnation is adhered to by a "minority left wing of Spiritualism." There is a similar tendency on the part of many Spiritual people to believe in reincarnation. Bishop F. Jones, the pastor of the Temple of Spiritual Truth, noted that this belief theoretically should be part and parcel of the doctrine of any Spiritual church, but although the notion of reincarnation is an explicit article of faith in some Spiritual groups (the Metropolitan Spiritual Churches of Christ and the Universal Ancient Ethiopian Spiritual Church of Christ, for example), in many instances acceptance or rejection of the idea is left to the discretion of individual members. Bishop Gilmore, the pastor of All Souls Christian Church No. 2 in Nashville, noted that she believes in reincarnation even though it is not an official teaching of her association.

Since Spiritual people tend to be quite eclectic and independent in forming their religious beliefs, it would be misleading to imply that their notion of reincarnation is necessarily always derived from the left wing of mainstream Spiritualism. Traditional African religions taught reincarnation, too, so there is the possibility, although admittedly remote, that acceptance of this concept among Spiritual people is somehow a survival of their African heritage (Genovese 1974:275). Perhaps a more likely explanation is the fact that some Spiritual people maintain or have had contact with one or more of a variety of occult groups other than Spiritualism in the larger society. Reverend Gilmore, for example, has over the years taken correspondence courses from the Mayan Order, an occult group headquartered in San Antonio, Texas. The founders of the Mayan Order claim to have rediscovered the teachings of the holy men who dominated the ancient Mayan civilization of Mesoamerica (Melton 1978, II:184–85). Although it is not clear whether this group served as the basis of Bishop Gilmore's belief in reincarnation, it is interesting to note that the concept is one of the central doctrines of the order.

For the most part, Spiritual people who believe in reincarnation tend to define it in a relatively loose manner. Although one member of the Temple of Spiritual Truth suggested that perhaps I was a philosopher during Biblical times because I hold a Doctor of Philosophy degree in this life, most Spiritual people seem to exhibit little interest in who they or others might have been in a previous existence. On the other hand, Bishop F. Jones holds a view of reincarnation that includes a rough resemblance to the Hindu concept of Nirvana, in which the transmigrating soul finds its resting place in the Godhead. It is his contention that the various saints of the Catholic pantheon have broken the cycle of reincarnation.

The Indian chief Black Hawk is probably the most renowned spirit guide in American Spiritualism. Mother Leafy Anderson was reportedly responsible for introducing Black Hawk into the "spiritualist" churches of New Orleans as the patron saint of the South (Tallant 1946:173–74): "Nearly all these spiritualist churches have statues of Black Hawk among the images of bona fide saints." Since the Voodoo groups in New Orleans incorporated various aspects of both Roman Catholicism and Spiritualism into their practices, it is not surprising that Black Hawk also became one of their saints. Kaslow's recent ethnographic work (1979, 1981) with Black Spiritual churches, which was done during approximately the same period as my own observations of Spiritual groups in more northerly environs, indicates that devotion to Black Hawk is still well and alive in New Orleans: "Black Hawk is honored in many of the churches, and a symbolic Indian statue may be placed on the main altar alongside or below Jesus and the Holy Family, or may be the centerpiece of a separate altar, usually decorated with a red cloth, red candles, plastic tomahawks, spears, bows and arrows, and photographs of Black Hawk on horseback" (Kaslow 1981:65).

Although Black Hawk is obviously an integral part of the Spiritual pantheon in New Orleans, I did not find any direct evidence that he is regarded as a significant figure in the various cities, including two in the South (Nashville and Memphis), where I visited Black Spiritual churches. Despite the fact that many Spiritual people named various Catholic saints, such as the Virgin Mary and Francis of Assisi, among their favorite spiritual intermediaries, none of my informants even alluded to Black Hawk. Furthermore, I never saw a statue or picture of Black Hawk in any of the Spiritual temples or the homes of Spiritual people that I visited.

Catholic Elements in the Spiritual Movement

The sanctuaries of many Spiritual churches more closely resemble those of Catholic churches than those of the Protestant groups that Black Americans have traditionally been affiliated with. It is difficult to determine whether the Catholic elements in the Spiritual movement were derived directly from Roman Catholicism or indirectly from Voodooism, which is generally regarded to be a syncretism of West African religion and Catholicism. Both routes of diffusion would seem equally plausible. At any rate, New Orleans appears to have been the place where elements from Spiritualism, Catholicism, and Voodooism merged and were reinterpreted. Unfortunately, the exact manner in which this blending of religious elements occurred is probably now impossible to reconstruct.

Despite the fact that peoples of African descent were converted in great numbers to Catholicism in many parts of the New World, this was not the case in most of North America. Comparatively few Black Americans today are members of the Catholic Church. A 1928 diocesan survey listed just over 200,000 Black Catholics in the United States; the 1939 diocesan census reported that this number had increased to 297,000 in just over a decade; in 1967, the number was reported to be 880,332 (cited in Feagin 1968). But since the United States Census Bureau reported over 22 million Blacks in 1970, it is quite obvious that the percentage of Blacks affiliated with the Catholic Church nationwide is small.

In contrast to the national pattern, the number of Black Catholics in southern Louisiana, where the Spiritual movement began, has

been substantial for some time. Following an order in 1724 by Bien-
ville, the founder of New Orleans, requiring all slaves to be instructed
in Catholicism, thousands of Louisiana slaves were baptized into
the Catholic Church (G. Simpson 1978:288). And even though the
church probably lost many Blacks following the Civil War, partly
because of slave rejection of the masters' religion, it seems that a
sizable minority of Blacks in Louisiana continue to function as at
least nominal Catholics. A survey of 309 families in the Black community of New Orleans in 1968–69 revealed that 90 percent of the
heads of households "claimed to hold membership in some church
or at least identified with some religious denomination"; of these,
60 percent claimed to be Baptist, 27 percent Catholic, 7 percent
Methodist, and 6 percent "other" (Thompson 1974:156–57). If we
can assume that these figures represent a rough reflection of the percentage of Black Catholics in New Orleans during the twentieth century, it would seem possible that Black Catholics joining the infant
Spiritual movement may have served to facilitate the incorporation
of Catholic elements into it. One account notes that Catholic
churches in New Orleans during the 1930s permitted Blacks to attend mass but usually required them to sit in the rear pews (*New
Orleans City Guide* 1938:82). This discriminatory practice may have
induced some Black Catholics to either establish or join Spiritual
congregations.

However the transfer occurred, Spiritual churches do make use
of many Catholic accoutrements, including crucifixes or crosses; statues of Jesus Christ, the Blessed Virgin, and the saints; incense burners; and holy pictures. The presence of an altar with various types
of religious paraphernalia is also quite common. In some Spiritual
temples it is as elaborate as those found in the older Catholic
churches; in the smaller Spiritual churches, altars (if present) tend
to be much more modest. Sometimes a small votive candle stand,
similar to those found in many Catholic churches, serves as a type
of altar. Items to be found on the altars include flowers, plants, bowls
and large jars filled with holy water, holy water sprinklers, and con-
tainers of holy oil. Prayers and rituals of various sorts are conducted
at the altar in many Spiritual churches, whereas in others the altar
seems to serve a chiefly decorative function. The space immediately
surrounding the altar is sometimes considered to be a sacred area
which may be entered only by certain sanctified or authorized in-

dividuals. Furthermore, like some traditional Catholics, some Spiritual people, particularly pastors and elders, have small altars in their homes at which they pray or meditate several times a day.

It is not uncommon to see Spiritual people engage in routine Catholic rituals, such as making the sign of the cross, genuflecting while passing before the altar, and burning incense and candles. For the most part, however, such rituals are interspersed with activities more typical of Black Protestant services, such as testifying, hymn singing, and shouting. I have never seen or even heard of anything resembling the Catholic mass occurring in a Spiritual church. As Raboteau (1978:272) notes, "the formal structure of the Catholic Mass, with each gesture and genuflection governed by rubric, did not allow the bodily participation and ecstatic behavior so common to Protestant services and so reminiscent of African patterns of dance and possession." Even some other type of reenactment of the Last Supper, common in many Protestant groups, seems to occur only occasionally, if at all, in most Spiritual churches. A possible exception to this pattern is the "love feast" that is occasionally conducted at St. Matthew's Spiritual Temple in Nashville. I observed this ritual event at one of the temple's regularly scheduled Friday night services. Elder Marcus blessed "bread" (actually crackers) and water by singing a prayer and making the sign of the cross over the sacramental elements. She gave everyone in the congregation a cracker and asked that it be held in the left hand. Each person then broke off small pieces from the crackers of others, and all the fragments were placed in a plate held by Elder Marcus. This procedure was followed by the participants' shaking hands with one another and saying the words, "I love you so much." They were then given water to drink from small paper cups. At the end of the ritual, Elder Marcus wrapped the cracker fragments in small tissue-paper bundles, which she distributed to the people in the congregation. She instructed them to crush the cracker fragments on Monday morning and place them outside their homes, and assured them that they would be sure to receive a blessing from the Lord.

Cultic activities focusing on the various saints in the Catholic pantheon are quite important in many Spiritual churches. As in Catholicism, the saints are considered intermediaries between an individual and God or the Spirit. According to Reverend Wilson, a medium at the Sacred Heart Spiritual Temple, one does not petition the saints themselves but instead asks them to take one's concerns to God. Since the saints are closer to God, they are often approached when the petitioner does not feel "spiritually strong or clean enough" to pray directly. Again like Catholic churches, many Spiritual congregations incorporate saints' names in their churches' names. St. Anthony helps the poor and those who are searching for lost objects; St. Jude works with impossible cases; Abraham is a source of blessings; St. Michael the Archangel is for general protection; St. Christopher is the guardian of the road; and the Blessed Virgin is the protector of all women and children. If a congregation is in the process of building a church, it should appeal to St. Joseph, the patron saint of builders and carpenters. Bishop Gilmore said that St. Martin de Porres, the traditional Catholic saint of peoples of African descent in the New World, is a favorite in her church. Spiritual mediums often rely upon selected saints as intermediaries in making contact with the Spirit. Bishop G. Jones, the assistant pastor of the Temple of Spiritual Truth, "works" primarily with the Blessed Virgin and St. Francis of Assisi.

Favorite saints appear to vary from congregation to congregation in the Black Spiritual movement. St. Joseph is particularly popular among the Spiritual churches of New Orleans; St. Joseph's Day, which falls on March 19, serves as a brief respite from the general abstinence of Lent for many New Orleanians. "The origins of this unusual holiday are in question, but anthropologist Ethelyn Orso points to evidence that the feast was begun by the Arbreshe Italians of Albanian descent whose ancestors lived in Sicily before moving to New Orleans" (Kaslow 1979:48). The celebration of St. Joseph's Day is an event that crosscuts racial and ethnic lines in New Orleans — involving, for example, various Black social and pleasure clubs as well as religious groups. In many of the city's Spiritual churches, special altars with food, flowers, candles, and statues are constructed in honor of St. Joseph, the patron saint of working people. Kaslow (1979:50–51) provides a colorful description of the St. Joseph's festivities in the Israelite Spiritual Church in New Orleans:

> Guided by Archbishop E. J. Johnson, the church serves as a center for other Spiritual congregations in the city, including one on Baronne Street in Central City. In fact, members of that uptown congregation were present at the ceremony this year, in as much as they had

not constructed their own altar for the first time in many years. The multi-tiered altar, centered just below the pulpit in this spacious modern church, was filled with a cornucopia, and a near life-sized statue of St. Joseph presided over it. Cross-shaped breads, pineapples, and homemade cakes of every flavor were in abundance, and festivity filled the air. Mother Magee, a vivacious church elder, welcomed guests and coordinated the entire celebration, which culminated in a buffet banquet which offered more appetizing dishes than could possibly be tasted, even in small quantities.

The burning of various types of candles (as well as incense) is an integral part of the devotional activities conducted by Spiritual people. Statues and candles are often viewed as vehicles that permit one to focus attention upon spiritual matters during prayer or meditation. Bishop F. Jones maintains that theoretically one could dispense with the use of such articles in establishing contact with the spirits, but they prove to be helpful devices in enabling most people to "concentrate" upon their sacred goals. Candles are occasionally distributed in some Spiritual churches, either for a donation or free of charge. In addition, most Spiritual advisors give blessed candles to their clients in order to assist them in acquiring a blessing. A red candle is generally associated with love or power, a blue candle with hope, a green candle with purity, harmony, and truth. Although many individuals view the burning of a black candle as a malevolent act, some Spiritual people argue that it may be used for various benign purposes, such as breaking a streak of bad luck. While color symbolism is not associated with candle burning in orthodox Catholicism, it is found in Voodooism and hoodoo (Tallant 1946; Hyatt 1970, I:797–99). Furthermore, while candle burning is an old European tradition, the worship of the divinities in the pantheons of various African religions was also filled with color symbolism (Cohen 1972:83, Raboteau 1978:77). Various European and Euro-American occult groups also place a strong emphasis on the burning of candles of various colors. *The Master Book of Candle Burnings* by Henri Gamache is a particularly popular source of information on the color symbolism of candles, the dressing of candles, and the variety of problems that can be overcome by burning them. Some Spiritual people purchase copies of this book in "candle stores." Other religious paraphernalia is obtained in occult stores serving the Black community, or in stores that stock Catholic religious supplies. Many

Spiritual people in Nashville, for example, frequent the Catholic store in the city's downtown area for this purpose.

During religious services, many Spiritual pastors, ministers, and elders wear garments resembling those of Catholic priests — even of those, such as monsignors and bishops, who hold high rank in the Catholic politico-religious hierarchy. It is particularly common to see officiants, both male and female, in Spiritual temples wearing a traditional black cassock, a Roman collar, and a colored biretta — perhaps blue, purple, or red. Some Spiritual ministers will wear a uniform that mixes several bright colors. A picture of a now deceased pastor of a large church associated with the Metropolitan Spiritual Churches of Christ in Detroit, for example, shows him wearing a red biretta topped by a bright blue pompom. Occasionally, particularly for special religious events, Spiritual pastors wear elaborate vestments similar to those worn by a Catholic priest while saying mass. In the Spiritual churches that have altar boys and/or altar girls, one finds them dressed much like their counterparts in Catholic churches.

Spiritual people do not restrict their religious clothing styles to those worn by Catholic clerics, however. The dress of some Spiritual officers is rather simple, resembling that of many Protestant ministers; others will choose quite elaborate, even regal uniforms. Long robes of a wide variety of colors, accompanied by elaborate turbans or other types of headdress, are popular with many females in Spiritual churches. In some instances a "crown" may be worn by a high-ranking Spiritual dignitary, such as a "King" or "Queen." Despite the fact that he is the pastor of a modest storefront church, even Bishop F. Jones anticipates the possibility of wearing a headdress more becoming than his ordinary biretta (which he calls a "bishop's cap"). He already has a design for the crown that he hopes to wear someday.

Voodoo, Hoodoo, and the Spiritual Religion

Of all the religious traditions that have been incorporated into the Spiritual movement, it seems to be the presence of Catholic elements that Spiritual people point to with greatest pride. In contrast, it may be argued that Voodoo and hoodoo constitute the underbelly of the Black Spiritual religion. Voodoo is probably one of the most feared and misunderstood religions in the world. In the minds of most people, both White and Black, Voodoo is associated with grotesque effigy dolls stuck with pins, which — through contagious magic — are to result in the downfall of some unsuspecting victim. As Murray (1980:298) notes, "This identification of Voodoo with illness-or-death-inflicting sorcery has even made its way into the anthropological literature, in which discussions of Voodoo revolve around the question of magically induced sickness or death."

While witchcraft is in a sense part of Voodoo, the same may be said of most magico-religious systems. The shaman or religious healer is invariably regarded in an ambivalent manner — that is, as one who may be the source of great goodness but who is also potentially quite dangerous. Even today, many people in our society view the Billy Grahams, the Oral Robertses, the Jerry Falwells with mixed feelings. Particularly in the Black community, there is a strong tendency to regard the preacher as a combination of saint and trickster. Various scholars have in passing noted the widespread mistrust of preachers and other religious figures in the Black community (Drake and Cayton 1945:617; Staples 1976:166). In the following remarks, Hannerz (1969:147) comments upon the reservation that many Blacks have about some of their spiritual leaders:

> Many have skeptical words to say about God's representatives on earth, and in particular about those in the ghetto. The unofficial image of the ghetto preacher borrows much from the notion that some people always turn human affairs into a game. For all his pious words on Sunday and in quite a few weeknight meetings, the preacher is seen by many ghetto dwellers as a con man in a silk suit and with a long white Cadillac, forever fooling around with the sisters and his own actions interpreted in this ready made fashion. There were those in the Winston Street neighborhood who suspected a preacher in a nearby storefront church of being both a moonshiner and a slumlord, although there was actually nothing to substantiate this. One of the preachers who hold forth on black radio stations on Sundays made a point in one of his broadcasts of denying the rumor that he had lost his ghetto church because he had used the money of his congregation to buy a new car. But even though ghetto dwellers may at times exaggerate the shady sides of the persons who are supposed to be their spiritual leaders, there are certainly examples among the

preachers of people with conspicuously worldly interests. Many of them, of course, are among those storefront church ministers and freelance prophets who are entirely self-made men or women as religious leaders and who operate free of the shackles of any larger established organization.[2]

Despite the prevalence of a certain cynicism among Blacks during both antebellum and postbellum times concerning the motives of some of their religious leaders, it is important to note, as Genovese (1974:262) correctly does, that "never did the blacks' criticism of their preachers run so deep or extend so wide as to discredit them as a group." In a very similar vein, while many Spiritual people admit to the presence of charlatans, con artists, "false prophets," and "lying preachers" in their midst, these are not viewed as a negation of the validity of the Spiritual religion.

Despite the fact that many Spiritual people are willing to grant that their religion share certain features with Catholicism, Black Protestantism, and even Spiritualism, they invariably deny that it has any connection whatsoever with Voodoo or hoodoo, both of which are regarded as "evil" and forms of sorcery. On the other hand, Spiritual people often admit that some perverse individuals in their midst have been known to go astray and do the will of "evil spirits." For the most part, they readily accept the negative stereotypes about Voodoo that are commonplace in the larger society. Taking this attitude into consideration, it indeed seems ironic that Spiritual people are often suspected by others in the Black community of being involved in malevolent activities.

Voodoo is known by a variety of terms, including *vodun, vodu, vaudoux,* and *vaudou.* It emerged among African slaves on the island of St. Domingue (present-day Haiti and the Dominican Republic) as a syncretism of West African religions and Roman Catholicism (Herskovits 1971; Metraux 1972; Simpson 1978). The term *vodun,* which is commonly used to refer to Haitian Voodoo, comes from Dahomey; it means "god" and serves as a generic term for all the deities (Herskovits 1971:140). As Herskovits (1971:153), who made

2. On one occasion when I attended a service at a Spiritual church in Flint, a young man who was also visiting admitted his skepticism about the motives of the rather flamboyant pastor of the congregation.

a thorough anthropological study of social and religious life in the Haitian town of Mirebalais, asserts, "*vodun* is neither the practice of black magic, nor the unorganized pathological hysteria it is so often represented to be." *Vodun* essentially is the folk religion of the Haitian people and, like many other religions, involves beliefs in a pantheon of spirits, rituals directed toward these spirits, and specialists who serve as intermediaries between the believers and the spirits. At the same time, however, most Haitians practice Roman Catholicism alongside *vodun* and see no incompatibility between the two. Following the classic distinction made by Redfield (1956), the former constitutes the Great Tradition imposed upon the society by a small ruling stratum; the latter is the Little Tradition, which tends to cater to the more immediate concerns of the masses of people.

Vodun focuses on the worship of the *loa*, which are essentially benevolent spirits. The most important *loa* are derived from the Fon of Dahomey and the Yoruba of Nigeria, but the names of some less popular *loa* come from deities in the Congo and other regions of Africa (Metraux 1972:27–30). In a list of 152 *loa* that G. Simpson (1978:65) collected in 1937 in a northern Haitian village, "27 bore the names of African gods, 18 appeared to be the variations of names of African gods, 6 had names derived from African tribal or place names, 9 were probably names of African origin, 57 seemed to be names of Haitian origin, 16 were names of Catholic saints, and 19 were of uncertain origin." The *loa* tend to be identified in some way with various Catholic saints — either as one and the same, as separate but mutually cooperative spirits, or as antagonistic beings.

Priests (called *houngans*) and Voodoo priestesses (called *mambos*) not only conduct ceremonies in honor of the gods and the dead but also engage in healing, divination, and evidently — at least on occasion — sorcery. The early leaders of the slave revolt against the French planters were practitioners of *vodun*. The new religion served as a rallying point for the slaves in the Haitian revolution, which culminated in the establishment in 1804 of an independent republic made up almost exclusively of peoples of African descent. Despite its tremendous regional differentiation on the island, it became the popular religion of the Haitian people.

Slaves from the islands of Martinique, Guadeloupe, and Saint Domingue were brought to Louisiana as early as 1716. Although

Voodoo was probably imported into Louisiana with these slaves, its principal impetus in the region apparently occurred around 1809 when French masters escaping the Haitian revolution brought slaves with them. "It is estimated that New Orleans at that time received about two thousand slaves and an equal number of free people of color" (Raboteau 1978:76). During the nineteenth century, Voodoo meetings — presided over by "queens" and "witch doctors"— catered to slaves, free Blacks, and some White women (Reinders 1961:241). While slaves constituted the bulk of rank-and-file Voodooists, the priesthood was made up almost entirely of "free people of color," principally mulattoes and quadroons (Asbury 1936:254). As a result of anti-Voodoo sentiment and legal action beginning about 1820 and surfacing periodically during the nineteenth century, Voodoo in New Orleans was forced to go into hiding.

The name of Marie Laveau is generally associated with the zenith of Voodoo in Louisiana during the nineteenth century, but a considerable amount of mystery and confusion surrounds this intriguing figure. In fact, it is not at all clear how many Maries there actually were. Tallant (1946) speaks of two, whereas Hurston (1931:326) maintains that there were three, "of whom the last, the daughter and granddaughter of the other two, was the most renowned." Furthermore, several other Voodoo queens may have borrowed the name. Even the burial site of Marie Laveau and the date of her death are in dispute, although the most widely held belief is that she is buried in St. Louis Cemetery No. 1 in New Orleans. Needless to say, this burial place has not only become a famous Voodoo shrine but also a popular tourist sight. At any rate, Marie Laveau or the Marie Laveaus added many Catholic elements to Voodooism and established a dynasty that reportedly unified Voodoo as it had not been earlier and has not been since (Tallant 1946).

After the passing of the Laveaus in the late nineteenth century, Malvina Latour unsuccessfully attempted to act as principal Voodoo queen (Asabury 1936:270). Voodoo in New Orleans disintegrated into a multitude of small groups, each with its own titular head. Although various small Voodoo groups have functioned during the present century, for the most part it appears that aspects of Voodooism in the United States became incorporated into the magical system called *hoodoo.* Kuna (1974–75) stresses the importance of making a distinction between Voodoo (or *vodun*) and hoodoo, noting that the latter, although a system of belief and therapy, is not a cult; nor does it engage in cult or group activities or worship. *Vodun* or Voodoo as a full-blown ceremonial complex is found in Haiti and still occurs sporadically or even regularly in various parts of the United States. Hoodoo (also commonly referred to as "conjure" or "rootwork") developed as a system of magic, divination, herbalism, and witchcraft among slaves in North America (Raboteau 1978:80). Since the more malevolent dimensions of Voodooism and hoodoo were sometimes directed by slaves toward their masters as a symbolic protest against oppression, it is not surprising that they became objects of intense fear.

Attempts to revive Voodoo have occurred in recent decades among both Blacks and Whites (Cohen 1972). While they appear to be catering primarily to a gullible tourist clientele, several curio shops offering and purporting to be dedicated to the preservation of Voodoo have appeared in New Orleans. A much more significant factor in the growth of Voodoo has been the large influx of Haitians into New York, Miami, and other areas of the country (Weidman et al. 1978; Jackson 1981).

Voodoo as a ceremonial system exists in only skeletal form in the United States; hoodoo as a magical system is a thriving component of the subterranean side of Black American culture, not only in rural areas but also in large metropolitan centers (Whitten 1962; McCall 1963; Maduro 1975; Snow 1979). The name is said to have derived from "juju," meaning *conjure*, but may also be a simple adulteration of "Voodoo" (Haskins 1978:66). Hoodoo Book Man, one of folklorist Harry Hyatt's (1970, II;1758) informants in New Orleans, stated that Hoodoo started when Moses gave up his divinely ordained status of prophet and wrote *The Seventh Book of Moses*. Whether or not this origin myth is commonly accepted by other hoodoo practitioners, *The Seventh Book of Moses* is apparently a type of hoodoo Bible which may be purchased in many candle stores. Since hoodoo lacks a set of religious ceremonies per se and a cultic following, its major foci are health, love, economic success, and interpersonal power.

The central figure in hoodoo is the rootworker, who goes under a wide variety of names. In rural areas of the South, he may be referred to as a "conjurer," "conjure doctor," "hoodoo doctor," "blood doctor," or "hungan." The urban counterpart of the hoodoo practitioner tends to avoid these titles, probably because of the negative connotations they carry, and is more likely to adopt labels such as "psychic," "spiritualistic reader," or "prophet" (Cooley 1977a:193). In their work with individual clients, hoodoo doctors use a wide variety of paraphernalia, including roots, herbs, candles, sprays, powders, oils, incense, and even statues of human beings. Although the rootworker once collected many of his materials in the field, he is now much more likely to obtain such items from occult stores and mail order houses. For the most part, the hoodoo practitioner employs techniques resembling those that the Voodoo priest or priestess utilizes in his or her work with individual clients.

Of all the traditions that have influenced the Black Spiritual movement, perhaps the impact of Voodoo and hoodoo is the most difficult to establish, particularly since Spiritual people deny their influence. Yet similarities do exist. As was already noted, it is often unclear whether various Catholic beliefs and practices found in present-day Spiritual churches were borrowed directly from Catholicism or indirectly from Voodooism. At any rate, both Voodoo and Spiritual ceremonies often exhibit many Catholic features, such as devotions to the Blessed Virgin and the saints; the making of the sign of the cross; the use of elaborate altars, crucifixes, statues, votive candles, and holy water; and anointing with holy oil. Furthermore, both Voodoo and the Black Spiritual movement are highly eclectic, flexible, and tolerant religions. Voodoo in Haiti as well as the United States progressively added more and more elements of Roman Catholicism.

Also, it has been noted that "a great many beliefs and practices in Haitian magic originate from Normandy, Berry, Picardy, or ancient Limousin" (Metraux 1972:269). Elsewhere anthropologist Francis Huxley notes that "French books on occultism creep into Haiti every year" and describes some of his Haitian friends who practice a mixture of Voodoo and European and Oriental occultism (quoted in Cohen 1972:57). Just as Haitian *vodun* has incorporated aspects of French mysticism, its counterpart in the United States has appropriated dimensions of American Spiritualism, such as the veneration of the spirit guide Black Hawk.

In addition to their eclecticism, Voodoo, hoodoo, and the Spiritual religion all place a strong emphasis on "mysteries" and "secrets": a set of magico-religious techniques and beliefs that are intended to provide an individual with "power" over his or her destiny (Metraux 1972:84). It has already been pointed out that the Universal Hagar's Spiritual Church prohibits student and graduate mediums from revealing many of the esoteric matters that are taught in its School of Mediumship and Psychology. Bishop F. Jones noted that certain "mysteries" have been revealed to him by the Spirit, some of which he may not reveal to anyone, not even his wife. He added that the Lord gives people "secrets" in order to help them with their problems and gives Spiritual leaders "special secrets" because others seek their advice and assistance. Yet Bishop Jones expressed the deepest contempt for Voodoo, arguing that it is "nothing but tricksters" and is practiced not only in Africa but among peoples of all colors. Spiritual pastors, elders, and mediums tended to be somewhat arbitrary and selective as to what secrets and mysteries they were willing to reveal to me (and presumably others). A case in point is the conversation that I had with the pastor of a congregation affiliated with Spiritual Israel Church and Its Army. After he explained to me that a white candle represents "purity" and a red candle "power," I asked the significance of a blue candle. The pastor replied, "I can't give you all my secrets," adding that "secrets are given only to me and my staff for strength."

An interesting link connecting Voodoo, Catholicism, and the Spiritual religion in New Orleans is St. Expedite (Tallant 1946:209–10). Many New Orleanians regard this saint, whose origins are obscure, as the most dependable one to appeal to when things must be done in a hurry. St. Expedite is usually compensated for his services by burning a candle and saying a prayer before his statues "but at other times, if you're a genuine Voodoo, by leaving a slice a poundcake, a new penny or sprig of green fern at his feet" (Tallant 1946:210). During the 1940s two Spiritual Churches in New Orleans bore the name of St. Expedite; at present there is at least one. Yet I did not find any churches that were named after him or informants who explicitly paid homage to him in the cities where I studied the Spiritual movement.

St. John the Conqueror, an important Voodoo saint, has also been explicitly incorporated into the pantheon of Spiritual churches in New Orleans (Kaslow 1981:66). John the Conqueror is an Afro-American transformation of St. John, the favorite disciple of Jesus Christ, and is also known as Dr. John, the protypical Voodooist, rootworker, or hoodoo doctor. During the nineteenth century, St. John's Eve was allegedly the night when Voodooists in New Orleans gathered at Bayou St. John and Lake Pontchartrain to engage in spectacular ceremonials. Many occult stores serving the Black community stock candles, roots, and other articles bearing the name of John the Conqueror.

Bibliomancy, or the practice of reading various scriptural passages for the purpose of solving personal problems, is an important part of Voodoo, hoodoo, and the Spiritual religion (Hurston 1931; Puckett 1926; Hyatt 1970, II; Weidman et al. 1978:608–11). Mediums affiliated with Spiritual churches often instruct their clients to read various scriptural passages, particularly in the Book of Psalms. Although the 23rd Psalm is the most popular and is used for a wide array of difficulties, certain others may be recommended for more specific problems or concerns. Reverend Arnold recommends Psalm 27 "when you fail," Psalm 91 "when you are in danger," "Psalm 121 "when leaving home for labor or travel," and Psalm 90 "when the world seems bigger than God." For a donation of two dollars, one may receive a cloth book marker, bearing a picture of Reverend Arnold, which lists these recommendations and others. Like practitioners of Voodoo and hoodoo, Spiritual people often also write down a request on a piece of paper and burn it before the image of a saint.

The use of a wide variety of amulets, talismans, charms, sprays, incenses, baths, floor washes, perfume oils, special soaps, powders, roots, and herbs are integral components of the ritual practices of Voodoo, hoodoo, and at least some Spiritual people. As has been noted already, many of these articles may be purchased from occult stores and mail order houses. In commenting on the items sold in such a supply store in Philadelphia, Winslow (1969:59) notes that "although the terms 'voodoo' or 'hoodoo' were not used in any advertisements about the store and its merchandise, nor were these terms used in any conversation with the operator of the store, the evidence suggests we are dealing with beliefs and practices derived from these systems." In addition, smatterings of Spiritualism, astrology, and other occult systems have been incorporated into the belief system revolving around the use of articles sold in such establishments. Among my informants I found a wide range of responses to the materials available in candle stores. When I showed one Spiritual pastor a catalogue that I had purchased from a shop in Atlanta that specializes in the sale of "occult-spiritual and religious supplies," he referred to most of the merchandise advertised in it as "junk" and noted that "these articles are not what they say." Yet this same man wears a talisman which, he claims, wards off evil. Similarly, when I showed the same catalogue to Bishop Gilmore, she confessed that she no longer buys the types of items advertised in it but added that many Spiritual people and churches do use them; in her church the decision of whether or not to do so is left to the discretion of individual members. Despite the fact that some Spiritual people view such articles with a considerable degree of ambivalence, Reverend Brown testified to the efficacy of many of them. It was not uncommon for me to see "jinx removing" candles or "Dr. Japo" anointing oil used in Spiritual churches or lying around in the homes of some of my informants.

Black Protestantism and the Spiritual Movement

As has been shown, the Spiritual religion embodies many aspects of mainstream Spiritualism, Roman Catholicism, Voodoo, and hoodoo. In many respects, however, it bears striking similarities to Black Protestantism. The typical Spiritual religious service closely resembles those in various Black Protestant groups (R. Simpson 1970; Williams 1974). Parallels can be seen in the style of singing and the content of the hymns, the emphasis on testimonies, the call and response pattern, the manner of delivering the sermon or message, the ritual of "opening the doors of the church," and the elaborate ceremony of taking up collections. The politico-religious organization of Spiritual churches, with its boards of ministers, deacons, missionaries, mothers, ushers, and nurses, also closely parallels that of many Black Protestant congregations.

It is difficult to determine whether certain features in the Spiritual movement were borrowed from the Baptists, the Methodists, or the various Pentecostal and Holiness sects. The following comments by Washington (1973:79) partly clarify the reasons for this difficulty: "In time, what was the special creation of Pentecostals and Holiness black sects became contagious among all lower class black congregations. The black Holiness people left the Baptist and Methodist churches because they could not exercise therein their gifts of the spirit, but their spirited ways returned to dominate the scene to the extent that black Baptist and Methodists now claim this heritage as their very own, failing to credit the special gifts of Pentecostals and Holiness types."

Although Spiritual churches share many elements with Baptist and, to a lesser degree, Methodist churches, they probably most closely resemble Black Holiness and Pentecostal sects in the style of their services. This is demonstrated by their emphasis on spirit possession, divine healing, prophecy, shouting, hand clapping, foot stomping, and tambourine playing. Many Spiritual people also refer to glossolalia, or speaking-in-tongues, as one of the "nine gifts of the Holy Spirit," but I have witnessed few instances of glossolalia in Spiritual churches.

It must be remembered that American Spiritualism emerged in part as a response to the severity of mainstream Protestantism (G. Nelson 1969). Consequently, it should not be surprising that Spiritualism retained dimensions of the latter's dogma, ritual, and organization, as Ellwood (1973:137) makes clear in the following description of his visit to a Spiritualist church with a White leadership and a congregation consisting of Whites, Blacks, and Chicanos:

> The typical Spiritualist church is designed like a traditional Protestant Church, with pulpit, altar holding open Bible, and stained glass windows, but with a perhaps garish maximum of such accoutrements as flowers, candles, cloth altar hangings, and sentimental pictures of the Master. There is an odd resemblance in taste to the cluttered Victorian parlor. This was true of the church I visited. It was a store front building, and had the conventional altar and portrait of Jesus. But the difference lay in the fact that behind the altar were the crudely painted symbols of the major religions of the world.
>
> The service opened with hymns, led by a short, stocky lady minister. . . . The hymns were of a sentimental type, such as "Blessed Assurance," and "In the Garden."

While there certainly has been a considerable amount of diffusion of religious elements between the White and Black versions of Protestantism, it seems more likely that the latter met the needs of Black Spiritual people more satisfactorily than the former. The somber tone of mainstream Protestantism that Spiritualism has tended to retain surely would have been far less appealing to lower-class Blacks, who have constituted the bulk of the adherents of the Spiritual movement, than the more exuberant style of evangelical Protestantism. It is doubtless impossible to reconstruct the manner in which Black Protestant elements were incorporated into the early Spiritual movement. In cities outside of southern Louisiana, such as Chicago, Detroit, Nashville, and Atlanta, it would seem that this process was a rapid one. In New Orleans, since many Blacks are Catholics, it may have been a somewhat slower but nevertheless inevitable process.

As in Black Protestantism, shouting or spirit possession became an important aspect of the Spiritual religion. Although spirit possession is not an acceptable pattern in Catholic religious ceremonies, it is a significant component of *vodun* or Voodoo. In contrast to Black Protestant groups, which view shouting simply as a state in which the Holy Spirit or Holy Ghost "fills" an individual, spirit possession in the Spiritual churches of New Orleans occurs on two levels (Kaslow 1981:64–65): in addition to Holy Spirit possession, members of Spiritual churches in that city may become possessed by a "spirit guide," such as one of the traditional Catholic saints or even Black Hawk. My own work with Spiritual churches suggests that the "spirit guide" form of possession that Kaslow observed may be restricted to those in southern Louisiana. When my informants spoke of spirit possession, they were referring to the type in which a person is filled with the Holy Spirit, or simply "the Spirit." It may be that the Black Spiritual movement tends to be more "Catholic" and "Voodooist" in New Orleans than it is in other parts of the country, whereas elements of Protestantism in the Spiritual religion are probably more pronounced in geographical areas outside of southern Louisiana.

Frazier (1974:67) maintains that the Spiritual movement is differentiated from the Holiness movement "by the fact that the former was not opposed to cardplaying, dancing, or 'sporting life.'" It is interesting to note that the pastor of St. Catherine's Spiritual Temple of Metaphysics, a storefront church in Detroit, made a similar comment when I asked him to compare Spiritual and Holiness churches. In noting that Holiness churches believe smoking and other "things of the world wrong," he added, "We don't see it that way."

Thompson (1944:45) mentions the absence of any formal regulations governing marital and sexual relations, the consumption of alcoholic beverages, and prevalence of amusement activities in the All National Spiritualist Church of God in Atlanta. Rev. Clarence

Cobbs, the late leader of the Metropolitan Spiritual Churches of Christ, was described by Drake and Cayton (1945:645–46) as a man who is "proud of his connections with politicians and policy kings, and does not attempt to conceal his love of good living, including attendance at the race track." They go on to remark:

> The Reverend Cobbs wears clothes of the latest cut, drives a flashy car, uses slang, and is considered a good sport. Such a preacher appeals to the younger lower-class people and to the "sporting world"—he's "regular." To the older people he offers the usual Spiritualist wares—advice in times of trouble, "healing," and good-luck charms—as well as a chance for self-expression in a highly organized congregation. . . .
> "Brother Cobbs" symbolizes the New Gods of the Metropolis. He is the alter-ego of the urban sophisticate who does not wish to make the break with religion, but desires a streamlined church which allows him to take his pleasures undisturbed.

While similar observations may be made about most Spiritual churches, my data indicate that they need to be qualified. Bishop Rogers, the pastor of Resurrection Temple, vehemently denounced the consumption of alcoholic beverages, social dancing, smoking, and premarital sex. Bishop Gilmore noted that her association, which broke away from a larger Spiritual association, is opposed to the same things and to theatergoing as well, although she does not personally feel that it is a "sin" to attend a movie. Other pastors and elders in Nashville and elsewhere, although they seldom emphasized this view during religious services, told me that Spiritual people should avoid the "ways of the world."

For the most part, however, Spiritual groups do not adhere to the puritanical morality subscribed to by many Holiness and Pentecostal sects. There are many similarities between sermons in Spiritual churches and those in Holiness and Pentecostal ones, but I found few references to the "wages of sin" or the threat of everlasting damnation in the former. The reason may be that many Spiritual people reject the traditional Christian concepts of heaven and hell. Reverend Brown, for example, noted that "hell can be right here," and Father Hurley taught his followers that heaven and hell are states of mind, existing in the here and now.

Most Spiritual people tend to be quite open about their enjoyment of the "good life." When Reverend Bloch announced to her congregation that there would be some "disco music" at an upcoming Hurley's Feast dinner, she commented, "You know, some of us need to do a little discoing." I have observed Spiritual men on several occasions openly smoking cigarettes outside the church building. Bishop F. Jones often carries a package of cigars prominently displayed in his shirt pocket. The elderly pastor of a Spiritual church in Nashville said that she not only approves of premarital sex (people "have to know what they are getting") and common-law marriage (it is "not good for man to be alone") but maintained that she would not perform a marriage ceremony for anyone who had not experienced coitus. Likewise, although he opposed extramarital sex, the pastor of St. Catherine's Spiritual Temple of Metaphysics said that there is nothing wrong with premarital sex and added that "sex is a beautiful thing."

Although most evangelical and probably mainstream Protestant groups vehemently object to homosexuality, at least some Spiritual people, if not many, take a "live and let live" attitude toward it. The pastor of one Spiritual church in Nashville was rumored by some to be gay. On another occasion, a Spiritual advisor asked me if I had seen any "sissies" when I visited a certain Spiritual temple because she had heard that some of its members were gay. Unfortunately, as the conversation that I had with one person indicates, discussion of the issue of homosexuality tended to be a sensitive topic which had to be discreetly approached in interviews with my informants. On the occasion of a pastor's anniversary in one Spiritual temple, a visiting organist came over to speak to the elderly woman I was eating with. First he kissed her on the mouth and, although we had never met, did the same to me, causing me to suspect that he might be gay. After he left, the woman told me that this man had been the temple's regular organist, but that he moved on to another church when he obtained a better-paying position there. I gradually moved our conversation to the topic of norms and taboos in her Spiritual group. Finally, I asked her about her association's stand on homosexuality. She evaded the question by noting that she has nothing personally against homosexuals. When I asked her if there were any gay people in her own congregation, another temple in the same association as the one that we were visiting, she politely refused to answer my question. A Black psychic who, although not formally affiliated with the Spiritual movement, is intimately familiar with it was more open to discussion. It was his contention that many Spiritual people view homosexuals in much the same way that many Blacks view mentally retarded individuals: that is, both are believed to have a "spiritual gift."

Overall, Spiritual groups appear to provide their members with a flexible and tolerant code of conduct. This perspective is perhaps best exemplified by the philosophy that Bishop F. Jones expressed to me concerning the behavioral patterns expected in his congregation. He noted, for example, that the decision of whether or not to drink alcoholic beverages was something that he left to the discretion of his members, so long as it did not interfere with church affairs. Although he does not have any particular objection to movies in general, he would prefer that his people refrain from attending "X-rated" films but reiterated that such decisions are personal matters. Bishop Jones emphasized that if a person is "really born again," there are certain things that he or she is not going to do. He stated that Spiritual churches permit people to "find themselves" and primarily urge them to search for "truth."

Religious Syncretism in the Father Hurley Movement

The Father Hurley movement is an example *par excellence* of the phenomenon of syncretism that is characteristic of the Black Spiritual religion. George W. Hurley belonged to a Spiritualist group for a brief period and adopted the *Aquarian Gospel of Jesus Christ,* a text widely used in various mainstream Spiritualist circles, for his own organization. Communication with the spirit world, including deceased loved ones, became an integral part of his movement at a very early stage in its development. Since Father Hurley was raised a Baptist, belonged to a Methodist group for a while, and later became a high-ranking elder in a Holiness sect, it is probably safe to assume that he incorporated organizational, ritualistic, and ideological features of Black Protestantism into his own organization. Unfortunately, the source of the Catholic elements found in the Universal Hagar's Spiritual Church today is unclear. Perhaps they were absorbed as part of the general process of Catholicization that occurred in the early stages of the Spiritual movement.

Like other Spiritual people, Hurleyites vehemently deny that their religion has anything whatsoever to do with Voodoo or hoodoo. Father Hurley complained to his followers that "I am accused of being one of the biggest hoodoo workers in the United States by my black brothers and sisters" (*Aquarian Age*, Jan. 1965). Yet like practitioners of Voodoo and hoodoo, Father Hurley emphasized the acquisition of "power" through the performance of a variety of magicoreligious techniques. It also appears that he condoned the use of the religious paraphernalia sold in occult stores. A Hagar's newsletter published during Father Hurley's lifetime advertised the sale of "John the Conqueror, Oriental, Dreaming, Bringing Back, Business, Love, Success and Concentrating incense." The advertisement went on to point out that "the Ethiopian Christmas is coming and you will need abundant success. Don't forget your Christmas cards and incense which we have on hand. Make order to Prophet George W. Hurley" (*Aquarian Age*, May 1939). Other advertisements informed readers that not only Father Hurley, "The Wonder of the World," could be consulted for spiritual counseling, but also Rev. Thomas Surbadger, who was listed as a "Native of Algiers." Many Spiritualists, psychics, and prophets who advertise their services in the Black community refer to themselves as natives of Algiers. While it is difficult to say exactly why Prince Surbadger did so, it is interesting to note that Algiers, the name given to a section of New Orleans located directly across the Mississippi River from the city's French Quarter, has the reputation of being the Voodoo capital of the country.

Father Hurley was by no means the first Black man to claim to be God Incarnate. As early as 1899, Blacks in the countryside of Savannah, Georgia, began to worship Dupont Bell, a self-proclaimed Son of God (Parker 1937:81–86). After Bell was committed to an asylum, other messiahs claiming to be God appeared in various parts of Georgia until as late as 1916. Various writers have maintained that George Baker, better known in later years as Father Divine, was born and raised in the general vicinity of either coastal Georgia or the nearby Sea Islands of South Carolina (Hosher 1936; Parker 1937; S. Harris 1971). It has been suggested that George Baker as a young man could not have failed to hear of his divine precursors (Parker 1937:86). At any rate, while seving as an assistant preacher in a Baptist church in Baltimore, Baker met and later became the disciple of Samuel Morris, a Black man who also claimed to be God. Around 1907, Morris took on the name of Father Jehovia and designated George Baker "the Messenger" (S. Harris 1971:7–8). The following year John Hickerson, also known as Bishop St. John the Vine, joined the team, which became a popular attraction in the Black community of the city. But Bishop Hickerson had a parting of ways with Father Jehovia and moved on to New York City, where he established the Church of the Living God, the Pillar and Ground of Truth (Parker 1937:98–101). In 1913 or 1914, the Messenger and a small coterie of his followers traveled in the South and became a particularly successful attraction in Valdosta, Georgia. Reportedly proclaiming himself to be the "Son of Righteousness" of God," the diminutive Baker was arrested on the premise that he was a public menace (Parker 1937:91–92; Mosely 1941: 106–08; S. Harris 1971: 9–11). The court declared that the Messenger should leave the state — which he did, along with some of his followers.

Around 1915, Baker arrived in New York and sought out his friend, St. John the Vine Hickerson. Bishop Hickerson was teaching his congregation the concept of the "in-dwelling God," the belief that God resides in everyone and therefore everyone is in essence God or part of God. The Messenger, who soon became Major Morgan J. Divine, decided to establish a communal household in Brooklyn with his followers (Burnham 1979:28). In 1919 Major Divine purchased a home in a residential area of Sayville, Long Island. Some of his followers, who found domestic jobs in the vicinity, lived there with their spiritual mentor. As his reputation grew, an increasing number of individuals came to worship with Father Divine between 1919 and 1932. "In the late fall of 1931 and the winter of 1932 Father Divine was in such demand at meetings in Harlem that he was traveling back and forth daily, a trip of about 120 miles" (Burnham 1979:29).

Although its beginnings were somewhat earlier, the Father Divine Peace Mission prospered largely as a response to the hardships that not only Blacks but Whites experienced during the Depression of the 1930s; it spread to many parts of the country, including Detroit — the home of Father Hurley — and California. Unlike most other predominantly Black religious leaders Father Divine attracted many White people, not only from the United States but also from other countries, including Canada, Australia, Germany, Switzerland, and Austria. Nevertheless, the Peace Mission at least prior to Father Divine's death in 1965, addressed itself primarily to the oppressive situation of Blacks in American Society.

Father Divine presented his program as a practical means of providing his followers with health, food, clothing, and shelter. Like his lesser-known rival, George W. Hurley, Father Divine "had no patience with pie-in-the-sky religion nor with a heaven in some imaginary place" (Burnham 1979:50). In order to provide jobs for his followers, he established an elaborate network of cooperative businesses: restaurants, stores, clothing factories, farms, and various other economic endeavors. His followers could live in sexually segregated but racially integrated communal hotels, or "heavens."[3] Father Divine was particularly committed to the civil rights and social welfare of Black people. His followers established a Righteous Government Movement during the mid-1930s. Of the fourteen planks in its platform, eight focused on racial issues and three on economics, education, and politics (Burnham 1979:38–46). In addition to establishing schools for both children and adults, Father Divine urged his followers to register and vote in political elections.

For several years during the 1930s, he maintained a warm relationship with the Communist Party. Father Divine purportedly said, "I stand for anything that will deal justly between man and man. The communists stand for social equality and for justice in every issue and this is the principle for which I stand. I am not especially representing religion. I am representing God on earth among men and I will co-operate with an organization that will stand for the right and will deal justly" (quoted in S. Harris 1971:202). Despite Father Divine's sponsorship of cooperative ventures and brief flirtation with the Communists, however, he was by no means a revolutionary but rather a reformer committed to working within the framework of a capitalist system. He was a staunch advocate of the Protestant ethic of work, self-support, savings and investments, and the sanctity of private property (Burnham 1979:51).

Although the Father Divine Peace Mission was similar to the established sects in the Black community in its emphasis on social reform efforts, it also took on some of the dimensions, at least in a subtle manner, of the Black messianic-nationalist sects. Essien-Udom (1962:32) makes this comparison between the two aspects of the

---

3. Father Divine, although himself marrying a White woman, appears to have attempted to avoid the emotionally laden issue of racial intermarriage by advocating a life of celibacy for his followers.

movement: "During its early stages he styled himself the "Messenger," implying that he was the 'Son' of God or a 'Prophet' of God. At that time he taught his followers that God is in every person, but later he changed from this conception of God to the idea that God is in Father Divine. He directed his appeal to both Negroes and whites. His teachings, like those of black nationalists, display the mood of alienation from the existing society." Despite the fact that Father Divine taught that color is of no consequence, he was a living testimony of the belief that "black is beautiful." After all, had not God decided to take on the body of a man who was not only short, squat, and bald but also black?

Another Black God was the more flamboyant but less famous Bishop Charles Emmanuel ("Sweet Daddy") Grace. In 1921 Daddy Grace, a Black Portuguese immigrant from the Cape Verde Islands off the coast of West Africa, established in Wareham, Massachusetts, and nearby New Bedford the United House of Prayer for All People of the Church on the Rock of the Apostolic Faith (Alland 1962; Robinson 1974). Growth in New England was slow, but Daddy Grace shortly thereafter found more fertile pastures in the South, particularly in Charlotte, North Carolina; Newport News and Norfolk, Virginia; and Washington, D.C. He opened a church in Brooklyn in 1930 and another in Manhattan in 1938. The sect also established congregations in several Connecticut cities, in Detroit, and in Los Angeles. It is not clear exactly when Daddy Grace was accepted by his followers as the Saviour and the spirit of Jesus Incarnate (Alland 1981:347–48), but Fauset (1971:26) indicates that Grace's divinity had become well accepted among his followers by at least the early 1940s; even during his lifetime, they said prayers, knelt, and genuflected — much as Hurleyites do — before the picture of their Saviour. At the time of his death in 1960, Daddy Grace was maintaining a lavish seventeen-room mansion, which also served as the headquarters of his church, at Logan Circle in Washington, D.C. Following legal disputes among various factions within the United House of Prayer for All People, Bishop ("Sweet Daddy") McCullough emerged as the leader of the sect (Robinson 1974).

Although it appears that Father Hurley never attracted such large followings as his contemporaries, Father Divine and Sweet Daddy Grace, his church apparently was at its zenith during the Depression and World War II, when the organizations of his divine rivals

were also at their height. Unfortunately, I have not been able to determine whether Father Hurley began to claim divine status before
or after Father Divine's Peace Mission became a national phenomenon. By at least 1933, however, he was teaching his followers that
he had learned at the age of thirteen years that he was the "second
coming of Christ." While it appears that Father Divine had proclaimed his own divinity as early as 1914, it seems unlikely that Father Hurley would have been aware of this claim before the early
1930s. On the other hand, having spent his early years in south
Georgia, George Hurley may have been familiar with the messiahs
of the area who claimed to be God. He may have even heard later
of the concept of the indwelling spirit that St. John the Vine Hickerson and apparently other Black preachers were teaching during the
1910s. While it is difficult to ascertain the exact source of Father
Hurley's claim that he was the incarnation of God, it is interesting
to note that his interpretation of the notion of Christ bears some
similarity to the one held by Father Divine. For Father Hurley,
"Christ" was an honorific position of sorts which the Spirit of God
assumed by taking on the bodies of various Black men throughout
the ages. According to Braden (1949:55), Father Divine seemed to
regard Jesus as "merely the temporal and physical embodiment of
the Christ." Just as God or Christ had occupied the body of Jesus
at one time, he came to occupy the body of a Black man in more
recent times.

Father Hurley reacted to the racism and social inequities of American society by incorporating various aspects of messianic nationalism, including a belief in a glorious Black history, a subsequent "fall"
from grace, and the imminent beginning of a new golden age for
Blacks. He also rejected, at least in theory, Black Protestantism and
the use of such terms as "Negro" and "colored" in referring to Black
people. Since variations of these ideas had been floating about for
several decades in the Black community, particularly among certain Black Jewish and Black Islamic or Moorish sects, it is difficult
to determine the sources of the messianic-nationalist themes that
Father Hurley adapted to his theology. The most important source
may have been the Garvey movement. By the 1920s, if not earlier,
George Hurley and some of the early members of the Universal Hagar's Spiritual Church had become members of Garvey's Universal
Negro Improvement Association (personal communication, Rev. G.

Latimer). Furthermore, Hurley was reportedly personally acquainted with Marcus Garvey. In fact, while the Universal Negro Improvement Association (U.N.I.A.) was not a religious organization per se, its meetings exhibited many of the characteristics of a religious service, and its membership included an appreciable number of clergy (Burkett 1978).

Marcus Garvey, the "Black Moses," was born in 1887 in Jamaica and established the U.N.I.A. in his homeland in 1914 with the aim of "uniting all the Negro peoples of the world into one great body to establish a country and Government absolutely their own" (quoted in Essien-Udom 1962:40).[4] Eventually the movement spread to hundreds of thousands, if not millions, of Blacks in other parts of the West Indies, the United States, Latin America, and Africa. Garvey taught his followers to be proud that they were Black, to cherish their African heritage, and to build for themselves their own civilization. He identified the oppressive conditions of Blacks in the New World with colonialism in Africa, maintaining that only when Africans were liberated would there be hope for Black people elsewhere.

In 1916 Garvey arrived in Harlem, and he established a branch of the U.N.I.A. in that community the following year. During the 1920s and even well into the 1930s, thousands of lower-class Blacks in cities such as New York, Chicago, Philadelphia, Detroit, and Washington, D.C., were Garveyites and apparently many more were sympathetic to Garvey's program. Between 1918 and 1933 the U.N.I.A. published *Negro World*, the leading Black weekly of the period, which reached a peak circulation of around 200,000 (Pinkney 1976: 44–45). In order to ameliorate the economic plight of Blacks, Garvey established a shipping line, cooperative factories, restaurants, stores, hotels, a moving company, and a printing plant. In 1925 Garvey was imprisoned on a conviction of using the mails to defraud. His sentence was later commuted by President Calvin Coolidge, but Garvey was deported as an undesirable alien in December 1927. He returned to Jamaica, tried unsuccessfully to revive the U.N.I.A. to pre-1925 status, and died in London in 1940.

Considering that Father Hurley and some of his early followers

4. Despite the fact that many Black Jews joined the U.N.I.A., they were unable to persuade Marcus Garvey to drop the term "Negro" or to adopt Judaism as the ancestral religion of Black people (Brotz 1970:101).

were Garveyites at one time, it is interesting to note that Garvey's movement "encouraged blacks to leave existing churches and to form new ones within the U.N.I.A. that were based on a black theology and on a willingness to join the struggle for self-determination" (Vincent 1971:18). Although I have not been able to determine the exact period during which George Hurley was a member of the U.N.I.A., it appears that the Garvey movement may have provided one more stream of ideas for his new religion. As Vincent (1971:221–22) indicates, Garveyism had a definite impact on a wide variety of Black groups:

> Among the hundreds of thousands, perhaps millions, of black people who had joined the Garvey movement, few were willing to reject the movement's philosophical, political, and cultural outlook. When the UNIA could no longer coordinate this sentiment, its members moved to build new organizations based upon what they considered important in their Garveyite experience. Columnist Samuel Haynes condemned these deserters bitterly in the *Negro World*. "Former Garveyites are now enrolled in the Moorish American Society, in the various Africa movements, most of them founded by ex-Garveyites themselves," wrote Haynes, who also saw a move of "thousands" to "new religious movements claiming to be associated with Garveyism. Former Garveyites see in Father Divine, evangelist George Wilson, Bishop Grace and others the incarnation of Marcus Garvey."

Perhaps as well as being the incarnation of God, Father George Hurley, the founder of the Universal Hagar's Spiritual Church, was in some ways the incarnation of Marcus Garvey. At any rate, some of the doctrines he taught bear a strong resemblance to those promulgated by the dynamic leader from Jamaica. Garvey, an inactive Catholic, viewed Blacks as God's chosen people and urged his followers to worship a Black God and a Black Christ (White 1978). Despite the fact that many preachers from among the lower-status Protestant congregations joined the U.N.I.A., an attack upon organized Christianity became an integral part of Garveyism. Although Garvey himself never became a member or directly controlled the sect, the African Orthodox Church, founded in New York by Rev. George Alexander McGuire (the chaplain general of U.N.I.A.), essentially started out as the religious component of the association. McGuire, a former Episcopal clergyman, urged Blacks to forget the image of a White God and instead worship a Black Christ and a

Black Madonna. Nine congregations of the sect are concentrated in New York and others are found in the Boston area, Chicago, Philadelphia, Miami, and Sydney, Nova Scotia (White 1978:171). While Garvey and Bishop McGuire regarded Jesus as a Black man, Father Hurley made a sharp distinction between Jesus and Christ and proclaimed himself to be the second coming of Christ the Savior and Black God of the Aquarian Age. Also, he discarded the saints of Catholicism, which are accepted by many other Black Spiritual groups, and elevated the prophets and patriarchs of the Old Testament to the status of Black Gods for their respective ages. Like Garvey, Father Hurley was a vitriolic critic of traditional Christianity, viewing it as a tool that Whites used to keep Blacks in a "deplorable condition." In commenting upon Black Protestantism once, he stated that "all of the black man's preaching, singing, and praying is a farce" (*Aquarian Age*, May 1939).

Ethiopianism, or the veneration of Ethiopia as an ancestral homeland, has played a major role in nourishing racial pride among Blacks of the New World. As Black writer Claude McCay (1940:176) put it, "To the emotional masses of the American Negro church the Ethiopia of today is the wonderful Ethiopia of the Bible. In a religious sense it is far more real to them than the West African lands from which most of their ancestors came." Garveyism was an important influence on Black interest in Ethiopia. According to King (1978: 49), Garvey "is generally thought to have used the word Ethiopia to mean the whole continent, and although this is certainly so in such usages as the 'Universal Ethiopian Anthem,' there is some evidence that he made a similar outreach to the historic empire as he did to President King's Liberia." Father Hurley, perhaps in part inspired by Garvey's thinking, often referred to Blacks as Ethiopians and Whites as Gentiles, and regarded himself, at least for a time, as the founder of the largest Ethiopian Spiritual church in the world.[5]

Like Garvey, Father Hurley expressed in his writings a strong disapproval of miscegenation and a certain contempt for "mulattoes,"

5. Another source of Ethiopianism in Father Hurley's thinking may have been the ideas of Father E. D. Smith, the founder of Triumph the Church and the Kingdom of God in Christ. Around the time that Hurley joined Triumph the Church, Father Smith moved to Addis Ababa, the capital of Ethiopia, and reportedly never returned to the United States (Wilmore 1972:212; Melton 1978, I:227–28). While it is not clear whether Smith or his followers subscribed to Ethiopianism, it would

many of whom he viewed as having betrayed their darker brothers
and sisters. However, he recognized that Ethiopians or Blacks may
be "high-brown, or chocolate-brown, mulatto, soot black, ebony
black" (*Aquarian Age*, April 1940). In contrast to Marcus Garvey,
who was relatively dark, Hurley's ambivalence about Blacks of mixed
ancestry may have been conditioned by his own relatively light com-
plexion, which is revealed in his photographs.

Another bit of evidence for the possible influence of Garveyism
is that the flag of the Universal Hagar's Spiritual Church carries the
same colors (black, green, and red) as did the U.N.I.A. banner. Finally, although Hurley's creation of a secret fraternal auxiliary within
his organization was probably largely influenced by Masonry, Garvey's Noble Order of the Knights of the Nile (established in 1922)
may have also served as an inspiration for the establishment of the
Knights of the All Seeing Eye (Vincent 1971:103).

The Moorish Science Temple and the Nation of Islam are messianic-
nationalist sects with which the Father Hurley movement may have
undergone a cross-fertilization of ideas and practices. The Moorish
Science Temple was established about 1913 by Timothy Drew in
Newark, New Jersey (Fauset 1971:41–42). Noble Drew Ali, as the
founder came to be known later, started Moorish temples in Harlem, Philadelphia, Pittsburgh, Chicago, Kansas City, Detroit, Lansing, and numerous southern cities. As a self-proclaimed prophet
of Allah, Drew maintained that Blacks are "Asiatics," or descendants
of a proud Moorish nation in Africa, and that following the destruction of Whites ("Europeans"), they will inherit a regal future. He
said that Christianity is a religion for the Europeans; Islam is the
religion of the Asiatics. Following the mysterious death of Drew in
1929, the sect split into several factions. Although no longer as prominent as in the past, Moorish Science temples can still be found in
Philadelphia, Chicago, Toledo, and other cities.

Shortly after the death of Nobel Drew Ali, Wallace D. Fard, a ped-
dler whose origins are mysterious, suddenly appeared in the Black
community of Detroit in the midsummer of 1930. Fard started conducting meetings in the homes of interested parties and shortly there-

---

seem that such a notion may have served as an impetus for his emigration. If indeed
this was the case, Father Hurley's version of Ethiopianism may have been in part
inspired by that of Father Smith.

after established a temple of Islam. He claimed to have come from the Holy City of Mecca and to be Drew Ali reincarnated (Essien-Udom 1962:55). Although Fard maintained that he was racially identical to Black Americans," his racial and national identity remains undocumented" (Lincoln 1961:10). He taught his followers that Blacks were the original people and that Black civilizations flourished long before those of Europe (Lincoln 1961.). Whites are "blue-eyed devils," the embodiment of evil. Through deceit and trickery, Whites enslaved Blacks and took away their native language (which was Arabic) and their true identity (as "Blacks" or "Asiatics" rather than as "Negroes"). The White slavemasters took away their Islamic religion and made them worship a pale-faced Jesus with blond hair and blue eyes. Between 1930 and 1934 Prophet Fard reportedly recruited several thousand followers, including many who had been Garveyites or Moorish-Americans (Essien-Udom 1962:56; Lincoln 1961:60). The organization that Fard started became so effective that within three years he was able to withdraw almost entirely from active leadership. During the first half of 1934, Fard disappeared as mysteriously as he had appeared. Elijah Muhammed, Fard's most trusted lieutenant, headed the faction that regarded the Prophet as none other than the incarnation of Allah. Apparently partly in order to avoid further conflict with the faction that did not accept this interpretation, he moved the headquarters of the Nation of Islam to Temple No. 2, in Chicago. As is well know, it was under the leadership of Elijah Muhammed that the Nation of Islam flourished, particularly during the 1960s, and grew to its present size, with temples in many cities throughout the United States.

While there are specific differences among the doctrines that Noble Drew Ali, Wallace D. Faid, and George W. Hurley espoused, their respective teachings exhibit some interesting similarities. All of these modern-day prophets insisted that Afro-Americans have a glorious but forgotten past and that they will soon rise to their rightful place in the world. In addition, each one of these men told his followers that they are not "Negroes," strongly urged them to reject Christianity, and attempted to instill in them a new ethnoreligious identity. Again, it is difficult to determine what impact, if any, the Moorish Science Temple and the Nation of Islam — at least in their early stages — may have had on the thinking of Father Hurley and his followers. One of the early temples of the Moorish Americans was located in Detroit and possibly predated Father Hurley's arrival in that city in 1919 and the establishment of the Universal Hagar's Spiritual Church in 1923. It would not be surprising if Prophet Hurley at least heard of the teachings of Drew Ali. On the other hand, by the time Prophet Fard had started his Temple in Detroit in the early 1930s, the Universal Hagar's Spiritual association apparently had established temples not only in southeastern Michigan but also in several other states. Given this fact, it is quite conceivable that Wallace Fard was in some way influenced by the teachings of Prophet Hurley. Considering the rapid growth of the new Black Muslim sect in Detroit during the early years of the Depression, however, it seems even more likely that Fard's doctrines had an impact on the thinking of George W. Hurley.

At best, we may only speculate about such matters until more data — assuming that any exist somewhere, perhaps in documents, newsletters, or the minds of elderly informants — are uncovered. At any rate, the religion that Father Hurley and his associates developed exemplifies the rich eclecticism of the Black Spiritual movement. Like other Spiritual groups, Hurley incorporated dimensions of mainstream Spiritualism, Protestantism, Catholicism, and perhaps Voodoo or at least hoodoo into his religious system. His creativity, however, went far beyond these. While the sources of all the strands in the religion that he developed cannot be definitely ascertained, it appears that he also included elements from Garveyism, certain messianic-nationalist sects, the Father Divine Peace Mission, and such occult systems as astrology and possibly New Thought and Theosophy.

General Observations on Religious Syncretism in Spiritual Churches

Anthropologist Erika Bourguignon (1970:190) has noted that "Afro-American religions, in their many forms, represent a mixing and merging of African and European traditions and often the formation of a new growth of belief and ritual, quite different from the sources from which they started." In that Spiritual churches have blended together elements from several traditions in such a way that they have created an essentially new and unique religious tradition, it may be argued that they are excellent examples of these transformational processes. Nor do I deny the presence of Africanisms in the Spiritual movement, or in other Black religious sects in the United States. In fact, I am tempted to suggest that the Spiritual movement is one of the more likely places in which scholars might find success in their search for African survivals in Black American culture.

At any rate, while eclecticism appears to be characteristic of many religious movements in the Black community, this tendency seems to be most pronounced among the Spiritual groups (Baer and Singer 1981). They exhibit a core that generally consists, to greater or lesser degree, of elements from Spiritualism, Catholicism, Protestantism, Voodooism, and/or hoodoo; elements from other traditions may be added to this basic core. It would be erroneous to argue that the Spiritual movement is merely a Black version of White Spiritualism. While elements of the latter are certainly present in the former, although probably less so today than in the past, the Spiritual religion is the product of a complex process of combination and transformation which has been one of many responses by Black Americans to their historical and social circumstances in a racist and stratified society. The decision of Spiritual people over time to refer to themselves as "Spiritual" rather than "Spiritualist" may in part be a semiconscious, if not at times conscious, recognition of this process.

Because of the decentralized structure of the Spiritual movement, the manner in which its diverse elements are merged is highly fluid and even idiosyncratic. Individual congregations affiliated with a particular Spiritual association exhibit considerable heterogeneity. Ultimately it seems that the pastor and the elders of a particular congregation determine its ritual and doctrine. Although the larger association may attempt to apply certain standards and regulations in order to constrain this tendency, in effect its power to enforce these is minimal. In fact, it is much more likely that a particular congregation (or assemblage of congregations) will break off from an association than it is that the latter will eject its own dissident components. The local congregation generally has the option of realigning itself with another association with which it perceives itself to be more compatible. If this option is not readily available or desirable, it may choose to become organizationally independent or to serve as the nucleus for the establishment of a new association.

The actual origins of the Black Spiritual movement are obscure. Although some Spiritual people do not appear to be particularly concerned with the origin of their faith, others claim to find its beginnings in antiquity. Bishop Gilmore, for example, maintained that the Spiritual religion goes back to the time of Moses. On the other hand, Bishop F. Jones, while arguing that the Catholic Church derives from the ancient Israelite priesthood, stated that the Spiritual movement was started by Jesus Christ.

As was noted earlier, it appears that American Spiritualism held an appeal for some Blacks in the deep South during the nineteenth century. Undoubtedly part of its appeal was rooted in the fact that both mediumship and communication with the spirit world, including the ancestral spirits, were integral parts of many traditional African religions (Mbiti 1969; Jules-Rosette 1980). In addition, the relatively egalitarian and democratic nature of Spiritualism, which resulted in a willingness on the part of its adherents (at least in some instances) to transgress the etiquette of the southern caste system, must have made a favorable impression upon Blacks.

Although Spear (1967) presents the only documented evidence that I have found of Spiritualist churches in the Black community prior to World War I, it is possible that similar congregations existed in other American cities besides Chicago during this period. Once Spiritualism became institutionalized among Black Americans, they apparently adapted it very quickly to the religious forms, primarily those of evangelical Protestantism, that they were most familiar with. While Spiritualism became wedded with Black Protestantism at a relatively early point in Chicago and probably elsewhere, it appears that its transformation in New Orleans constituted the process by which the Spiritual movement took on its highly syncretistic nature. Spiritualism in New Orleans served as a respectable cover for Voodoo, just as the latter had used Catholicism for much the same purpose. The Spiritualist and the Voodooist had similar ends in that they were both intent on making direct contact with various kinds of spirits, in public settings as well as private ones.

Ironically, Catholicism, which lacks a concrete institutional form by which direct communication with the spirit world may be established, ultimately provided an aura of respectability for both Voodoo and Spiritualism. Although Spiritualism initially served this function for Voodoo, it too has had a tainted image in both the larger society and in the Black community. On the other hand, Catholicism, at least in New Orleans, was a respectable religion. In fact, some Blacks entering the middle class have used Catholicism as a vehicle of upward social mobility (Feagin 1968). In a not too different vein, lower-class and working-class Blacks joining Spiritual churches are able to enjoy the prestige of Catholicism, at least vicariously, by adopting its overt features. While Spiritual people today adamantly deny the existence of Voodoo or hoodoo elements in their religion and express a certain ambivalence about being identified with mainstream Spiritualism, they generally express pride in the similarities between their beliefs and practices and those of Catholicism.

In a sense, Voodoo in the United States, contrary to both popular and scholarly thinking, has not so much disappeared as it has become transformed, at both a group level and an individual level. Voodoo degenerated from a religious system to a strictly magical system — that is, it became a part, perhaps the larger part, of hoodoo. In its diluted form, Voodoo continues to thrive discreetly and quietly as part of the underside of Black American culture. At the collective or group level, despite the spotty existence of Voodoo temples in various parts of the country, it has essentially been transformed into a component of the Spiritual movement. Much as Hurston argued was often the case in New Orleans, McCall (1963:361) maintains that "hoodoo has been assimilated to the bewildering variety of store-front spiritualist churches in its truly religious aspects, leaving a heavy residue of sorcery and fetishism as the remaining native elements."[6] This transformation has by no means been a simple one, but has involved the addition of several other religious traditions, primarily Catholicism and Protestantism. Voodoo, a product of the Afro-American experience in the Caribbean and in Catholic Louisiana, was exposed to and even further transformed by Black Protestantism. Ironically, while the Spiritual movement constitutes in the minds of many Black Americans a disreputable part of their religious experience, Voodoo is viewed by Spiritual people as the unmentionable dimension, better repressed and forgotten, of their re-

---

6. McCall (1963:364) views "hoodoo" as the North American counterpart of *vodun* and *obeah* in Haiti, *shango* in Trinidad, *candomble* and *macumba* in Brazil, *santeria* in Cuba, and *cumina* in Jamaica.

ligion. This is not to say that Voodooism is any more disreputable in an absolute sense than any other religion. Black Americans, however, have come to accept many of the stereotypical views of Voodoo held by people in the larger society.

Kaslow and Jacobs (1981:31) note that although the specific identification of Catholic saints with African deities that is part of *vodun* or Voodoo has been lost by the Spiritual churches in New Orleans, the functional relationship has persisted. Like the *loa* in *vodun*, the saints, along with certain Indian spirits such as Black Hawk, are viewed as "spirit guides" who may take possession of individuals. Some people claim that they can actually identify the "spirit guide" in control by observing the external behavior of the possessed individual. Although many Spiritual people in Nashville, Detroit, and other cities pay homage and direct petitions of various kinds to the saints, the cult of the saints does not appear to have taken on the elaborate form that it has in southern Louisiana, the region of the country where *vodun* was first introduced. In this respect, as Kaslow (personal communication) notes, the Spiritual churches in New Orleans much more closely resemble the Afro-American religions of the Caribbean and South America, where a cultural fusion of African deities and particular Catholic saints occurred. It is interesting to note that in the case of one Spiritual group, the Father Hurley movement, the Catholic cult of the saints has been completely eliminated. In its place we find the worship of Father Hurley himself and the creation of a new category of saints: the deceased patriarchs and prophets of the Universal Hagar's Spiritual Church.

In comparing the practice of spirit possession in the Spiritual churches that I visited in more northerly environs with that in New Orleans congregations, we find a similar process by which another aspect of Voodooism has undergone transformation. In this instance, the item of congruence exists between Voodoo and Protestantism rather than between Voodoo and Catholicism. As was noted earlier, spirit possession may involve either a "spirit guide" or the "Holy Spirit" in New Orleans, whereas elsewhere — at least as far as I know — it involves only the Holy Spirit. Again, just as Voodooism has been forgotten by the Spiritual people of New Orleans, possession by the "spirit guide" has been forgotten by their counterparts in other regions of the country.

Although Spiritualism initially served as a protective cover for

Voodoo in New Orleans, Spiritual groups, while not necessarily deny-ing any connection between their religion and mainstream Spiri-tualism, tend to downplay this dimension of their development. The term "Spiritualist" was contracted to "Spiritual," and some congre-gations and associations have even dropped the word and begun to identify themselves instead with Baptist or Holiness churches. As we have seen, syncretism does not simply involve the addition of elements but also often results in reinterpretation or transformation of them. In the case of the Spiritualist aspects of the Black Spiritual movement, there has been a decline — in some instances, the virtual disappearance — of the séance, which has been traditionally associ-ated with Spiritualism. A renowned French anthropologist provides us with some insights that may make this trend more comprehensi-ble. In attempting to explain why various Afro-Brazilian sects have been selective in their appropriation of aspects of *spiritism*, which is essentially the Latin American counterpart of North American Spiritualism, Bastide (1978:261) makes the following observations: "Spiritism is a somber religion. The room is dimly lighted and lu-gubrious. The believers sit on benches, eyes closed, heads bowed in concentration. The only sound is an occasional sniff or gulp, a breath caught and held like the breathing of a woman in labor straining to deliver the spirit. The African religion is a joyous one, celebrated in an atmostphere of music, singing and dancing, festivity; faces re-flect sheer gladness."

In a similar vein, I suspect that it is because mainstream Spiri-tualism is a somber religion and Black American religion is a joyous affair that there has been an appreciable decline of the séance in the Spiritual movement. The functional equivalent of the séance is now a part of the prophecy session or the bless service. The acting medium makes contact with the Spirit or the "spirit guides" in a brightly lighted room rather than in a semidark one. Hymn sing-ing, testifying, and ecstatic dancing may serve as interludes between the various messages that the medium receives from the spirit world. When I attended religious services in Spiritual churches, I was re-peatedly asked by the members whether I was having a "good time." Congregations in the Spiritual movement and probably in many other Black religious groups are continually reminded that ritual events are to be joyous occasions. Apparently, an emphasis on joy is an old theme in Afro-American religion. According to Wilmore

(1972:16), "The dominant motif of slave religion was affirmation and enjoyment — even carnal pleasure." At any rate, when the saints do not appear to be sufficiently exuberant, they are often cajoled by the pastor or one of the elders to "get the Spirit." As one prominent member of Sacred Heart Spiritual Temple often exclaimed to her congregation, "Let's have church!"

Although I earlier suggested some possible connections between the Black Spiritual movement and African religion, it is not so much my intention to reopen the venerable debate between Melville J. Herskovits and E. Franklin Frazier on the matter of African survivals in Black American culture as to suggest some possible directions for research along these lines. Herskovits (1941) argued that New World Black cultures exhibit a great number of African traits, particularly in the area of religion. Conversely, Frazier (1949), while admitting the existence of African retentions in Latin America and the Caribbean, maintained that the process of slavery and the passing of earlier generations born in Africa destroyed almost all traces of African cultures among the Blacks of North America. Despite the fact that it has now been several decades since Herskovits and Frazier stated essentially diametrically opposed positions on the issue, few new insights have been shed on the question. If anything, Herskovits's position has gained a certain credibility, particularly among Black cultural nationalists, while Frazier's position has diminished in popularity. The irony of this trend is that Herskovits was a white anthropologist, whereas Frazier was a Black sociologist.

The search for the possible existence of Africanisms or African survivals in the New World will have to be done by scholars who, like Herskovits, are well acquainted with both African and Afro-American cultures. Unfortunately, I cannot claim any expertise on African cultures; others more competent in this regard will be needed to conduct painstaking comparative research. Nevertheless, in reading the literature on what are often called "spiritual," "spiritualist," "spiritist," and *aladura* churches in West Africa, particularly Nigeria and Ghana (Parrinder 1953; R. Mitchell 1971; B. Wilson 1973:168–195; Mullings 1979), I have noted some striking similarities between these groups and those found in the Black Spiritual movement in the United States.

In his description of the Sacred Cherubim and Seraphim Society, one of the many independent and syncretistic spiritualist sects

Religious Syncretism   157

in West Africa, Parrinder (1953) mentions various practices that are
common to Spiritual groups in this country, including the making
of the sign of the cross; the use of candles, incense, and holy pictures of the Catholic variety; and an emphasis on the Holy Spirit
and glossolalia (the latter being more common to Black Pentecostal
churches in the United States than Spiritual churches). H. Mitchell
(1975) notes the importance of direct revelation in the form of visions, dreams, possession, healing, divination, and the use of holy
water and candles in the *aladura* (meaning "owner of prayer" or
"praying man") churches in Nigeria. Like Spiritual churches in
America, many of the *aladura* churches attract people who are seeking the spiritual resources necessary to achieve a satisfactory life in
the here and now, which includes financial security, good health,
and freedom from fear of witchcraft and attacks by magic. In many
instances, successful divination influences the client of a prophet to
join his or her congregation. Like Spiritual advisors in the United
States, some *aladura* prophets may be extremely busy with clients
during the week but minister to only small congregations on Sunday mornings. The diagnostic and treatment procedures applied by
the *aladura* prophets, which include prayer, divination, and the use
of religious articles (such as holy water and holy oil), are similar
to those employed by prophets and advisors affiliated with the Spiritual movement in the United States.

In her study of the Church of the Messiah, a "spiritual" or "spiritualist" sect in Labadi, Ghana, Mullings (1979:75) found the same
utilitarian concerns typical of Spiritual people in this country, as
she notes in the following passage:

> The overriding theme of most sermons is salvation. In attempt-
> ing to delineate the indigenous meaning associated with salvation,
> I found that although church members occasionally allude to other-
> worldly phenomena, most associate salvation with divine assistance
> in solving everyday problems of "unbeez" ("unbusiness" or unemploy-
> ment), family relations, and health. This was not only my observa-
> tion, but also that of the founder, who noted "Here in spiritualist
> churches, most people come with the simple aim of acquiring some-
> thing from the church — getting healed or getting their requests an-
> swered by the Lord." To the congregation, then, the importance of
> salvation concerns help with everyday problems. The Christian God
> is held to be the source of benevolent power that may be brought

to bear on solving problems. The sermons tell the congregation how salvation, resulting in help with problems, can be achieved.

Healers in the Church of the Messiah and various other spiritualist churches in Labadi, like many Spiritual mediums in the United States, prescribe the repetition of the Psalms and prayers, the burning of candles, and bathing with holy water in attempting to treat the problems of their clients.

Finally, one finds the same suspicion in West Africa as in Black American communities concerning purported petty economic exploitation on the part of prophets and pastors (R. Mitchell 1971:75). "The business aspect of spiritualist churches is recognized by the townspeople of Labadi, who frequently verbalized their belief that most founders are in the church solely for the purpose of making money. . . . Among spiritualist church-going population, this belief takes the form that the founders of the other spiritualist churches are primarily concerned with this financial aspect" (Mullings 1979: 81).

How are we to account for many of the striking similarities that we see between the spiritual or *aladura* sects of West Africa and the Black Spiritual groups in the United States? One possibility, of course, is that Spiritual churches have retained many Africanisms, perhaps more than other religious groups among Black Americans. The fact that the Spiritual movement has incorporated or even in a sense transformed the Voodooism of southern Louisiana would support this argument. If indeed this is the case, it may be said that the Spiritual movement more than any other religious groups found among Blacks in the United States resembles the various Afro-American sects in the Caribbean and in South America.

On the other hand, it must be noted that the contact Africans have had with both the Protestant and Catholic traditions of the European colonial powers may have transformed their religions in ways not too different from what occurred in the New World when the slaves here came into contact with Christianity. Just as many Afro-American sects, including the Spiritual groups in the United States, evolved into highly syncretistic religions, contact with the West through colonialism triggered religious syncretism in many parts of sub-Saharan Africa.

Furthermore, as Jules-Rosette (1980:283) points out, "The relationship between Africa and America also involves a two-way exchange. Religious beliefs which crossed the Atlantic under the slave trade ultimately returned to Africa in modified form. The nineteenth century colonialization and repatriation movement marked the large-scale beginning of this two-way exchange. Garveyism and Pan Africanism in the twentieth century marked similar cultural exchanges." Various Black Protestant groups, particularly of the Holiness and Pentecostal varieties, have sent missionaries from this country to Africa (B. Wilson 1973). At least one Spiritual association, the Metropolitan Spiritual Churches of Christ, Inc., has affiliated congregations in Liberia and Ghana, and it is possible that other Spiritual groups from the United States have also been involved in missionary activities in African nations.

CHAPTER 5

The Spiritual Movement
as a Response to Racial Stratification

THIS CHAPTER will focus on the contradictory role of the Spiritual movement among Black Americans. It will be argued that on the one hand, it serves compensatory and ameliorative functions at the individual level and as a mechanism by which otherwise isolated persons residing in Black urban ghettoes are integrated into a social group that provides them with a sense of community and dignity. On the other hand, the Spiritual movement encourages its adherents and clients to accept mainstream American values and goals, such as material success and individual achievement — an orientation that unwittingly discourages critical examination of the process of victimization experienced by many Blacks in American society and often results in the objects of this process blaming themselves for their problems.

Black Americans have adopted a wide variety of strategies — economic, political, social, and (or primary concern to us here) religious — in coping with their structural position in the larger society. The religious strategies that churchgoing Blacks have developed to deal with racism and social inequality are exemplified by the four general types of sects that Singer and I have delineated (Baer and Singer 1981).

To recapitulate briefly: (1) the *mainstream denominations*, particularly the large middle-class Baptist and Methodist congregations, have adopted a reformist strategy that attempts to create improvements for Blacks by working within the system and accepting the "American Dream." The majority of lower-class Blacks with a religious orientation have turned to (2) various *conversionist sects*, such as the multitude of small Baptist, Holiness, and Pentecostal "storefronts" that proliferate in the Black neighborhoods; these groups tend to accommodate their members to their structural position in the class system by adopting puritanical and expressive behavioral patterns and offering an other-worldly salvation. While also incorporating puritanical attitudes, (3) the *messianic-nationalist* sects, such as the Black Muslim and the Black Jewish groups, have constructed countercultures that rejected many of the values and goals of the larger society, worked toward utopian communities (Singer 1979), and often developed chauvinistic cosmologies. While various Spiritual groups incorporated dimensions of the conversionist and messianic-nationalist sects, they primarily sought their salvation in (4) a *thaumaturgical/manipulationist strategy* that promised the "good life" and the benefits of the "American Dream" in return for the performance of certain magico-religious acts and adherence to a philosophy of positive thinking.

It appears that the early Black Spiritual or Spiritualist churches attracted largely lower-class individuals. For the most part, Spiritual groups still make their greatest appeal to this segment of the Black community. Nevertheless, some Spiritual congregations have outgrown the storefront stage and attract a broader spectrum of the Black populace: in addition to large numbers of lower-class individuals, these larger congregations also include relatively affluent working-class and middle-class persons. St. Cecilia's Divine Healing Church No. 2 in Nashville, the United House of the Redeemer in Indianapolis, and the Spiritual Temple of Metaphysical Science in Memphis are examples of such congregations among the Spiritual churches that I visited. From its humble beginnings as a storefront on the South Side of Chicago, the First Church of the Deliverance, now the headquarters of the Metropolitan Spiritual Churches of Christ, developed into a large congregation which cuts across socioeconomic lines. In a footnote, Drake and Cayton (1945:646) state that "an analysis of 10 percent of the 2,000 members of this church reveals that they were recruited largely from among former Baptists and Methodists, tend to be slightly above Bronzeville's average in education, and are considerably younger than most lower-class church members."

Although I did not systematically collect specific data on the social composition of the Spiritual churches that I visited, my observations indicate considerable variability in sex and age, as well as in class. Like most churches in the Black community, although prob-

ably even more so, Spiritual congregations are characterized by a
heavy preponderance of female members. In most cases, even if the
pastor is a man, female members will outnumber males by at least
two to one. The age composition of most Spiritual churches today
shows a heavy concentration of middle-aged and elderly individuals,
but there is a relatively high percentage of adolescents and young
adults in some. This seems to be particularly true of the larger
churches — such as the United House of the Redeemer in Indianapolis, which has a young and flashy pastor.

It is important to point out that Spiritual churches, probably like
many other congregations in the Black community, tend not to be
neighborhood churches; instead, the members frequently come from
many Black sections of the city. Spatial proximity is not nearly as
important in determining membership in a particular congregation
as are the style of the pastor and kinship or social ties among the
members. Finally, while Spiritual churches still provide a haven for
recent migrants from rural areas, more often than not they attract
individuals who have been residents of urban areas for some time,
if not their entire lives. This pattern should not be surprising when
one considers that the vast majority of Black Americans now live
in cities. Overall, it appears that the Spiritual movement appeals
to people who are still attracted to many features of traditional Black
religion but who also want to enjoy the pleasures of urban life. Furthermore, while only a few individuals in the Black community actually become regular members of Spiritual churches, others rely
upon their services periodically for blessings and spiritual advice.
Since many in the latter category prefer to keep their involvement
in the Spiritual movement anonymous, it becomes extremely difficult to determine just how extensive the appeal of the Spiritual religion may actually be.

The Role of Spiritual Churches in the Black Community

The role of Spiritual churches in the Black community is complex,
multifaceted, and paradoxical.

How do these churches meet the needs of some Blacks, who continue to be the victims of a racist and socially stratified society? First,
although Fauset (1971:9) viewed Spiritual groups as an atypical reli-

gious category, many of the observations that various social scientists have made of Black religion in the United States in general would also apply to them. For example, like many other religious sects, Spiritual churches are compensatory in that they substitute religious status for social status. In this regard, there is a strong functional similarity between Spiritual groups and other Black religious groups.

> Giving Blacks a sense of recognition and somebodiness is important in a society where all Blacks are regarded as inferior vis-à-vis all Whites. Even on an objective index of status most Afro-Americans fall into the bottom level. Hence, the janitor can elevate his self-esteem via his role as a superintendent of the Sunday school. The domestic servant can gain appreciation by serving as leader of the church choir and the railroad porter could achieve a sense of importance and prestige in his role as a senior deacon. Because the Black church has provided a place where individuals could participate and be accepted and valued by standards of their own community rather than that of the White majority, it has preserved the self-respect of many Blacks who would have been otherwise overwhelmed by their dehumanizing experiences. (Staples 1976:167)

Similarly, an individual of humble standing in the larger society may be recognized in a Spiritual church as a bishop, minister, elder, deacon, or prophet who can communicate with the spirit world. The observation that Black churches are overflowing with apprentice ministers and "jackleg preachers" is particularly valid in the case of Spiritual churches, which provide their adherents with a wide variety of opportunities to display their abilities and talents (Johnstone 1975:276). And since Spiritual churches are generally regarded as being among the lowest echelons of Black religious organizations, it is interesting to note that some of them attempt to compensate for their marginal status by creating quasi-royal positions, such as King, Queen, Prince, and Princess. The leader of one of these groups is no longer an ordinary person but a "Royal Elect Ruler," a "King of All Israel," the potentate of some other regal kingdom, or perhaps even a god or goddess of a new age.

Largely because many other avenues of social advancement have been traditionally closed to Blacks, some of them have resorted to the ministry as a means of obtaining upward mobility. While many Spiritual pastors probably have similar ambitions, in most instances any improvement in their socioeconomic status as a direct result of religious endeavor is at best modest. Nevertheless, the pastors of some of the larger Spiritual congregations and the heads of some Spiritual associations have become self-made success stories who serve as living testimonies to their flocks of the efficacy of the Spiritual religion. A case in point is Rev. Mary Arnold, the pastor of St. Cecilia's Healing Churches No. 1 and No. 2. With only $55, she started what became one of the largest Spiritual churches in Cleveland, and went on to establish the largest Spiritual church in Nashville and to become the overseer of a small Spiritual association. Unlike most Spiritual pastors and advisors, she is financially successful, able to support herself on the salary from her Cleveland congregation, "love offerings," and counseling activities. Reverend Arnold told me that she advises from fifty to one hundred clients during the course of a typical week (in fact, on two of the three occasions that I went to interview her in Nashville, many people were waiting their turns outside her consultation room), and it is generally known that the standard donation for seeking her help is $10 (although she sometimes receives less or more). The monetary compensation that she derives from her position permits Reverend Arnold to maintain two homes and an elegant wardrobe, and to fly back and forth between Cleveland and Nashville at least twice a month.

Women have often compensated for their relative powerlessness cross-culturally by participating and even sometimes rising to positions of leadership in sectarian religious movements. During the nineteenth century in the United States, women played a prominent role in the establishment of Seventh-Day Adventism, Spiritualism, and Christian Science, for example. In light of the fact that the ministry has been one of the main avenues of social mobility in the Black community, it becomes particularly understandable why males may attempt to monopolize positions of religious leadership for themselves. In her discussion of the Baptist churches in a rural area of Mississippi, Powdermaker (1939:272–76) notes that the large majority of those who attend services and revival meetings, "shout," and "get religion" are women; furthermore, the women organize the activities of the churches and assume financial responsibility for its maintenance. Yet the preachers and the officers are invariably men. We see a continuation of this pattern among the Baptist and Methodist churches of Bronzeville and other large cities (Drake and Cay-

ton 1945:631–32). Since the male preachers of the Baptist and Methodist churches rely upon the women for the bulk of their regular attendance, financial support, and general church work, they maintain
a constant surveillance for any attempts on the part of the women
to challenge their subordinate status. Consequently, as Drake and
Cayton (1945:632) observe, "The ban on women pastors in the regular churches has increased the popularity of the Pentecostal, Holiness, and Spiritualist churches where ambitious women may rise to
the top."

My own data support the contention that the Black Spiritual
movement provides an alternative for ambitious women who would
be barred from the upper echelons of the politico-religious hierarchy
of other Black religious groups. Many female members of Spiritual
churches told me that they were attracted to the Spiritual movement because it provided them with the opportunity to preach,
whereas this was denied to them in Baptist congregations. Of the
thirty-five Spiritual churches that I visited in various cities, seventeen had female pastors. Six of the eleven Spiritual churches in Nashville had female pastors during the period of my fieldwork in that
city.

In the case of Sacred Heart Spiritual Temple, although the present pastor is a man, its founder was a woman (who served as pastor
until illness and old age forced her to retire), and the actual leader
of the congregation is Evangelist Anderson, the dynamic and forceful
middle-aged daughter of the founder. (Ironically, according to one
informant, the only reason that Reverend Smith was chosen to be
pastor was that the majority of members wanted a male in this position.) At the Temple of Spiritual Truth the pastor is a man, but his
wife acts as assistant pastor and coordinates most of the religious
and financial affairs of the church. On the other hand, at St. Cecilia's Divine Healing Church No. 2 the assistant pastor is Rev. Mary
Arnold's husband; and although there are many males among the
ministers and deacons, they appear to assume a position subordinate to the female ministers and assistants. The fact that Rev. Mary
Arnold is the "main drawing card" of St. Cecilia's is demonstrated
by the 50 percent drop in attendance when her husband conducts
the Sunday morning service. When I asked two deacons why fewer
people are present at services presided over by Rev. George Arnold,
they confessed that they have also wondered about this pattern, but

attempted to assure me that the assistant pastor himself was not disturbed by it.

In addition to being pastors, many women in Spiritual churches are elders, mediums, and healers. Nevertheless, the chances for men to achieve a prominent position in a Spiritual church are still greater than those for women: in almost any given Spiritual temple, more of the desirable offices are occupied by males than by females — even though it is the women who generally do the bulk of the work required to maintain the church. It seems that the women feel they must make this concession to the men in order to ensure their continued involvement in the congregation.

As is the case for most religious groups in the Black community, an analysis of Spiritual churches would be incomplete if we did not recognize their integrative dimensions — that is, their ability to create a sense of *Gemeinschaft* or *communitas*. Individuals and families who would otherwise be isolated in the impersonal environment of the city become part of a fictive-kin network of "brothers" and "sisters." During times of personal or familial crisis, the congregation may provide moral and even financial support, despite its limited economic resources. Religious services, annual associational conventions, pastor's anniversaries, musical performances, banquets, suppers, picnics, visits to other churches, and other events constitute a major portion of the social activities of many Spiritual people. Group cohesiveness, although not always actualized, takes precedence over religious dogma in these churches. Although some Spiritual pastors will, if pressed, admit to a belief in the superiority of their own religious systems, they generally downplay "denominationalism" and may even refer to their congregations as "interdenominational." Spiritual churches provide their members with a meaningful social identity and a set of important primary relationships with others. Although Williams (1974:185) made the following remarks about a Black Pentecostal church in Pittsburgh, they apply to many Spiritual churches as well:

> We must not allow our economic mythology of scarcity . . . in which those with little access to possession of, and control over economic goods are conceived as underprivileged, deprived, and poverty-stricken — to contaminate our preconception of social life among the poor. This mythology will help us to understand why some of the poor deny, defile, and defy the values in the larger society. But poor

people throughout the land within organized groups of intensive interaction and complex networks of social intercourse will continue
to cherish life — lived in their style and with their own perspectives
of the world.

Many social scientists have commented on the cathartic aspects
of Black religion (Jones 1939; Clark 1965; Fauset 1971; G. Simpson
1978). Like many other Black sects, Spiritual groups provide their
members with a variety of opportunities to ventilate their anxieties
and frustrations. Testimony sessions, which occur during most services and spontaneously from time to time, are occasions when members express their dependence on the pastor and the congregation;
they are expected to unburden themselves of recent disappointments
and crises. Individuals who begin to cry at this time are given moral
support with responses such as "that's all right" or "tell it." Shouting
— involving trancelike behavior, dancing, falling backwards, running back and forth, leaping over pews, or even rolling on the floor —
is actively encouraged by the ministers and apparently also serves
a cathartic function. Although shouting may occur at almost any
time during the course of the service, it often appears to be triggered by certain events, such as an especially emotional sermon,
loud music, or the pastoral anointing and laying-on-of-hands of an
elder.

Despite the foregoing functional similarities between the Spiritual
movement and Black Protestant groups, it is the emphasis on the
manipulation of one's present condition through the use of magico-
religious practices that tends to distinguish the former from the more
conventional religious sects among Black Americans. The belief that
events can be controlled by magical practices is found in all walks of
life, but especially among the poor. The following remarks by Whitten (1962:322) are particularly relevant to our discussion of the thau-
maturgical/manipulationist orientation of the Spiritual movement:

> The proclivity of the American Negro to cope by magical means due
> to his social, political, and economic position in the greater Ameri-
> can social structure may well be another crucial factor. Malinowski,
> among others, has presented evidence for the hypothesis that the
> greater the uncertainty regarding the means to an end, the greater
> the tendency to cope by magical means. Due to his suppressed social
> position a Negro can find little satisfaction by coping directly with

his frustrations and dissatisfactions. Misfortunes that befall him may have no real solution, though magical practices or the relegation of problems to magical causes may offer at least partial satisfaction by relieving some anxiety and tensions.

The acquisition of the "good life" and the "American Dream" (or at least a larger slice of it) are central concerns of Spiritual people as they are for others of low socioeconomic status. The intended function of magical ritual is to put people in touch with supernatural power. According to Murphy (1979:170), magic usually promotes a sense of self-assurance and "produces the illusion that people are masters of their fate, controllers of their environment and not its pawns."

As has already been noted, the techniques with which Spiritual people attempt to manipulate their destiny include burning votive candles, praying before the image of a saint, the use of a wide array of occult articles, and public or private divination by a medium.

Spiritual churches also conduct special services, often referred to as "demonstrations," during which thaumaturgical techniques for obtaining spiritual power or a blessing are revealed. Bishop Stewart, the pastor of the now defunct St. Joseph's Spiritual Church in Nashville, was particularly well known for her "cabbage demonstrations," which took place annually on November 24. Members of the congregation would each bring a head of cabbage to be blessed at the church, and Spiritual people in other southern and midwestern states would send cabbage heads to St. Joseph's through the mail. After the cabbages were blessed, they were taken home or returned by mail to those who sent them. Three days later the cabbages were to be cooked and eaten during the course of the day before sunset. Each time an individual consumed part of the cabbage, he or she was to ask for a blessing: for example, money, a new house, a new automobile, or success in love.

Some Spiritual leaders also have developed elaborate metaphysical systems which they combine with other aspects of the Spiritual religion. For example, the pastor of Unity Fellowship in Nashville places great emphasis on the power of positive thinking and prescribes a number of rituals intended to raise the level of one's "consciousness." One of these, referred to as the "prosperity and money treatment," involves reciting the following words three times: "Large

sums of money and big financial surprises now come to me for my
personal use. I use them wisely."

Although the majority of Spiritual people are poor, others —
particularly many of those who belong to the larger churches —
appear to be relatively affluent working-class or middle-class individuals. The appeal of the Spiritual religion for the latter is not as
apparent as it is for the less advantaged, but Frazier (1974:84–85)
has observed that members of the "new Negro middle class" are often
fascinated by "'spiritual' and 'psychic' phenomena." Perhaps part
of the appeal of the Spiritual religion for certain upwardly mobile
Blacks is that its "positive-thinking" ideology serves to validate their
achievements. As increasing numbers of Black Americans acquire
well-paying white-collar and blue-collar jobs (but are kept socially
segregated from mainstream American life), it may be that some
of them will be attracted to the larger Spiritual congregations. The
phenomenal growth of St. Cecilia's Divine Healing Church No. 2
in Nashville and the United House of the Redeemer in Indianapolis
may reflect such a trend. In both congregations, the more successful members are quickly promoted to positions of leadership and
responsibility and are presented as living proof of the efficacy of the
Spiritual religion.

It is apparently the appeal of thaumaturgical and manipulative
rituals that prompts many individuals who are not regular members
of Spiritual groups to attend services in these churches or visit Spiritual prophets and advisors privately. In his elaborate discussion of
Haitian Voodoo, Metraux (1972:25) notes that it is a "practical and
utilitarian religion which cares more for earthly than for heavenly
goings-on." In a similar vein, the Spiritual religion concerns itself
with the concrete problems and needs of its adherents and clients.

The Spiritual Movement as a "Client Cult"

My analysis of the role of Spiritual churches thus far has emphasized the various ways that they attempt to meet the needs of their
members. Through its complex of mediums, however, the Spiritual
movement serves a somewhat larger and more intangible clientele
comprising persons who, while not actually joining one of the
churches, do seek out certain services that Spiritual prophets and

advisors offer. In other words, Spiritual churches serve two, more or less discrete, types of clients: (1) actual members of Spiritual congregations and (2) free-floating individuals who seek the services of a medium, sometimes by visiting a Spiritual church for a bless service or prophecy session, but more often through private counseling. The latter category includes members of other Black religious groups, the unchurched, and even some Whites.

As is indicated by Table 5, the complex of Spiritual prophets and advisors who serve this twofold clientele constitutes a variant of Black ethnomedicine. My typology recognizes that Black folk healers function in both public and private settings and that they may or may not affiliate their healing practice with a religious group.

Table 5. A Typology of Black Folk Healers*

A. Independent Healers (work only in private settings)

   1. neighborhood practitioner
   2. rootworker
   3. Spiritualist
   4. magic vendor

B. Cultic Healers (work in both public and private settings)

   1. evangelistic faith healer
   2. Voodoo priest or priestess
   3. Spiritual prophet or advisor

---

*Reproduced by permission from Hans A. Baer, "Prophets and Advisors in Black Spiritual Churches: Therapy, Palliative, or Opiate?" *Culture, Medicine, and Psychiatry* 5: 145–70.

The neighborhood practitioner is generally an older woman who serves as a local consultant for common ailments and is well versed in the use of roots and herbs (Jordan 1975). Although she may occasionally receive monetary compensation for her services, the neighborhood practitioner is more likely to receive thanks or a gift of food. The rootworker, who may also be referred to as a "conjurer," "conjure doctor," or "hoodoo doctor," is probably the most renowned character in Black ethnomedicine. He or she has a detailed knowledge of the use of roots and herbs, and possesses the ability to interpret signs in nature as good or bad omens. Like the Spiritualist, the hoodoo doctor solves personal problems, heals ailments, and provides a variety of magico-religious articles for clients. The Spiritualist is an individual who has received a "call" from God to help people communicate with the spirit world (Jordan 1975). He or she may be affiliated with an occult supply store or operate on a strictly individual basis. Magic vendors either own or are employees of occult supply stores, and while they generally are not healers per se, they offer advice as to the appropriate articles for overcoming various conditions or ailments (Hall and Bourne 1973).

The most common type of cultic healer in Black ethnomedicine is probably the evangelistic faith healer, who is generally a prominent member of a fundamentalist congregation. He or she resorts to techniques such as praying, the laying-on-of-hands, anointing with holy oil, and giving a client a blessed handkerchief or apron. The Voodoo priest or priestess in many ways resembles the hoodoo doctor, but serves also as an important religious functionary in a Voodoo cultic temple. As we have already seen, techniques used by Spiritual mediums have much in common with other healing traditions in the Black community. Furthermore, the complex of prophets and advisors in Spiritual churches is analogous to other alternative health systems that serve various minority groups, such as *curanderismo* among Mexican Americans, *espiritismo* among Puerto Ricans, *santeria* among Cuban Americans, and a variety of traditional healing practices among American Indians.

The activities of a complex of prophets and advisors in the Spiritual movement tends to contradict one of the generalizations that Stark and Bainbridge (1979:125–26) make concerning the nature of what they term "client cults." Stark and Bainbridge are among those who distinguish between the "sect" and the "cult": they define a sect as a schismatic group that has had earlier connections with a well-established mainstream denomination or church, whereas they view the cult as "something *new* vis-à-vis the other religious bodies of the society in question." They do not delineate subtypes of the sect, but do argue that "three degrees of organization (or lack of organization) characterize cults."

Since the Black Spiritual movement fulfills their definition of a cult better than that of a sect, their classification of cults is pertinent to our discussion. The "audience cult," which often simply involves individuals attending lectures or learning about cult doctrines through magazines, books, newspapers, radio, and television, is the most diffuse and least organized variety. "Client cults" tend to propagate their doctrines primarily by way of a dyadic relationship between a therapist (or consultant) and a client (or patient): "Considerable organization may be found among those *offering* the cult service, but clients remain little organized." Finally, "cult movements" are full-blown religious movements with a relatively well-defined set of beliefs and rituals and a more or less identifiable membership or following. As occurred in the case of Scientology, client cults may evolve into cult movements.

The Black Spiritual churches combine the essential elements of the "client cult" and the "cult movement." Indeed, some independent prophets or readers have organized a private counseling practice into a storefront church and even affiliated it with a Spiritual association. On occasion, individuals who seek assistance from pastors or mediums actually join the congregation that the latter belongs to. Bishop F. Jones, for example, stated that a fair number of the members of the Temple of Spiritual Truth joined the group after he had successfully treated them.

However, Stark and Bainbridge (1979:128) maintain that "client cults seem almost never to serve a low-status market, if for no other reason than that they charge for their services." In fact, while Stark and Bainbridge present no evidence for their assertion, they claim that Spiritualists draw on middle- and upper-class clients. While it is true that some relatively affluent Blacks as well as Whites seek out the services of Spiritual prophets and advisors, my intensive interviews with eight advisors in Nashville as well as more casual interviews and conversations with other Spiritual mediums indicate that the majority of those who consult them are lower-class individuals (Baer 1981a). Low socioeconomic status is probably characteristic also of most clients of Voodoo doctors, rootworkers, and independent Spiritualists in the Black community. A lack of adequate financial resources does not necessarily prevent a lower-class individual from seeking out the services of some sort of folk healer, particularly if he or she feels that his investment will result in a handsome return.

In contrast to the professional psychotherapist (or even the cultic therapist affiliated with a religious movement such as Christian Science or Scientology), the Spiritual medium is a "poor person's psychiatrist" whose services tend to be congruent with the economic means and the world view of his clients. Whereas the former may charge $50 or more for a consultation, the latter tends to provide his clients advice for a nominal donation or a fee of a few dollars. The professional therapist may be a member of a higher social stratum and a different ethnic group; the Spiritual advisor tends to have the same humble origins as his or her clients and consequently shares a common etiology of disorder with them. Furthermore, the Spiritual advisor meets clients in surroundings they are familiar with rather than in an impersonal office complex filled with white middle-class faces. Even when the Spiritual advisor, imitates the trappings of such a forbidding environment, as does Rev. Mary Arnold, the effect is probably not the same, because the client knows he or she is visiting a charismatic and successful healer who has *arrived*, despite the barriers that the system creates for the poor and for various minority groups in their attempts to obtain economic security.

Spiritual advisors are generally empathetic, warm, and compassionate individuals who are well acquainted with the problems of their clients. In the process of counseling, the advisor presents solutions that are realistic in terms of both the standards of the client's culture and the opportunities available to poor Blacks. Although Spiritual advisors view some illnesses as predominantly physiological and others as predominantly psychosocial in nature, their approach to healing tends to focus on the latter. Even when a physical ailment is recognized, the Spiritual advisor's tendency is to resort to psychotherapeutic techniques — laying-on-of-hands, anointing with holy oil, or giving the client a blessed handkerchief or apron — rather than to use physical treatments, such as the prescription of roots and herbs.

The therapy provided by Spiritual mediums is by no means a panacea that will solve all the problems faced by their clients. While most Spiritual advisors are sincere, some apparently are exploitative, either in terms of what they promise a client or expect as a financial compensation for services or both. Perhaps the most problematic dimension of their approach is a strong tendency to deemphasize or overlook social forces that may be contributing to their clients' problems, an issue which I will explore in greater detail later in this chapter. Further study needs to be conducted on the efficacy of the treatment prescribed by Spiritual advisors—yet all of these reservations concerning the therapy provided by Spiritual mediums can also be applied to a greater or lesser degree to conventional professional psychotherapy.

The Dual Nature of the Black Spiritual Movement: Accommodation versus Protest

The relation between religion and political activism is a paradoxical and often contradictory one. While Karl Marx's assertion that religion is the "opium of the people" is well known, he was also cognizant of its emancipatory potential. For the most part, however, Marx viewed religion as "the self-consciousness and self-feeling of a man who has either not yet found himself or has already lost himself again" (Marx and Engels 1964:41). He argued that in the case of primitive peoples, religion emanates from the awe that they experience in their encounter with nature—a view not unlike that of anthropologist Paul Radin. Of course, it must be noted that religion in primitive societies also serves as an expression of social solidarity and cultural identity, and in some instances possibly as a form of ecological adaptation. In general, Marx directed his cursory remarks on religion to class societies rather than primitive societies: in the former, religion is primarily a by-product of social alienation and secondarily a source of it. Although Marx recognized that throughout history ruling classes have used religion as a mechanism of social control, he regarded it primarily as an attempt to ease the pain, at least for the moment, of living in an exploitative and fragmented society. The price that the masses must pay for the solace of religion is a form of "false consciousness" that obscures the real root of their suffering, namely a stratified social system, and prevents them from arising against their oppressors.

Marx succinctly summarized the dual nature of religion in the following statement: "Religious distress is at the same time the *expression* of real distress and the *protest* against real distress. Religion is the sigh of the oppressed creature, the heart of a heartless world, just as it is the spirit of an unspiritual situation" (Marx and Engels 1964:42). Unfortunately, Marx had very little further to say about the protest function of religion. In the case of capitalist society, while he did not claim that the bourgeoisie necessarily imposes its religious ideology upon the proletariat, Marx explained the acceptance of similar religious notions among the working class as a product of the cultural hegemony of the ruling class as well as the alienated condition of the proletariat, which made them all the more receptive to such ideas. In other words, religion is the result of inequity, oppression, and human misery more than the generator of these conditions.

It was actually Engels more than Marx who elaborated upon the matter of religious protest. According to Engels, until the nineteenth century class struggles had been "carried out under religious shibboleths" and were usually "concealed behind a religious screen" (Marx and Engels 1964:98). Although initially he viewed religious movements as reactionary responses to oppression, Engels later applauded the progressive nature of primitive Christianity and, as is made apparent in the following remarks, likened it to the working-class movement of his day:

> Christianity was originally a movement of oppressed peoples: it first appeared as the religion of slaves and emancipated slaves, of poor people deprived of all rights, of peoples subjugated or dispersed by Rome. Both Christianity and the workers' socialism preach forthcoming salvation from bondage and misery; Christianity places this salvation in a life beyond, after death, in heaven; socialism places it in this world, in a transformation of society. Both are persecuted and baited, their adherents are despised and made objects of exclusive laws, the former as enemies of the human race, the latter as enemies of the state, enemies of the religion, the family, social order. (Marx and Engels 1964:316)

In part guided by Marx and Engels's recognition of the dual nature of religion, a significant debate in the literature on Afro-American religion addresses the matter of whether it has been accommodative or emancipatory. Particularly in recent years, various scholars have argued that religion has performed an ideological function in Black resistance in various regions of the Americas, including the United States, Brazil, Colombia, Haiti, and Jamaica (Wilmore 1972; Bastide 1978; Taussig 1979; Laguerre 1980; H. Campbell 1980). In contrast, however, Eugene D. Genovese, the renowned historian of North American slavery, makes a distinction between the religion of Blacks in the United States and of those in other parts of the Americas. It is his contention that "religion (Islam, voodoo, or Afro-Catholic syncretisms) proved to be an essential ingredient in slave cohesion and organized resistance throughout the hemisphere, but in the United States the enforced prevalence of Protestant Christianity played an opposite role" (Genovese 1974:402–03). Christianity was primarily used by slaveowners as a mechanism of social control which served to ensure docility in the behavior and thinking of their slaves. In compensation for their miserable condition under the oppressive institution of slavery, Blacks were to be consoled by the promise of some ill-defined form of deliverance from their woe.

For the most part, however, scholars have come to recognize that religion among Black Americans, both before and after the Civil War, has functioned both as an opiate and a form of social and political protest, yet there is little consensus as to the relative weight of each of these dimensions in Black American religion. In his penetrating historical analysis of slave religion in North America, Raboteau (1978:317–18) appears to give roughly equal weight to its accommodative and rebellious components:

> Slave religion has been stereotyped as otherworldly and compensatory. It was otherworldly in the sense that it held that this world and this life were not the end, nor the final measure of existence. It was compensatory to the extent that it consoled and supported slaves worn out by the unremitting toil and capricious cruelty of the "peculiar institution." To conclude, however, that religion distracted slaves from concern with life and dissuaded them from action in the present is to distort the full story and to simplify the complex role of religious motivation in human behavior. It does not always follow that belief in a future state of happiness leads to an acceptance of suffering in this world. . . .
>
> To describe slave religion as merely otherworldly is inaccurate, for the slaves believed that God had acted, was acting, and would continue to act within human history and within their own particular history as a peculiar people just as long ago he acted on behalf of another chosen people, biblical Israel. Moreover, slave religion had a this-worldly impact, not only in leading some slaves to acts of external rebellion, but also in helping slaves to assert and maintain a sense of personal value — even of ultimate worth. The religious meet-

ings in the quarters, groves, and "hush harbors" were themselves frequently acts of rebellion against the proscriptions of the master.

The first quantitative analysis of the relationship between religiosity and militancy among Black Americans was done by Gary Marx (1970). When various dimensions of religious involvement — for example, the subjective importance given to church attendance — were examined, it was consistently found that religiosity was inversely related to civil rights militancy. Among the interviewees who identified themselves as "very religious," 39 percent of those with a temporal orientation were militant, whereas only 15 percent of those with an other-worldly orientation were militant. On the basis of this distinction among the religious, it is argued that for many of the former category, "religion seems to facilitate or at least not to inhibit protest" (G. Marx 1970:374). Overall, other-worldly religiosity tends to inhibit civil rights militancy, while temporal religiosity is more likely to promote, but does not guarantee, militancy. Remarking on the nature of the other-worldly orientation of various religious Blacks, G. Marx (1970:374) laments that "until such time as religion loosens its hold over these people or comes to embody to a greater extent the belief that man as well as God can bring about secular change, and focuses more on the here and now, religious involvement may be seen as an important factor working against the widespread radicalization of the Negro public."

More recently, Nelsen and Nelsen (1975) have called into question the contention that religion tends to have a dampening effect on political activism among Black Americans. They present empirical data suggesting that "blacks were more likely than whites to embrace a more vigorous role for the church as an agency claiming their allegiance and as an institution making pronouncements and taking a protest stance" (Nelsen and Nelsen 1975:99). Arguing that Marx does not control for sectarianism, they make a distinction between this variable and orthodoxy. Following Demerath (1965), they maintain that the sectarian is more adverse to participation by a minister in community affairs and controversial issues than the conventional church member. On the basis of a sample of 405 interviewees in Bowling Green, Kentucky, Nelsen and Nelsen demonstrate that orthodoxy is positively associated with militancy; sectarianism, negatively associated. By utilizing religiosity style indices, they present evidence indicating that "a churchlike orientation inspires militancy, while a sectlike orientation acts as an opiate for militancy" (Nelsen and Nelsen 1975:123). In assessing the overall impact of religion on political activism among Black Americans, Nelsen and Nelsen (1975:136) conclude that "Black religion serves in part as a channel through which feeling about society can be voiced and protest expressed in a routinized way."

Historical and social scientific research on Black religion attests to its multifaceted character. Unfortunately, statements as to whether Black religion tends to be an opiate or an inspiration for militancy often overlook its diversity. Although G. Marx in his sample makes fine distinctions among those respondents with conventional religious affiliations (that is, Episcopalian, Presbyterian, Catholic, Methodist, and Baptist), he lumps those who belong to various "sects and cults" in one category. In light of his concern with militancy among religious Blacks, it is important to note that there may exist considerable variation of political attitudes and behavior among adherents of unconventional religious groups. One might, for example, expect a member of a messianic-nationalist sect, such as one of the Black Islamic groups, to be much more militant than a member of a conversionist sect, such as a small Holiness or Pentecostal storefront church. Similarly, Nelsen and Nelsen (1975) fail to recognize that some religious sectarians fully *expect* their leaders to speak out on political issues. Undoubtedly, such behavior on the part of Elijah Muhammed and particularly Malcolm X attracted many young lower-class Blacks to the Nation of Islam. While indeed many sects in the Black community, as in the larger society, tend to be apolitical, one must be careful not to assume that they all are. In a sense, many Black religious groups emerged as a protest to racism and social stratification in American society.

Yet while Black sects and denominations have secured some autonomy for Black Americans, the extent to which they have stimulated social change is not entirely clear. Even though slave religion provided Blacks with a certain degree of solace and comfort during the antebellum period, evidently it never developed a full-blown, politically militant millennialism. In some instances, religion inspired slave rebellions, but these generally resulted in even closer control over all aspects of slave life. As Genovese (1974:254) aptly points out, the Black slaves of the New World transformed Christianity into a "religion of resistance — not often of revolutionary defiance, but of a spiritual resistance that accepted the limits of the politically possible." On the other hand, slave religion "laid the foundations of protonational consciousness" which eventually blossomed in the Black messianic-nationalist sects and the Black mainstream denominations during the twentieth century (Genovese 1974:284). The emancipatory dimension of contemporary Black religion, however, may be a limited one. The messianic-nationalist sects are relatively small and are outside the mainstream of Black religion. Furthermore, despite their often militant rhetoric, messianic-nationalist groups sometimes move toward a position of accommodation vis-à-vis the larger society (Parenti 1964). For example, since the death of Elijah Muhammed in 1975, the Nation of Islam, now known as the American Muslim Mission, has dropped its racist posture toward Whites and moved toward a more orthodox form of Islam. The mainstream denominations in the Black community, while criticizing the racist features of American society, have for the most part ignored the intricate relationship between racism and capitalism. In reality, much more research is needed on the question of whether Black religion is an opiate or a source of political inspiration for its people. What follows is my examination of this issue for the case of the Black Spiritual movement.

I have argued that Spiritual churches have in large part responded to racial stratification in American society by adopting a thaumaturgical/manipulationist strategy. Despite certain similarities between the Spiritual movement and Black Protestantism, it is the emphasis on manipulation of one's present condition through the use of magico-religious rituals and the acquisition of esoteric knowledge that tends to distinguish the former from some of the more conventional religions among Black Americans. For the most part, members of Spiritual churches do not adhere to the puritanical morality and the other-worldly perspective of many conversionist sects. Even when other-worldly dimensions are present in Spiritual churches, they generally are overshadowed by more temporal concerns. Spiritual churches tend to emphasize the acquisition of the "good life" along with its worldly pleasures. Since the conventional avenues of achieving success and economic prosperity are not readily open to its adherents, the Spiritual movement promises that they may be achieved instead by obtaining spiritual power to receive a blessing. The Spiritual religion concerns itself with the concrete problems of its adherents or clients by attempting to provide them with the spiritual means of acquiring needed finances, employment, health, mental tranquility, love, or the improvement of a strained personal relationship. In fact, many Spiritual people repeatedly note that heaven and hell are states of the human mind — the former being a result of a positive attitude and the latter of negative thinking.

Various anthropologists have come to regard many aspects of Black culture as adaptive mechanisms which have enabled the majority of Black Americans to survive against seemingly insurmountable odds in a hostile environment (Valentine 1972; Stack 1974). Mithun (1976) cites the extended family and an existential philosophy exhibited in music, dance, religion, folklore, verbal styles, and cooperative networks as examples of strategies that Blacks have devised to deal with the ambiguities of their condition. The Spiritual religion, with its complex of prophets and advisors, may be included among the various strategies for coping with the social realities of living in a stratified and racist society. Like many other Afro-American religions, such as Voodoo in Haiti and in the United States, *shango* in Trinidad, and *batuque* in Brazil, the Black Spiritual movement provides Blacks with a theology for existence and survival (G. Simpson 1978; Leacock and Leacock 1975). It is a pragmatic religion with a strong temporal orientation in that it emphasizes the acquisition of health, love, economic prosperity, and interpersonal power.

However, while the Spiritual religion appears to provide an important coping mechanism for a certain segment of the Black community, it also exhibits a maladaptive dimension in that it unwittingly encourages its adherents and clients to accept existing socioeconomic arrangements. This pattern is particularly evident in the type of advice that Spiritual pastors, elders, and mediums give in sermons, sermonettes, prophecy sessions, and private consultations: to a considerable degree, it appears that the counseling provided in these settings focuses on individualistic concerns and does not call for larger social structural adjustments. This is not to say that Spiritual leaders never make note of the need for social cohesiveness among members of a specific congregation or within the Black community in general. Nor do I wish to downplay the importance of the mutual support network found in many Spiritual churches. For the most part, however, the Spiritual movement provides certain people with thaumaturgical techniques by which they hope to solve their personal problems. In essence Spiritual pastors, elders, and mediums promise their members and clients improvement in their lives if they engage in various magico-religious practices, develop a positive attitude, and overcome negative thoughts.

The following examples of the kind of instruction that pastors, mediums, and elders often give their congregations will illustrate this accommodative side of the Spiritual movement (all names of persons and churches are fictitious).

At a demonstration conducted at Unity Fellowship, Mother Bates, the temple's "divine healer" gave the congregation the following advice in conjunction with her healing prayer: "You can be a millionaire in your mind. Whenever you need money, God will give it to you. Just ask him."

During a Sunday afternoon service at St. Cecilia's Divine Healing Church No. 2, Reverend Arnold told her congregation, "Children, you don't have to suffer. You don't have to be in dire need. It is the way you think that is the problem. . . . I know that you can make yourself suffer. Look at me. If I could get you to think big, you would have everything."

During another service, Reverend Arnold spoke of the unrealized potential of the subconscious mind: "Your mind had a whole lot of power which you do not use. . . . The subconscious mind has to bring out inspiration. Some of you have in the subconscious mind hate and jealousy. . . . Think of whom you have mistreated. Ask for forgiveness. I don't have no hate. I don't care what kind of car you drive." Referring to the few Whites present in her congregation, Reverend Arnold noted that they were aware of the poor housing that Blacks have been forced to live in. She assured her followers that "God can give us big fine houses."

Reverend Walton, the "Royal Elect Ruler" of a Spiritual church in Michigan, discussed the need to overcome negative thoughts if one wishes to succeed in this life. In large part, the following words were a response to his dissatisfaction with what he considered to be the reluctance of his members to be generous in contributing to his "consecrated offering" at a Sunday afternoon service: "We're getting slack in paying our dues. If you don't pay the rent, we will be outside. It

is not sanctification that pays the bills. Everyone has got a penny somewhere. I am not taking my money to pay the bills of the church. . . .
Don't allow yourself to become glad of your present condition. A lot
of us is glad we are broke. The reason that we don't have more is
because of our negative thoughts. Wishing don't get anything. First
you got to have a positive mind. You is your worst enemy. . . . God
promised to give everything. Money is out there for you to get. God
works through mind and money. . . . Some of you are scared to obey
me. I want all of you to get a prosperous spirit. People say the prophet
beg too much. I don't beg. You don't give. Some of you makes pledges
to Rev. Ike. You better put your trust in what you know is right." Rev.
Walton tells his congregation that the previous evening he "put on
one of my finest suits and cut glass" and attended a banquet with
some "millionaires." "I want some millions. Jesus did not deal with
no poor folk. Those people he picked were professional people —
lawyers, doctors, and fishermen. Jesus was a wealthy man. They gam-
bled for his garment."

Reverend Swanson, the pastor of another Spiritual church in
Michigan, spoke of the need for people to make contact with the Divine Mind: "We are going to talk to you about the Aquarian Age —
the age of advancement. This is the age of new knowledge. . . . You
cannot go up by keeping the old ideas. The mind is all you have. Just
as you think, you become. You are a miniature universe. We are trying to rise above and live in the consciousness of Divine Mind. You
are a divine power. There is not anything that you cannot do if you
want to do it bad enough. The mind never dies. This is not a church.
The church is in you."

According to Frank (1973:314–15), all persons seeking psychotherapy are demoralized in some way — that is, they have lost confidence
in their ability to cope with the pressures of everyday problems,
whatever their sociocultural milieu, and consequently are "prey to
anxiety and depression . . . as well as to resentment, anger, and other
dysphoric emotions." Psychotherapy can restore morale by enabling
the patient to change his perceptions and behavior, which in turn
enables him to overcome obstacles that at at one time seemed insurmountable. Similarly, as I have argued elsewhere, the techniques
used by Spiritual leaders in dealing with the everyday problems of
their followers and clients, either during religious services or in private consultations, may help some people to ovecome a state of "de-

moralization" (Baer 1981a). As is made apparent by the examples presented above, a common theme in this effort is the notion that one has to think positively and overcome negative modes of thought. The emphasis on positive thinking is evident not only in public prophecy sessions and private consultations, but also in sermons, testimonies, and commentaries of various types. Spiritual leaders continually remind their clients that they must believe in themselves, and that if they do not, no one else will.

The advice that Spiritual leaders impart to their followers and clients tends to focus on individualistic concerns. Life in modern America, particularly in large urban areas, is characterized by increasing privatization, or what John Wilson (1978:358–59) terms "individuation." The positive-thinking approach, whether expressed in a secular form such as that of Dale Carnegie or a religious form such as that of Norman Vincent Peale, has had great appeal in American society. In essence, the emphasis on positive thinking in the thaumaturgical/manipulationist sects in the Black community is a Black version of its counterpart in the larger society.

This approach to problem solving has a maladaptive dimension for Blacks, however, in that it tends to deny "political conflict by stressing the importance of individual over society, the insignificance of social arrangement and plans, and the irrelevance of group conflict beside the paramount importance of the individual" (J. Wilson 1978:356). In this regard, the approach of Spiritual leaders is similar to that of conventional psychotherapists, who often urge their clients to muster the psychic resources necessary to adjust to the demands of society. Again as is apparent from the examples cited above, there is often a tendency on the part of the Spiritual pastors, elders, and mediums to engage in what amounts to "blaming the victim." Instead of pointing out how social and economic forces may be at the root of many of their followers' and clients' problems, this approach holds the individual responsible for his or her own failures.

As Marvin Harris (1980:381–82) so aptly notes, the tendency to blame the poor for their plight is not by any means restricted to the more affluent strata of society: "The poor or near-poor themselves are often the staunchest supporters of the view that people who really want to work can always find work. This attitude forms part of a larger world view in which there is little comprehension of the conditions that make poverty for some inevitable. What must be seen as a system is seen purely in terms of individual faults, individual motives, individual choices. Hence, the poor turn against the poor and blame each other for their plight."

The question that inevitably arises is why lower-class Blacks who are victimized by the existing social relations in American society would come to accept a belief system which in some ways is inimical to their self-interests. In this regard, we must consider a well-known passage in *The German Ideology* where Marx and Engels declare that the "ideas of the ruling class are, in every age, the ruling ideas." Some time later, Antonio Gramsci went on to develop this idea in his concept of "hegemony." In an overview of the concept, Femia (1975:30) observes, "Gramsci states that the supremacy of a social group may manifest itself in two forms: 'domination,' which is realized through the coercive organs of the state, and 'intellectual and moral leadership,'" which is objectified in and exercised through the institutions of civil society, the ensemble of educational, religious, and associational institutions." The latter of these two forms of supremacy constitutes hegemony—the situation in which one class exerts control of the cognitive and intellectual life of society by strictly cultural means as opposed to coercive ones. A consequence of hegemony is that the dominant group obtains the consent of the various subordinate groups to their own domination. In essence, as Bauman (1976:68) points out in the case of capitalist society, the world view of the dominant group or ruling class becomes so thoroughly diffused among the masses that it becomes the "commonsense" of the entire society:

> Capitalism, like any established system, has a powerful edge over any of its potential adversaries in that its very reality, the structure of the everyday situations which it creates for the individual, reaffirms and reinforces the capitalism-sustaining brand of commonsense even without an open intervention of refined intellectual arguments. It lends the habitual patterns of conduct a spurious air of naturalness and eternity; and it stamps everyday routine as rational behavior, having previously established the value of rationality as a supreme criterion of worthiness. Moreover, the ruling class can rely on the fact that its culture, once established, defines all imaginable improvement as an advance in acquisition of this very culture. Even a powerful thrust toward amelioration, therefore, can hardly fracture the cul-

tural foundation of the current hegemony; if anything, it will rather reinforce it by adding a new strength and popularity to its constituent value-patterns.

Cultural hegemony in large measure is achieved and maintained by a subtle process of education, which involves not only the schools but the mass media and popular literature. Since these agencies of socialization are generally controlled by the dominant group, it is not surprising that they would communicate their image of social reality. In mainstream America, the emphasis on individualism promoted by these organs is so pervasive and all encompassing that it even influences the perceptions and attitudes of individuals and groups living on the margins of our society.

In this regard, the Black Spiritual movement unwittingly contributes to the "cult of private life" which is championed by such agencies of socialization as the family, the schools, the media, advertisers, social workers, and psychotherapists, and which serves to legitimize the existing social system (Greisman and Mayers 1977: 61–62). According to this perspective,

> the source, if not the cause, of mental disorders is invariably traced to the client himself and/or his friends and relations. Society-at-large does not, and cannot, figure significantly in these treatments, although the collective ill-effects of living day-to-day in advanced industrial society have been repeatedly demonstrated. Thus psychology, counseling, and allied techniques further privatize the individual, leading her or him to search for exclusively existential solutions, more sophisticated avoidance mechanisms, and tried and true adjustment techniques. Marcuse's remark about "shrinks" being so-called because they shrink minds to manageable proportions is appropriate as social problems are telescoped into personal ones.

Although many Blacks, like other social groups on the lower rungs of the American class system, may sense a contradiction between the ideal definition of reality and the starkness of their own lives, they often are unable, in large part because of the hegemony of mainstream beliefs, values, and attitudes, to locate the source of their discontent. The individualistic orientation of American culture is rooted so deeply that most people are unable to recognize that larger social forces play a strong influence in shaping their destinies.

Unlike the messianic-nationalist sects, most Black Spiritual groups tend not to identify external enemies or oppressors, and their members often fault themselves for the miseries that they experience. Characteristic of many people in working-class communities, as Parkin (1971:90) has noted, is that they "generate a meaning-system which is of purely parochial significance, representing a design for living based upon localized social knowledge and face-to-face relationships" and fail to adopt a "macro-social view of the reward structure and some understanding of the *systematic* nature of inequality." In like manner, Black Spiritual churches deflect attention from the social and economic roots of the problems of their members and clients and thus conform to the Marxian notion of religion as an opiate or a device that leads the downtrodden to accept their plight.

On the other hand, to view the Spiritual movement merely in this light would do injustice to its dualistic nature, which exhibits some subtle and even occasionally overt elements of social protest. Although these elements are not as pronounced as the accommodative ones, they do surface from time to time in comments made by Spiritual leaders during religious services that allude to the racist and class structure of American society. The following examples (again using pseudonyms) indicate some degree of racial and class consciousness on the part of Spiritual people:

> During his sermon at a Sunday morning service, Reverend Thomas, the pastor of the Cathedral of Spiritual Science in Memphis, made several references to social injustice. In decrying the prevalence of police brutality in Black ghettoes, he maintained that "the police are in charge of order but they do not know how to control themselves. They come up with falsehoods in order to arrest whom they want to." He also turned his attention to international relations between the advanced industrial nations and those of the Third World, noting that "the trouble with the world is that some countries are trying to control others." Referring specifically to the political situation in Iran and comparing the social inequality there to that in the United States, he noted that most Iranians are "more poor than some of us here."

At a Sunday morning service, Reverend Gibson, the pastor of St. Jude's Spiritual Church, urged her tiny congregation to vote for Jane Eskind, the Democratic candidate who was running against the Republican incumbent, Howard Baker, for the United States Senate in the fall of 1978. Ironically, her comments also contained an accommodative dimension in that she viewed Blacks as being incapable of effectively promoting their own political interests. Taking a picture of Eskind from the temple's altar, Rev. Gibson told her congregation, "I am hoping that this lady be elected. She would be a big aid to the Black race. They don't want her to be elected because she is a Jew and a woman. . . . Baker is for the rich man. I am praying that she get elected because the Black race needs help. Jane Eskind is going to win. After she gets elected, we ain't going to appreciate it. The reason that I said that she is going to win is because God said that she is going to win. They don't want a Catholic as president because he would help the Black folks. . . . We are down on one another rather than for one another. The White man will help us ten times more often than the Black man."

The assistant pastor of a Spiritual temple in Pittsburgh included several comments on international tensions in her sermon, noting the conflict between China and Vietnam at the time, and predicted that the world was heading for another war. As she was about to read a passage from the Book of Revelations, she complained about White dominance in the larger society and in international relations: "This is The Man's world. I don't know how many little children didn't get bread so that he could have that Cadillac."

Prophet Adams, the male pastor of Calvary Spiritual Temple (a small storefront church in Detroit), made the following remarks during a Sunday morning sermon: "What is wrong with people? They want to live in the gutters and hog pens of life. What is wrong with the Arabs? They have greed. What is wrong with the money changers in this country? They have greed. They are going to fight over this oil. Our President would be a better man if he knew who he was."

Social protest in Spiritual churches usually takes a more subtle form. In his discussion of the belief in Indian spirits among the Spiritual people of New Orleans, Kaslow (1981:64) alludes to their symbolic meaning: "Black Hawk is regarded as a warrior who can cause justice to be done, and his intercession is frequently sought in court cases, or in seeking the release of loved ones from prison. The role of the Indian as an opponent of white domination is an expression of protest against status inferiority in the larger society." Protest is also inherent in the widespread belief among Spiritual people that heaven and hell exist in the here and now. Members of Spiritual churches often pride themselves that unlike other religious individuals and groups they do not subscribe to the other-worldly notion of salvation that they often refer as pie-in-the-sky religion. While it may be argued that the means that members of Spiritual churches use in attempting to attain heaven on earth are in large part accommodative, the refusal to wait for one's social rewards in some nebulous afterlife suggests some degree of nonacceptance of existing social relations.

Also, Spiritual people in large part have come to reject certain conventional notions of how to achieve success — namely, by abiding by the precepts of the Protestant work ethic. This does not mean that Spiritual people do not work hard; as is generally true of poor people, many of them do. On the other hand, thanks to the cultural hegemony of mainstream ideals, they value the benefits of the "good life" and the prestige symbols of the American Dream. Lower-class Black Americans share in the cultural goals of the larger society, especially in an era of mass education and communication, and their behavioral deviation from the alleged means of obtaining these objectives cannot be simply attributed to what some refer to as the "culture of poverty" (O. Lewis 1966). Ethnic groups generally have been enculturated into the dominant values long before they have achieved structural assimilation into American society (Gordon 1964). As Valentine (1968) notes, the values and aspirations of the poor may be very similar to those of middle-class people, but must become modified in practice because of the situational stresses that the former experience in every-day life. Many Spiritual people have come to realize that hard work in itself does not guarantee upward social mobility or security in American society. Since many Blacks in America are denied access to the strategies that can result in some modest degree of social advancement, many Spiritual people have come to reject mainstream platitudes about the Protestant work ethic that function to legitimize the American system of racial stratification. This is not to say that members of Spiritual groups do not see any merit in work, but rather that they recognize that financial success is dependent on more capricious factors. What these other factors are, as I have already noted, is often not clear in the minds of Spiritual people. Hence the tendency on their part to resort to thaumaturgical/manipulationist techniques, emphasizing a positive attitude and magico-religious rituals, in the attempts to cope with their marginal position in American society.

A Black God's Response to Racial Stratification

The elements of accommodation and protest characteristic of the Spiritual religion are perhaps best exemplified in the Father Hurley sect. George W. Hurley reacted to the racist and stratified nature of American society by combining elements of the thaumaturgical/ manipulationist sects and the messianic-nationalist sects in the Black community. Like his better-known contemporary, Father Divine, he taught that God had taken the form of a Black man of humble social origins. Father Hurley even went one step further by boldly asserting that God throughout the ages had appeared in the form of Black men and that all the great religious prophets of history had been Black. In addition, whereas the southern White segregationists maintained that Blacks were the offspring of Cain and consequently cursed with dark skin and servitude, Father Hurley argued that it was Whites instead who bore the curse of Cain.

On occasion, Father Hurley went so far as to hint that the prevailing caste system of American society would be reversed at some time in the not-too-distant future. He predicted that the White-dominated Protestant religion is "going to be swept into oblivion" and claimed that the time "has come for black people" (*Aquarian Age*, Dec. 1952). An unsigned article in one Hagar's newspaper boldly declared that Blacks are "superior"to Whites (*Aquarian Age*, Nov. 1939). For Father Hurley, hell constituted a condition of "hatred, jealousy, segregation, lying, robbery, stealing, disease and poverty" and sin translated into "hatred, prejudice, jim-crowism and segregationism" (*Aquarian Age*, April 1969; Feb. 1975; Oct. 1938). Like other messianic nationalists, he expressed his protest against the dominant White group by rejecting its notions of racial superiority, religious truth, and morality.

We can probably only speculate as to how Father Hurley was regarded by the White power structure in Detroit and the other American cities where temples of the Universal Hagar's Spiritual Church were located during the 1930s and the 1940s. As has been true in the case of the Nation of Islam and other Black messianic-nationalist sects, it would seem that the Father Hurley sect, at least in Detroit, must have come to the attention of law enforcement agencies and been the object of their surveillance at some time or another. Undoubtedly, as is indicated by the fact that no Hagar's temples were established in the Deep South until the 1960s, Father Hurley and his message would not have been tolerated by the White power structure in cities in that region of the country.

It is very difficult to determine the threat that George Hurley may have perceived from the larger society in preaching his radical brand of religion. A perusal of his writings, however, suggests that at times he may have realized how inflammatory his remarks were and felt a need to demonstrate some degree of conciliation. In contrast to his suggestions that "the top rail shall go to the bottom, and the bottom rail to the top," he also argued that what Blacks essentially desired was the same economic opportunities as Whites (*Aquarian Age,* June 1939). Father Hurley proclaimed an "age of equal rights" for all peoples (*Aquarian Age,* Aug. 1942); he also maintained that "we must be as one, both nationally and spiritually, black and white alike" (*Aquarian Age,* April 1954). In his opinion, the Constitution of the United States guarantees "freedom and liberty for all mankind, regardless of race, creed, or color" (*Aquarian Age,* June 1968). He even urged Whites, or Gentiles, to discard their Protestant traditions and to "serve God in spirit and truth" (*Aquarian Age,* Dec. 1952).

It is possible that the war effort of World War II, with its heavy emphasis on patriotism and total national commitment, caused Father Hurley to tone down some of his earlier virulent rhetoric. Even prior to American military involvement in World War II, however, he expressed his avid admiration and support of both President Franklin D. Roosevelt and Eleanor Roosevelt. Of the latter, Father Hurley approvingly wrote, "Mrs. Roosevelt is truly a woman of this New Age for she has left her throne and visited the slums and passed by alleys where poor ragged black nappy-headed children and dirty faced white children in rags are living, and has patted them on the head" (*Aquarian Age,* Aug. 1940). With respect to the President, to whom he referred as "his excellency," Father Hurley wrote, "He is a man with the gift of inspiration and divination, divinely inspired by a Mighty God, and God is righteous force dwelling not only within him, but within all mankind" (*Aquarian Age,* Aug. 1940). During the war, Father Hurley pledged the loyalty of his followers to the United States government.

In contrast to many Black messianic-nationalist sects, Father Hurley did not provide his followers with an extensive system of cooperative and communal institutions intended as programs of self-help. Nor did he for the most part emulate the programs of his more famous rival, Father Divine, who, in order to provide food, clothing, shelter, and jobs for his followers, sponsored elaborate feasts and an elaborate network of cooperative business, inexpensive restaurants, and racially integrated hotels or "heavens." Instead, Father Hurley's response to the problems of his people tended to take on a thaumaturgical/manipulationist orientation. The lesser-known Black god, who like Father Divine was born and raised in Georgia and in the violence and racial repression of the post-Reconstruction era, offered his followers an elaborate system of rituals, incantations, and occult knowledge intended to provide them with spiritual power to overcome their degradation. Hurleyites were and still are urged to direct their prayers for prosperity and security in this life to their deity.

The problems of poverty and life in the urban ghettoes of the industrial North were to be overcome through "meditation" and "concentration"—that is, by believing in oneself, thinking positively, and discarding all feelings of despair and hopelessness. Father Hurley taught his followers that their only hope for lifting themselves from their "deplorable condition" was to develop their "innate forces, to think, to will, and to imagine" (*Aquarian Age*, April 1940). During the height of the Depression, he offered a version of the same faith in the power of positive thinking that people like Dale Carnegie and Norman Vincent Peale would later offer to the White masses and Rev. Ike has more recently presented to the Black masses. According to George Hurley, only when one has learned that God is Spirit and resides in every man and woman may one begin to achieve his or her potential. Like others in the Black Spiritual movement, Father Hurley provided the saints of his earthly kingdom with a wide array of "secrets" and "mysteries" by which they could attempt to gain control over their destinies. Instead of political and economic solutions, it was to be spiritual or metaphysical power that would redeem the Ethiopians in America.

In the meantime, while his followers were awaiting the fruits of their magico-religious practices, Father Hurley provided them with an elaborate politico-religious organization of offices and auxiliaries within which they could achieve a religious status far greater than any status they might expect to obtain in the larger society. A man or woman who in everyday life might be a janitor or a domestic servant could become a Prince, Princess, Reverend, Master, Madam, Professor, or Saint in the Kingdom of God. By attending the School of Mediumship and Psychology or becoming an initiate of the Knights of the All Seeing Eye, one could have access to all the secrets and mysteries of the universe, thus setting oneself off from mere mortals. And one could come to the realization that even if one's present condition is "hell," one's spirit will go through a never-ending process of reincarnation, making it possible to obtain salvation not in some ill-defined afterlife, but in a future glorious earthly existence.

After the death of Father Hurley in 1943, the messianic-nationalist tone of his religion became considerably muted. As a colleague and I have noted, such a shift is not necessarily unusual:

> In spite of their often revolutionary stance, messianic-nationalist groups not uncommonly move toward a position of accommodation vis-à-vis the dominant society. As early as 1964, Parenti noted that the Nation of Islam was "manifesting a growing inclination toward a *modus vivendi* with the larger community . . . " Parenti (1964: 182–83). This shift accelerated rapidly following the death of Elijah Muhammed in 1975. Under the guidance of Wallace E. Muhammed (a.k.a. Inman Warith Deen Muhammed), the group, now known as the American Muslim Mission (A.M.M), dropped its anti-White ideology and moved toward a more orthodox practice of Islam. In the last few years, the A.M.M. has begun to exhibit a noticeable introversionist tendency. . . . This change is the result of a growing middle-class orientation of the A.M.M and its members. As this example reveals, worldly success — a goal implied in the messianic-nationalist desire for political-economic independence — can result in a muting of the more rebellious inclinations that exemplify this type of sect. (Baer and Singer 1981:7)

Hurleyites, of course, continue to worship their Black god and reject the notion of a fair-skinned Jesus Christ and the White saints of Roman Catholicism. The Ethiopian Christmas and New Year are still observed, but current Hagar's leaders for the most part do not strike out against institutional racism with nearly the same vengeance that Father Hurley did at a time when it was much more dangerous to do so.

Several association newspapers of the late 1960s suggest a brief but generally mild resurgence of Black nationalism in the group. A column on "Afro-American History" appeared regularly in the *Aquarian Age* during this period. One relatively new member wrote that Blacks are "not Negroes but Asiatic people," and that not only Indians but also Blacks were in the Americas prior to its discovery by Columbus (*Aquarian Age*, June 1968). He also claimed that technological innovations by Blacks included the elevator, photography, the telegraph, the refrigerator, golf clubs, the telephone, and the electric light bulb. Later, this same individual argued that separatism is necessary for Black power, that integration is a "dead topic," that God has called Black people throughout the world to be "his chosen people, the Original Jews," and that they are "predestined to build a new government" (*Aquarian Age*, March 1969). A perusal of Hagar's newspapers during this time also suggests, however, that some members took a more cautious stance toward the revival of messianic nationalism in their group. In an article entitled "White Power or Black Power?" another person wrote, "The answer is neither" (*Aquarian Age*, March 1968). He went on to state that time is the "only 'curative' for this racial scramble that the United States is involved in," that the Book of Revelation teaches that "all nations are created from one blood," and that Blacks and Whites "will one day march together." A third author wrote that "so-called leaders tell us to unite and be ready to fight," but although acknowledging that Black Power and unification are "good," warned Hurleyites that "fighting against people without having anything to fight with" is not desirable (*Aquarian Age*, June 1968). He noted that the White power structure owns and controls the factories, and that ultimately power is created with money. Therefore, the most effective means by which Blacks could bring about social change was to exert "green power" or "spending power." In concluding his article, the author reminded his readers that Blacks and Whites are "all brothers."

In contrast to the diluted version of messianic nationalism found in the group today, the thaumaturgical/manipulationist orientation that Father Hurley incorporated into his cosmology has continued to be a central concern. The sect also exhibits the dualistic combination of elements of accommodation and protest that is characteristic of Spiritual churches. This combination of oppositional elements

was particularly apparent in the following remarks that Reverend
Blaine, a middle-aged Hagar's pastor who is well-known for her intimate knowledge of the Spiritual religion, made at a Sunday morning service in her temple:

> Anything that you do, you should investigate. We were brain-
> washed into thinking God was so far away from us. That is the reason
> that we are so far back today. We fell short of our spiritual educa-
> tion. . . . We would take our earnings and take care of the minister.
> We bought him a car when he did not have a car. . . .
>
> You must be able to motivate your mind. We lost our prestige by
> following someone else's religion. I have found many people who have
> a mental problem. Father Hurley was born at the proper time, when
> people were at their lowest, when there was lynching and confusion.
> Father Hurley told people to think for themselves. He told you that
> you have six million brain cells to think with. Jesus brought the truth
> but man covered up the truth. People did not know that they have
> a right to the Tree of Life and to hold material things.
>
> The Spirit elevated Hurley as our prophet. He began to say that
> he was the second coming of Christ and had talks with Adam, Abra-
> ham, and Jesus. They were all a type of Christ. Adam was the God
> of the Adamic Age. Abraham came at the proper time. He picked
> it up and carried on for 2,001 years. The Spirit reincarnated itself
> in Jesus after it left Abraham. In 1884, a child was born. Father Hur-
> ley began to prophesize, heal the sick, and raise the dead. Father Hur-
> ley was seeking something to help his people. . . .
>
> The mind is governed by the Spirit. Father Hurley said that man
> can create heaven and hell and told you to remove all doubt out of
> your mind. . . . If you are poor, you are poor. All you have to do is
> to believe. All things are yours if you want them. He didn't teach
> you that you have a place to go. Education helps but the Spirit will
> make it alive. . . .
>
> We as a spiritually minded people are too idle. Plan what you are
> going to do. Through positive thinking, you are able to overcome all
> negative conditions. When you say you are poor, you are poor. When
> you say that you are rich, you are rich. If you have health, you have
> everything. Those material things are for your happiness. I should
> let my mind expand to its fullness. . . .
>
> Father Hurley was a radical man in his day. He stood for his peo-
> ple. He taught us that no one is better than another, whether he is
> white, black, or blue. . . . The United States has forgotten about the
> little people. We have been taking tokens. The people in Iran are not

satisfied with tokens. They have challenged the United States. . . .
Everyone has a right to live and to live comfortably. We all have to
pull off that intellectual self and be that spiritual self.

As Rev. Blaine's remarks suggest, the Universal Hagar's Spiritual
Church has in many ways become a typical Spiritual sect, despite
the tendency on the part of its members to disassociate themselves
from the larger Spiritual movement. The elements of accommodation and protest present in her words, however, are typical not only
of the dualistic nature of the Spiritual movement, but also of Afro-
American religion and religion in complex societies in general.

The Evolution of the Black Spiritual Movement

From the evidence available to us, it appears that the Spiritual
movement emerged during a period when many poor Blacks began
to migrate in massive numbers from the rural areas of the South
to the cities of the North as well as the South. Industrialization and
urbanization have not been processes exclusively characteristic of
the United States or other advanced capitalist societies. Furthermore,
Afro-Americans in other countries besides this one have been affected
by these two phenomena. For example, similar trends have had an
impact on Afro-Americans in Brazil:

> Industrialization might have brought the blacks an opportunity
> to earn a living and a channel of upward mobility. But they were
> slow to benefit from it, being held back at first by economic compe-
> tition from poor whites and immigrants. They were therefore not im-
> mediately integrated into the social class system of the capitalist re-
> gime. They formed a kind of subproletariat, and the development
> of urbanization, which destroyed their traditional values without pro-
> viding new ones in exchange, meant for them only a stepping up of
> the process of social disintegration. One might say that as the city
> developed, it had two successive effects on the Negro: first a disinte-
> grative impact and then a reintegrative one, as he finally gained a
> foothold in the class system, particularly in the construction and
> mechanical fields. (Bastide 1978:295)

Bastide goes on to describe *macumba*, a syncretistic Afro-Brazilian
sectarian movement that includes elements from African, Amerin-

dian, Catholic, and spiritist religions, as "an illustration of what happens to the African religions during a period when traditional values are being lost." His analysis of *macumba* is enlightening because its development exhibits some striking parallels with that of the Spiritual movement in this country. This is not to imply that the two movements are identical but rather to note that they may be viewed as adaptations to industrialization and urbanization on the part of Afro-Americans in two different areas of the New World. Bastide maintains that *macumba* served initially to provide recent arrivals in the cities of Brazil with some sense of cultural unity and social solidarity in an otherwise insecure, chaotic, and fluid universe. Although *macumba* still exists within the context of various socio-religious groups, in large part it has become an "individualized" movement. "Almost every priest invents new ritual forms or new spirits, and the fierce competition between cult groups is reflected not in greater fidelity to the past, as it is in Bahia, but in the very opposite: aesthetic or dogmatic innovations" (Bastide 1978:296). Today, *macumba* has to a large degree evolved from a collective ritual activity to an individual one, which places great emphasis on solving the personal problems of the poor by means of magical consultations. In some cases, *macumba* even "leads to social parasitism, to the shameless exploitation of the credulity of the lower classes, or to the unleashing of immoral tendencies that may range from rape to murder" (Bastide 1978:300).

While the Spiritual movement continues to exist and in some instances thrive in many cities in the United States, like *macumba* it seems to have passed its zenith. Time and time again I have heard Spiritual people speak of earlier days when their temples attracted larger numbers than they do today. It is not at all unusual to find Spiritual congregations whose founding pastors cater to a flock of middle-aged and elderly members. This is not to overlook the fact that some Spiritual churches are headed by relatively young and dynamic individuals who attract a large proportion of adolescents and young people. My observations, however, suggest that the latter type are considerably less common than the former. Furthermore, various studies have indicated that an increasing percentage of young Blacks exhibit a lower level of religiosity than do their parents and grandparents (Hamilton 1972:208). Although religion continues to be a significant aspect of life in the Black American community, it has been superseded in many of its functions by a variety of secular organizations and pursuits.

Just as *macumba* has undergone a process of devolution from a collective religion to a "client cult" which caters chiefly to the individualistic concerns of a wide variety of people, the Spiritual movement has to some extent undergone a similar metamorphosis. Both apparently have, since their respective beginnings, appealed to clients who have wished to restrict themselves to the private dimensions of their religion. Nevertheless, both started out as substitutes for the loss of community that certain rural migrants experienced upon arrival in urban areas. Over the years, whereas most Spiritual churches seem to have witnessed an appreciable decline in the number of regular members, many of the mediums associated with them still retain a fair number of clients seeking private counseling. While the Spiritual movement is by no means dead as a collective endeavor, it has to a large degree evolved into a system of magical therapy that attempts to provide its clients with individualistic solutions to their problems of living.

Given the paucity of historical data on the Spiritual movement, it is difficult to generalize about its overall evolutionary trajectory. However, there seems to be a tendency on the part of some of the larger Spiritual congregations to emulate the established sects or mainstream denominations in the Black community. In some ways, for example, the United House of the Redeemer in Indianapolis and St. Cecilia's Divine Healing Church No. 2 in Nashville exhibit such a pattern of development. Both congregations crosscut socioeconomic lines and, while still finding their greatest appeal in the lower class of their respective communities, have attracted some upwardly mobile working-class Blacks. Reverend Arnold has made it relatively easy for middle-class Blacks to join her church while retaining membership in a respectable Baptist or Methodist congregation — by permitting them to become associate members. It is possible that some middle-class Black members of mainstream denominations find her church attractive because it provides them with a certain degree of social recognition that they would not otherwise receive. One woman with a bachelor's degree and a relatively well-paying professional position admitted to me that she regards St. Cecilia's as a training ground for her ambition of becoming a religious leader. Although she retains regular membership in one of the prominent Black Bap-

tist churches in Nashville, she believes that her position at St. Cecilia's provides her with a unique opportunity to learn about the
inner workings of a successful religious organization.

Both Reverend Arnold and Reverend Brown tend to disassociate
themselves from most of the Spiritual congregations in their respective communities. In one of my interviews with Reverend Arnold,
she expressed some reluctance to categorize her congregations in
Nashville and Cleveland as Spiritual. In fact, her husband, in a separate interview, identified St. Cecilia's as a "Holiness" church devoted
to the "scientific study of Jesus Christ," and complained that many
of the Spiritual churches in Cleveland are involved in what he termed
"black art." Although the United House of the Redeemer is affiliated
with a large Spiritual association, as was noted earlier, Reverend
Brown considered the possibility of listing his congregation under
another heading than "Spiritual" or "Spiritualist" churches in the
telephone directory. Many Spiritual churches, even when the term
"Spiritual" is part of their formal names, prefer to be listed under
such categories as "interdenominational," "nondenominational," or
"various denominations," so as not to be associated with other Spiritual groups. Reverend Brown took an even more explicit step toward respectability by becoming a member of a Black interdenominational ministerial organization, among whose members he must
constantly deal with the negative image of Spiritual churches. In
addition, Reverend Brown is also a student at a non-Spiritual theological school. The training that he is receiving there may plausibly
move him to shift the religious orientation of his congregation away
from that typical of the Spiritual movement and closer to mainstream Black Protestantism. At any rate, it is apparent that some
of the larger Spiritual congregations are undergoing a process of
"denominationalization"—that is, becoming more and more like the
mainstream denominations in the Black community.

While it is not clear whether the smaller Spiritual churches are
also emulating the patterns of the mainstream denominations, there
is reason to believe that some of them are in the process of model-
ing themselves after the conversionist sects: the smaller Baptist
churches and the wide variety of Holiness and Pentecostal groups.
Such a trend is most apparent in the tendency of some Spiritual
churches to include the term "Holiness" (as opposed to "Spiritual")
in their formal name and/or to refer to themselves as a "Holiness"

group, despite the fact that they retain many of the beliefs, rituals, and normative patterns characteristic of other Spiritual congregations. Some Spiritual groups have, at least in theory, adopted some or many of the puritanical proscriptions that are generally part and parcel of the conversionist sects' beliefs. Although the status of the conversionist sects is considerably lower than that of the established sects or mainstream denominations in the Black community, it is generally regarded to be higher and more respectable than that of the Spiritual groups. Consequently, the adoption of the trappings of the conversionist sects serves as one strategy by which some Spiritual groups attempt to diminish or mitigate the stigma associated with the larger movement of which they are a part. This tendency is perhaps best exemplified by the attempt of St. Cecilia's Divine Healing Church No. 2 to achieve the respectability of the mainstream denominations by first going through the intermediate step of taking on some of the dimensions of the conversionist sects.

CHAPTER 6

Some Concluding Observations

TRADITIONALLY, religion has served socially unifying and regulating purposes in human societies. In fact, this was very much the role of religion in the early Puritan settlements on the eastern seaboard of North America. These communities, despite their autocratic nature, were characterized by a social economy rather than a capitalist economy, a fairly equitable distribution of property and land, and relatively little class conflict. As Howe (1981:118) cogently demonstrates, subsequent religious development in America involved the disappearance of the integrative features of religious experiments such as that of the Puritan commonwealth:

> The development of commodity production, in which social exchanges were determined by the market, laid to rest the possibility of religious regulation of social relations. On the other hand, precisely this development ensured that there could no longer be a truly common religio-social vision. The clarification, in particular, of differences and antagonisms in the everyday world of economic and political existence was reflected in increasing differentiation in religious life. The religious community split along class and ethnic lines, with churches acquiring a relatively internal homogeneity of membership—especially as the more enthusiastic churches gained lower-class adherents in the Revivals of the eighteenth and early nineteenth centuries (e.g., Baptists and Methodists), and as fundamentalism acquired a lower-class complexion. . . . In general, it increasingly became the case that the rich prayed with the rich in churches led by the rich responding to the personal problems of the rich (in, for example, the Episcopalian church). And likewise for the rest of society, though it is not likely that ethnic and class differences were reflected so clearly elsewhere as in the Black fundamentalist churches of the South.

Although many Blacks are now found in the urban areas of the industrial North, religious life in this country still continues to be divided along racial lines. The assertion that 11:00 A.M. on Sunday morning is the most segregated hour in American society is probably as valid today as it ever was. According to one source, only 10 percent of Black Americans worshipped with Whites in 1964 (Reimers 1965). Furthermore, undoubtedly the majority of Blacks who do worship in predominantly White congregations — such as those affiliated with Episcopalian, Congregational, Presbyterian, and Roman Catholic churches — are middle class. Even Blacks who are members of White-controlled religious groups — such as the Church of Christ, the Seventh-Day Adventists, and the Jehovah's Witnesses — often find themselves in all or nearly all Black congregations. Of course, many early religious congregations in the United States were integrated at least in membership, but generally not in spirit: Blacks in such groups were for the most part relegated to the sidelines and to the balconies. Consequently, the segregated nature of American religion is one that Blacks reluctantly chose in many instances, in order to worship not only in their own style but also with a sense of dignity and independence.

Bearing these observations in mind, it may be argued that much of what one finds in Black religion is a response to the racism and stratification inherent in our sociocultural system. Powerless groups have often utilized religion as a way of coping with social reality, and in this regard Black Americans are no exception. At the same time, it must be noted that the variety of strategies manifested in their religious response has contributed to the religious diversity found in the Black community. As was noted at the beginning of this book, it is impossible to speak of *the* Black Church, since there is a wide range of religious sects and denominations among Black Americans. Winter (1977:265) even suggests that "the variety of religious preferences among the Negro or black minority in the United States clearly rivals that found among the white majority." While Black religion was characterized by a considerable diversity during the nineteenth century, it was particularly during the early decades of the present century that a multitude of religious sects, some of which vehemently rejected traditional Christianity, emerged among Black people in this country. In large measure, these were a response to the displacement of many Blacks from the rural South and the stresses accompanying the processes of urbanization and industrialization that permitted the rapid expansion of American capitalism.

This book has attempted to draw attention to and examine the role of a neglected religious movement in the Black American community. In part, I have hoped to illustrate a portion of the richness and diversity of the Black religious experience in this country — an experience which has been only superficially recorded and recognized. The Spiritual movement described in this work was one of a multiplicity of transformations of the rural Black church of the South. The religious sects that emerged in the Black community after the turn of the century provided a means of preserving rural religious and social forms and cultural values, and served as a defense against the anonymity of the city and the large mainstream congregations whose style catered to the needs of the Black bourgeoisie more than to those of the newly arrived migrants from the South. Like the rural Black churches, these sects often served to sublimate the frustration of their adherents into emotionalism; they created meaning out of meaninglessness and self-respect out of the degradation of racial oppression and economic exploitation. In many instances, these groups provided opportunities for ambitious men and women of humble origins to demonstrate and perfect their leadership talents. Finally, all of these sects — Holiness, Pentecostal, storefront Baptist, Muslim, Judaic, and Spiritual — promised their followers some type of salvation: other-worldly, temporal, or a combination of the two.

While Spiritual churches exhibit many of the same characteristics as other religious groups in the Black community, and serve similar functions, they are distinguished from the others by their highly syncretistic nature and their thaumaturgical/manipulationist orientation in dealing with the structural situation faced by Blacks in the larger society. Spiritual churches in this country are excellent examples of religious syncretism and in this regard resemble many Afro-American religions in the Caribbean and South America. The Spiritual movement demonstrates the ability of Black Americans to take components from a wide variety of belief systems in order to create a new religion that meets their needs. In addition to combining elements from Spiritualism, Catholicism, Black Protestantism, and Voodoo and/or hoodoo, Spiritual churches often add features from Islam, Judaism, New Thought, and other esoteric systems.

Although Spiritual churches perform a number of significant roles for certain segments of the Black community, perhaps their greatest appeal lies in their emphasis on magico-religious rituals that promise people spiritual power over their destiny. It is apparently for this reason that to a considerable degree the Spiritual movement constitutes a "client cult" for many Blacks who do not belong to specific Spiritual congregations but choose to attend certain Spiritual religious services or seek private counsel from Spiritual advisors. Spiritual churches attempt to provide immediate release from the stresses that powerless, poor, and alienated Blacks feel as a result of their position in a racist and class-conscious society. In some cases, they instill a sense of confidence in and validate the achievements of upwardly mobile Blacks who are in the process of entering a more affluent social stratum.

Black religion has been characterized by a dual consciousness in that it has fostered both accommodation and protest. Marble (1981: 40) captures the essence of this contradictory dimension of Black religion when he notes that "the conservative tendencies within black faith reach for a Spirit which liberates the soul, but not the body," whereas "the radical consciousness within black faith was concerned with the immediate conditions of black people." The juxtaposition of these opposing themes of protest and accommodation is present in all Afro-American religions, both in this country and in other regions of the New World. Certain messianic-nationalist sects have emphasized the first; Spiritual churches have given more attention to the second. Yet protest against the larger society has often been couched in Spiritual people's rejection of the myth that hard work in itself guarantees material prosperity. Some Spiritual groups, such as the Universal Hagar's Spiritual Church and Spiritual Israel Church and Its Army, have heightened their critique of American society by adding aspects of messianic-nationalism to thaumaturgical strategies. For the most part, however, such groups have offered a limited critique of the larger society by focusing primarily on its racist dimensions without recognizing how these are intricately connected to the political economy of capitalism.

According to Howe (1981:114), "the history of religion in America is replete with examples of the withdrawal of groups from 'normal' society to pursue individual and collective ideals of the good religious life (e.g., Mormons, Mennonites, and Hutterites)." Parallel groups in the black community include Father Divine's Peace Mission during the Depression, the Nation of Islam under Elijah Muhammed and Malcolm X, and a wide array of Holiness and Pentecostal sects that reject the moral standards of the larger society. Despite such introversionist strategies among both Whites and Blacks, the dominant pattern in American religious life has become one of privatization or individuation. This statement does not mean to deny that the theme of communalism came to an end when Blacks became an urban people. To a large extent, the strong sense of group identity expressed in Black evangelical churches of the rural South was kept alive in the economic enterprises of various messianic-nationalist sects and the religious inspiration that leaders of mainstream congregations in the Black community, such as Martin Luther King, provided for the civil rights movement. In more recent years proponents of Black theology, such as Albert Cleage and James Cone, have attempted to keep the collective dimensions of Black religion alive.

Nevertheless, the pattern of individuation so characteristic of many White religious groups has become a strong part of Black religion. A stress on individual rather than collective salvation is particularly pronounced among thaumaturgical/manipulationist sects — the bulk of which fit into the Spiritual category that has been the primary concern of this book. The solutions that Spiritual churches provide for their members tend to be compensatory and accommodative rather than corrective. Instead of encouraging Blacks to seek social change or challenge the existing political economy and system of racial relations, the Spiritual movement strives to alleviate their alienation from society by promising financial success or the restoration of personal conflict in return for the enactment of certain magico-religious rituals. While the Spiritual religion appears to provide an important coping mechanism for a segment of the Black community, at best its benefits tend to be ameliorative. The problems that its adherents and clients experience in most cases will not be eliminated until there has been a drastic transformation in the social structure of American society.

Epilogue

S
ince the appearance of the first edition of *The Black Spiritual Movement,* I and a few other scholars have written about African American Spiritual churches. My own research has explored aspects of the movement in various parts of the country, whereas the work of Jacobs and Kaslow (1991), Estes (1991, 1993), and Berry (1995) has focused primarily upon Spiritual churches in New Orleans—an important center in the movement and one where the pattern of religious syncretism is most pronounced. My own published research has further explored three topics. These are: first, mini-ethnographies of Spiritual congregations in two small southern cities (Baer 1985); second, the Metropolitan Spiritual Churches of Christ (Baer 1988a); and third, the "battle of the sexes" within the Spiritual movement (Baer 1993).

Mini-Ethnographies of Spiritual Churches in Hattiesburg, Mississippi, and North Little Rock, Arkansas

In the course of my teaching stint in 1981–83 at the University of South Mississippi, I conducted ethnographic research on the Hattiesburg branch of Spiritual Israel and Its Army (Baer 1985). The Hattiesburg temple is one of the newer branches of Spiritual Israel. It was established in 1973 when Elder Alma Jones (pseudonym) accompanied a fellow Spiritual Israelite to a funeral in Hattiesburg. Although she had once sworn that she would never live in

Mississippi because of its long history of racism, Bishop Haywood persuaded her to spread the message of the Spiritual Israelite faith to this part of the Kingdom. A year after her first visit to Hatties-burg, Elder Jones returned in her car with her belongings and a mere $180 in her purse. Services of the new branch were initially conducted in the home of Hattiesburg's first convert to the Spiritual Israel Church. Later, apparently because this convert left the church, services were conducted in the home of another member. From there the temple shifted its meeting site to an unoccupied house, then to a church building, and finally to the location where I conducted my research. Elder Jones attracted a core member-ship of about two dozen people over the next several years, many of whom were interrelated by marriage or descent. Although some individuals came and went and occasionally reappeared, she could count on her core members not only to attend services regularly but to provide the financial and physical support required to make the Hattiesburg temple a going concern. In addition, the temple established a mission in a small town about ninety miles southeast of Hattiesburg, where the pastor and perhaps another church officer conducted a service once a month. Some of the preachers belong-ing to a local Baptist ministerial association reportedly regarded her as a threat because they feared she might attract members from their flocks and because she was a woman preacher.

In addition to her role as pastor, Elder Jones served as a prophet, healer, social worker, employment counselor, and friend of the members of her congregation. She describes herself as a "messenger of the covenant" and as an instrument for helping people help themselves. For those seeking private consultations, she gives "readings" as well as advice from the Spirit on how to deal with problems of everyday living. Like many people in the Spiritual movement, Elder Jones rejects a puritanical lifestyle but rather recommends moderation. With respect to premarital sex, she admits that she "would not buy a pig in a poke." While Elder Jones tells her members that "Israel should follow the laws of the land" with respect to marriage, she notes that it would be permis-sible for a Spiritual Israelite, as did the ancient Israelites, to prac-tice polygamy in African countries where this custom is legal. In the summer of 1982, Elder Jones moved to a city in the Pacific

Northwest where her daughter resided. She planned to establish a mission in what would become the westernmost outpost of the Spiritual Israelite kingdom.

Reverend Mother Martha Calloway (pseudonym), a custodian at the university, succeeded Elder Jones as the pastor of the Hattiesburg temple. She had served as the assistant pastor for several years. She was assisted in the running of the temple by the Deacons' Board, the Mothers' Board, the Nurses' Board, the Pastor's Aide Society, the Building Fund Committee, and the Utilities Board. Auxiliaries may have their own internal hierarchies. For example, the Mothers' Board includes the following categories in rank order: the "gold cape mothers," the "bride mothers" (who wear a doily), the "blue cape mothers," the "white cape mothers," and the "light blue cape mothers." The last grade includes recent graduates from the Daughters of Zion or the Junior Mothers' Board. In addition to discussing the history and sociopolitical organization of the Hattiesburg temple, my ethnographic account presents composite portraits of its Sunday morning services and Friday evening "bless services" (Baer 1985).

About a year after assuming my present position at the University of Arkansas at Little Rock, I conducted some fieldwork at the Damascus Spiritual Church in North Little Rock. Bishop August Harris (now deceased) served as the pastor of the congregation as well as the overseer of a small association consisting of four congregations. Bishop Harris was born in Mississippi and reared in Stuttgart—a small city in the Arkansas Delta. She grew up in the Spiritual faith and established a Spiritual church in Scott, Arkansas, in the late 1940s but moved it to North Little Rock around 1975. Bishop Harris once frequently visited Spiritual churches in various parts of the country, including Chicago, but had lost contact with them. She said that she did not agree with certain practices in the Spiritual movement, such as when members "make their leader like their God." Bishop Harris referred to herself a "healer" and noted that at one time she saw clients "all day long." She had reduced the number of clients that she saw to between ten and twenty-five a week. Bishop Harris added that most of her clients were not members of her congregation; some were teachers, professors, and lawyers.

The Metropolitan Spiritual Churches of Christ

Since 1984 I have also conducted ethnographic and archival research on the Metropolitan Spiritual Churches of Christ—the largest of the Spiritual associations (Baer 1988a). Although Metropolitan never approached the size of African American mainstream denominations (Baer and Singer 1992), its politico-religious organization suggests that it has undergone a process of institutionalization. Metropolitan is divided into regional councils (e.g., the Southwestern Michigan and Indiana Council and the Northeastern Regional Council). The association also has a board of directors, national boards (choir, youth choir, nurses, ushers, Sunday School, acolytes, missionaries, and ministers), and convenes annual congresses in cities around the country. Unlike its mainstream denominational counterparts, it does not have the financial capability of establishing a publishing board, seminaries, and colleges or universities.

In keeping with the process of institutionalization, Metropolitan has moved away, as have most other Spiritual groups, from the Spiritualist practice of conducting séances. According to Tyms (1938:117), the Mother Church in Kansas City in the 1930s housed a "room of mediumistic readings" where "contact is made with those of the past who give the assurance of immortality." Although Metropolitan's "Declarations of Truths" assert "that intelligent communications exist between the Spirit World and the physical world," this statement appears to be more of a relic of the past than a reflection of current practice. Although pastors and other mediums belonging to Metropolitan continue to give messages in public bless services or deliverance services and private consultations, the Spirit of God acts as their source much more often than a deceased loved one or even a Catholic saint.

In shifting more toward the model of the African American mainstream denominations, most Metropolitan congregations have shed some of their Catholic paraphernalia. Cobbs requested in 1968 that congregations remove statues of the Catholic saints, an edict with which the First Church of Deliverance abided. Conversely, while the Mother Church discarded some of its statues in May 1986, I saw a large statue of the Sacred Heart of Jesus on the front altar of the sanctuary and a statue of the Blessed Virgin in the outer courtyard leading into the sanctuary. While the altar in Cornerstone Church in Baltimore holds vigil candles and a small tabernacle and two vigil stands sit in the front of the sanctuary, statues of the saints were not present when I visited this congregation in August 1987.

Institutionalization has by no means transformed Metropolitan into a denomination. While the larger congregations in the association have some relatively affluent members, most of these congregations continue to be working and lower-class Blacks. While Metropolitan has a short "Statement of Purpose" and a short "Declaration of Principles," both of these allow for considerable flexibility in doctrines and rituals for individual members or congregations. At best, Metropolitan has evolved into what Yinger (1970:266–73) terms an "established sect" or, following Wallis (1974), a "centralized cult."

There appears to be some evidence that, since perhaps the late 1950s or early 1960s, Metropolitan has undergone a certain degree of stagnation. Like the larger Spiritual movement, Metropolitan appears to have passed its zenith. Several subjects observed that many Metropolitan congregations do not attract the crowds they once did. When I attended services at both the Alpha and Omega Church in Detroit and the Metropolitan Spiritual Church in Kansas City, the number in attendance was only a fraction of seating capacities. While First Church of Deliverance still attracts a relatively large number to its services, one Metropolitan leader noted that "First Deliverance is not the church it was when Cobbs was there."

The factors contributing to the decline in popularity of the Spiritual congregations both within and outside of Metropolitan are not entirely clear but may be related to the generally apolitical and thaumaturgical posture of most Spiritual groups. The Spiritual movement grew during a period when African Americans were migrating in great numbers to the cities. The movement underwent tremendous growth during the Great Depression, at a time when Black mainstream churches had undergone a process of "deradicalization" (Wilmore 1983). While some Blacks continue to migrate from rural to urban areas, migrations on the scale of those between the two World Wars are a thing of the past. Most African Americans are now urbanites. Furthermore, despite considerable variation among Black mainstream congregations in their expression of social protest, many of them began to exhibit heightened activism beginning in the late 1950s and early 1960s. The messianic-nationalist sects, particularly the Nation of Islam under the leadership of Elijah Muhammad and Malcolm X, generally provided even more militant forums for protest activities among religious Blacks. Some African American Pentecostal congregations, particularly those affiliated with the Church of God in Christ, assumed an openly political posture toward institutional racism and economic exploitation. In contrast, Spiritual churches, including those belonging to Metropolitan, continued to adhere to a thaumaturgical approach for dealing with the problems faced by African Americans in the larger society. Yet, this strategy probably produced limited results and, consequently, disillusionment with the efficacy of the Spiritual movement in addressing the vagaries created by racism and capitalism. As Stark and Bainbridge (1985:109) observe, thaumaturgical strategies are "very vulnerable to disproof" since magic "deals in specific compensators that promise fulfillment in the empirical world." Thus, institutionalized religions tend to eschew magic, leaving it instead to part-time practitioners (e.g., shamans and prophets) operating on the fringes of society.

While the Spiritual movement in general has been in a period of decline, some young, relatively well-educated Spiritual ministers are attempting to revitalize the stagnating congregations that they have inherited from elderly or deceased pastors by further "streamlining" the movement. In essence, they have discarded many of the traditional thaumaturgical practices (e.g., praying before the statue of a Catholic saint, burning candles, using incense sprays and floor washes) but retained or recast manipulationist practices (e.g., positive thinking, raising one's consciousness) historically associated with New Thought. At the same time, these ministers encourage their members to obtain additional education and vocational skills. The Redeeming Church of Christ in Chicago illustrates these trends. Rev. Southerland, its pastor, created a job placement program for his members, many of whom are young, and invites outside speakers, such as myself, to participate in his "academic program."

"The Battle of the Sexes" within the Spiritual Movement

Although women generally have not established separate religious organizations in state societies, certain religious movements have historically served as a "vehicle for the assertion of alternative roles for women" (McGuire 1987:109). As I noted in the first edition of this book and elsewhere (Baer 1993), the Spiritual movement, even more so than the Holiness-Pentecostal movement, has provided African American women—many of whom belong to a "triple minority"—with their most accessible route for achieving positions of religious leadership. Women generally started the earlier Spiritual churches in cities such as Chicago, New Orleans, and Nashville. Of some fifty active Spiritual congregations that Kaslow and Jacobs (1981:33) identified in New Orleans, "Approximately three-fourths of the pastors are women." Of the forty-two Spiritual congregations that I visited between 1977 and 1987, nineteen had female pastors. Despite the relatively elevated position of women in Spiritual churches, the "battle of the sexes" has continued within the Spiritual movement.

While in theory and often in practice, either males or females may assume positions of religious leadership in Spiritual churches, males sometimes attempt to assert dominance over females. These efforts in a movement consisting overwhelmingly of women take three forms: first, the royal kingdom; second, the male pastor-female assistant pastor team; and third, the male pastor as figurehead.

Males as opposed to females generally establish kingdoms. This was the case for three Spiritual associations discussed in this book, namely Universal Hagar's Spiritual Church established by Father George Hurley, the Mt. Zion Temple established by King Louis H. Narcisse, and Spiritual Israel Church and Its Army established by W. D. Dickson. The founders of other African American religious kingdoms, such as the Peace Mission founded by Father Divine, the United House of Pray for All People established by "Sweet Daddy" Grace, the Oyotunju Village in South Carolina established by Oba (King) Afuntola or Walter Serge, outside of the Spiritual movement per se, also appear to all have been formed by males (Baer and Singer 1992). However, as we see in the case of the Universal Hagar's Spiritual Kingdom and the Peace Mission, women may assume royal leadership once the kingdom has been established.

While many of the congregations in the Metropolitan Spiritual Churches of Christ have female pastors, the heads of the association have always been males. In selecting Mattye B. Thornton (known as the "Little Missionary") as his assistant pastor in 1929,

Clarence Cobbs established a model emulated by many other male pastors in the Metropolitan Spiritual Churches of Christ whereby the pastor is male and the assistant pastor is female. Male dominance at the First Church of Deliverance was manifested by the fact that in 1979 the Trustee Board consisted of fifty-two men and the Lady Trustees consisted of twelve women (First Church of Deliverance 1979:6). The Temple Spiritual Temple exhibited the male pastor–female assistant pastor pattern in the form of a husband-wife team.

Women sometimes rebel in instances where males attempt to assert dominance. When Thomas Watson, the senior bishop of the Spiritualist Church of the Southwest, "decided that women should no long be bishops, and demoted Junior Bishop Johnson to 'Reverend Mother Superior,' she formed shortly thereafter the Everlasting Gospel Eternal Life Christian Spiritual Churches of Christ" (Kaslow and Jacobs 1981:99). Like Clarence Cobbs, the Rev. Lucius Hall, the head of the First Church of Love and Faith, Inc. (which he formed as a schism from the Metropolitan Spiritual Churches of Christ in the course of a succession crisis following Cobbs's death), had a female, the Rev. Romano Joseph, as an assistant pastor for several years. While the source of their parting-of-the-ways is not clear, she started her own congregation on the West Side of Chicago and is generally regarded to be Hall's rival.

In virtually all Spiritual churches, females greatly outnumber males, sometimes by a ratio of as high as nine to one. Because of the disproportionate number of female members, women in Spiritual churches make concerted efforts to encourage males to belong, often by granting them religious offices. Spiritual women generally are not interested in establishing matriarchal congregations but rather sexually egalitarian ones. In order to induce males —often their spouses, nephews, and brothers—to join, they may make certain concessions that may eventually culminate in males attempting to assert dominance. As noted earlier, a case in point occurred at the Sacred Heart Spiritual Church in Nashville when Elder Smith was elected to be the pastor in the early 1970s after the female founder of the congregation had to step down due to poor health and age. Despite his formal leadership, Evangelist Anderson, the founder's daughter, functioned as the informal leader of the congregation.

As the Spiritual movement underwent a process of institutionalization, women came to play a less significant role in many of its larger associations, despite their playing a highly instrumental role in the establishment of the earliest African American Spiritualist or Spiritual churches. As Falk (1985:xvii) asserts, "as religious movements evolve, women appear to be less and less the agents of change and more and more its victims." Further study is needed to determine why male-headed associations are more likely to develop into bureaucratic and institutionalized structures, such as the Metropolitan Spiritual Churches of Christ, than are female-headed associations.

Other Scholars on Spiritual Churches

Whereas I have presented a broad overview of Spiritual churches based largely on ethnographic research in Nashville, Detroit, Flint, the New York metropolitan area, and various other cities, most of the research touching upon Spiritual churches by other scholars has focused upon New Orleans. An exception is a book by Davis (1985:69–73, 142–51) on the African American sermon in which he examines how this ritualistic event is performed by several ministers, one of whom is King Louis Narcisse. In *The Spiritual Churches of New Orleans* (1991), anthropologists Claude F. Jacobs and Andrew J. Kaslow greatly expand upon a relatively inaccessible monograph titled *Prophecy, Healing, and Power: The Afro-American Spiritual Churches of New Orleans,* which they wrote for the National Park Service (Kaslow and Jacobs 1981). In addition to conducting participant-observation on the mother church of the Israel Universal Divine Spiritual Churches of Christ headed by Archbishop Ernest J. Johnson, they visited seventeen other Spiritual congregations in New Orleans. While it remains debatable whether either New Orleans or Chicago or even some other site constitutes the birthplace of the African American Spiritual movement, Jacobs and Kaslow demonstrate that New Orleans served as the crucible for the infusion of Roman Catholic and Voodooist elements into what undoubtedly became the most syncretistic African American religion in the United States. Indeed,

Spiritual churches in New Orleans look more like Afro-Caribbean sects akin to Haitian vodun than they look like other African American religious groups in the United States as a whole. As elsewhere, most Black Spiritualist groups in the city had come to refer to themselves as "Spiritual" by the 1930s and 1940s.

In addition to an elaborate discussion of the Spiritual belief system, Jacobs and Kaslow describe in detail worship services and the strong emphasis on spirit guides, possession, healing, and prophecy, as well as the sociopolitical organization of Spiritual churches in New Orleans. They provide a social profile of the adult core and elite membership of the Israelite Spiritual Church and the Goodwill Spiritual Church (pseudonym). Whereas only 27.3 percent of the members in Israelite (one of the older Spiritual churches in New Orleans) were reared in the Spiritual tradition, 75.0 percent of those in the much newer Goodwill congregation were. Only 33.3 percent of Israelite's members, and none of Goodwill's members, came from rural areas. St. Mark's (pseudonym) "consists entirely of recent rural migrants, almost all of whom are middle-aged women on fixed incomes" and of Baptist origins (Jacobs and Kaslow 1991:177). Using an occupational profile of the membership of Israelite and Goodwill, Jacobs and Kaslow (1991:183) describe "the churches' membership as composed largely of working-class and low-income individuals, with some in the middle class."

As in much of the rest of the country, the Spiritual religion in New Orleans emerged almost exclusively as a woman's movement, but men have increasingly assumed positions of leadership as the movement has undergone institutionalization. Indeed, the heads of New Orleans' two largest Spiritual associations, the United Metropolitan Spiritual Churches of Christ and the Israel Universal Divine Spiritual Churches of Christ, are males. Nevertheless, as elsewhere, women continue to play an active role in Spiritual churches.

As opposed to the 1920s and 1930s, when the number of Spiritual churches in New Orleans grew to almost one hundred, Jacobs and Kaslow were able to identify only some fifty Spiritual congregations in the Crescent City during the early 1980s, a finding that indicates, as I have discovered elsewhere, that the Spiritual movement has entered a period of decline in recent decades. As they observe, "despite current members' exuberance, the churches constitute a movement that belongs to an earlier era, when their services of healing and prophecy had mass appeal for a population that was denied access to education, social services, and prosperity" (Jacobs and Kaslow 1991:211–12).

Jacobs and Kaslow provide a useful model of the "variability of worship and belief" in Spiritual churches, illustrating the possible variations that individuals and congregations may choose. Whereas some lean toward Catholic beliefs, emphasizing the saints and the sacraments, others may stress practices associated with American Spiritualism and Voodoo, such as séances and conjuring, and yet others may place great emphasis on evangelical and Pentecostal elements, such as prophecy and healing.

Jacobs and Kaslow's book is strong on describing historical, ideational, ritualistic, and organizational dimensions, but it tends to be weak in providing a theoretical analysis. In passing, they adopt a phenomenological or interpretive perspective in their analysis of healing and prophecy by arguing that Spiritual churches provide their members and clients with a meaning system that allows them to transcend the harsh realities of most of their lives. Although Jacobs and Kaslow recognize that Spiritual people are members of an exploited and oppressed racial minority, they only occasionally comment on the role of the religion in addressing the vagaries of lives in a racist and class-based society. As Keesing (1987:166) observes in his critique of symbolic or phenomenological approaches in anthropology, "cultures must be situated historically, viewed in a theoretical framework that critically examines their embeddedness in social, economic, and political structures."

A few other scholars have focused on various aspects of Spiritual churches in New Orleans. David C. Estes, an English professor at Loyola University of New Orleans, examines the chanted sermon as preached by Archbishop Lydia Gilford, the pastor of the Infant Jesus of Prague Spiritual Church (Estes 1991) as well as the ways that female Spiritual ministers ritually validate their religious authority (1993). Journalist Jason Berry (1995) presents a detailed account of the Black Hawk motif in many New Orleans Spiritual congregations, particularly the Eternal Life Spiritualist Church established by Mother Leafy Anderson. In his overview of African American religion, Anthony B. Pinn (1998:44–53) presents a brief ethnographic overview of the Voodoo Spiritual Temple in New Orleans—a congregation that was established by Priest

Oswan Chamani and Priestess Miriam Williams (Chamani) in 1990. In contrast to most Spiritual people who either deny or downplay Voodooist elements in their religion, "Priestess Miriam sees no functional distinction between Voodoo, Spiritualism, Santeria, Christianity, and so on" (Pinn 1998:47).

Suggestions for Further Research

The African American Spiritual religious movement no longer constitutes a neglected dimension of African American religion, as it did prior to 1980. Still, it has not received nearly the amount of attention as African American mainstream churches such as the National Baptist conventions and the African Methodist Episcopal Church (Lincoln and Mamiya 1990); various messianic-sects, such as the Nation of Islam, particularly under the leaderships of Elijah Muhammad and Malcolm X, and its successor organizations, the American Muslim Mission under the leadership of Wallace D. Muhammad and the reconstituted Nation under the leadership of Louis Farrakhan; and various conversionist or Holiness-Pentecostal sects, particularly the Church of God in Christ. As I told members of the Redeeming Spiritual Church on the South Side of Chicago, *The Black Spiritual Movement,* including this second edition, covers only the tip of the iceberg for a fascinating religious movement that represents the creativity of African American people in attempting to address the injustices of institutional racism and the inequities of American capitalism. The work of Jacobs, Kaslow, Estes, and Pinn provides a rich overview of various aspect of the Spiritual movement in New Orleans. Nonetheless, in-depth research on Spiritual churches in cities such as Chicago, Detroit, Atlanta, Memphis, the San Francisco–Oakland Bay Area, as well as in small cities and towns is badly needed in order for us to more fully understand this unique religious movement that continues to baffle many people, scholars and laity alike. It is ironic that, despite the strong presence of women in the Spiritual churches, no female scholars have published anything on the movement. One can only hope that the paucity of research by female scholars on Spiritual churches will soon be addressed so that new insights will be revealed.

References

Alland, Alexander, Jr.

1962   "'Possession' in a Revivalistic Negro Church." *Journal for the Scientific Study of Religion* 1:204–13

1981   To *Be Human: An Introduction to Cultural Anthropology.* New York: John Wiley.

Ammerman, Nancy

1987   *Bible Believers: Fundamentalists in the Modern World.* New Brunswick, N.J.: Rutgers Univ. Press.

Aquarian Age

1935ff.   Publication of the Universal Hagar's Spiritual Church. Asbury, Herbert

1936   *The French Quarter.* Garden City, N.Y.: Garden City Publishing.

Atkinson, P.

1990   *The Ethnographic Imagination: Textual Construction of Reality.* London: Routledge.

Baer, Hans A.

1976   "The Levites of Utah: Development of and Recruitment to a Small Millenarian Sect." Ph.D. diss., Univ. of Utah.

1980   "An Anthropological View of Black Spiritual Churches in Nashville, Tennessee." *Central Issues in Anthropology* 2 (2):53–68.

1981a   "Prophets and Advisors in Black Spiritual Churches: Therapy, Palliative, or Opiate?" *Culture, Medicine, and Psychiatry* 5:145–70.

Baer, Hans A. *(continued)*

1981b   "Black Spiritual Churches: A Neglected Socio-Religious
         Institution." *Phylon: Atlanta University Journal of Race
         and Culture* 42:207–23.

1985   "Black Spiritual Israelites in a Small Southern City:
         Elements of Protest and Accommodation in Belief
         and Oratory." *Southern Quarterly* 23(3):103–24.

1988a   "The Metropolitan Spiritual Churches of Christ: The
         Socio-Religious Evolution of the Largest of the Black
         Spiritual Associations." *Review of Religious Research*
         30:140–50.

1988b   *Recreating Utopia in the Desert: A Sectarian Response
         to Modern Mormonism.* Albany: State Univ. of New
         York Press.

1993   "The Limited Empowerment of Women in Black
         Spiritual Churches: An Alternative Vehicle to Reli-
         gious Leadership." *Sociology of Religion* 54:65–82.

Baer, Hans A., and Merrill Singer

1981   "Toward a Typology of Black Sectarianism as a
         Response to Racial Stratification." *Anthropological
         Quarterly* 54:1–14

1992   *African-American Religion in the Twentieth Century:
         Varieties of Protest and Accommodation.* Knoxville:
         Univ. of Tennessee Press.

Baer, Hans A., and Merrill Singer, eds.

1988   *Black American Religion in the Twentieth Century.*
         Special Issue of *Review of Religious Research* 29(4).

Barker, Eileen

1984   *The Making of a Moonie: Choice or Brainwashing?*
         Oxford: Basil Blackwell.

Baron, Harold M.

1976   "The Demand for Black Labor." In *Racial Conflict,
         Discrimination and Power: Historical and Contempo-
         rary Studies,* ed. William Barclay, Krisha Kumar, and
         Ruth P. Simms, 190–202. New York: AMS Press.

Bastide, Roger

1978   *The African Religions of Brazil: Toward a Sociology
         of the Interpenetration of Civilization,* trans. Helen
         Sebba. Baltimore: Johns Hopkins Univ. Press.

Bauman, Zygmunt
   1976   *Socialism: The Active Utopia.* London: George Allen & Unwin.
Berry, Jason
   1995   *The Spirit of Black Hawk: A Mystery of Africans and Indians.* Jackson: Univ. Press of Mississippi.
Bourguignon, Erika E.
   1970   "Afro-American Religions: Traditions and Transformation." In *Black America,* ed. John F. Szwed, 190–201. New York: Basic Books.
Braden, Charles Samuel
   1949   *These Also Believe. New* York: Macmillan. Broom, Leonard, and Norval Glenn
   1965   *Transformation of the Negro American.* New York: Harper and Row.
Brotz, Howard M.
   1970   *The Black Jews of Harlem.* New York: Schocken. Burkett, Randall K.
   1978   *Garveyism as a Religious Movement: The Institutionalization of a Black Civil Religion.* Metuchen, N.J.: Scarecrow Press.
Burnham, Kenneth E.
   1979   *God Comes to America: Father Divine and the Peace Mission Movement.* Boston: Lambeth.
Burns, Thomas A., and J. Stephen Smith
   1978   "The Symbolism of Becoming in the Sunday Service of an Urban Black Holiness Church." *Anthropological Quarterly* 51:185–204.
Campbell, Colin
   1972   "The Cult, the Cultic Milieu and Secularization." In *A Sociological Yearbook of Religion in Britain, vol. 5,* ed. Michael Hill, 118–36. London: SCM Press.
Campbell, Horace
   1980   "Rastafari: Culture of Resistance." *Race and Class* 22: 1–22,
Carter, Harold A.
   1976   *The Prayer Tradition of Black People.* Valley Forge, Pa.: Judson Press.

Clark, Elmer T

1965   *The Small Sects in America.* Nashville: Abingdon.

Clifford, James

1986   "On Ethnographic Allegory." In *Writing Culture: The Poetics and Politics of Ethnography*, ed. James Clifford and George March, 98–122. Berkeley: Univ. of California Press.

Cohen, Daniel

1972   *Voodoo, Devils, and the Invisible World.* New York: Dodd, Mead.

Cooley, Gilbert E.

1977a   "Boot Doctors and Psychics in the Region." *Indiana Folklore* 10:191–200.

1977b   "Conversations about Hoodoo." *Indiana Folklore* 10: 201–15.

Cox, Oliver C.

1976   *Race Relations: Elements and Dynamics.* Detroit: Wayne State Univ. Press.

Crane, Julia, and Michael Angrosino

1984   *Field Projects in Anthropology: A Student Handbook.* 2d ed. Prospect Heights, Ill.: Waveland Press.

Crapanzano, Vincent

1976   "On the Writing of Ethnography." *Dialectical Anthropology* 2:69–73.

Davidman, L.

1991   *Tradition in a Rootless World: Women Turn to Orthodox Judaism.* Berkeley: Univ. of California Press.

Davis, Gerald L.

1985   *"I Got the Word in Me and I Can Sing It, You Know":* A Study of the Performed African-American Sermon. Philadelphia: Univ. of Pennsylvania Press.

Demerath III, N. J.

1965   *Social Class in American Protestantism.* Chicago: Rand McNally.

Dillard, J. L.

1973   "On the Grammar of Afro-American Naming Practices." In *Mother Wit from the Laughing Barrel: Readings in the Interpretation of Afro-American Folklore*, ed. Alan Dundes, 175–81. New York: New Garland.

Dollard, John
  1937   *Caste and Class in a Southern Town.* Garden City,
            N.Y.: Anchor Books.
Dougherty, Molly C.
  1978   *Becoming a Woman in Rural Black Culture,* New
            York: Holt, Rinehart and Winston.
Drake, St. Clair
  1965   "The Social and Economic Status of the Negro in the
            United States." *Daedalus* 94:771–846.
Drake, St. Clair, and Horace R. Cayton
  1945   *Black Metropolis.* New York: Harcourt, Brace.
DuBois, W. E. B.
  1903   *The Souls of Black Folks: Essays and Sketches.* Chi-
            cago: A. C. McClurg.

Ebony 1
  1960   October:69.
Edmonson, Munro S.
  1960   "Nativism, Syncretism, and Anthropological Sci-
            ence." In *Nativism and Syncretism,* ed. Munro S.
            Edmonson, 133–202. New Orleans: Middle Ameri-
            can Research Institute, Tulane Univ.
Ellwood, Robert S., Jr.
  1973   *Religious and Spiritual Groups in Modern America,*
            Englewood Cliffs, N.J.: Prentice-Hall.
Essien-Udom, E. U.
  1962   *Black Nationalism: A Search for Identity in America,*
            Chicago: Univ. of Chicago Press.
Estes, David C.
  1991   "Preaching in an Afro-American Spiritual Church: Arch-
            bishop Lydia and the Traditional Chanted Sermon."
            In *Cultural Perspectives on the American South.* Vol.
            5, *Religion,* ed. Charles Reagan Wilson, 79–102. New
            York: Gordon and Breach, Science Publishers.
  1993   "Ritual Validations of Clergywomen's Authority in
            the African American Spiritual Churches of New
            Orleans." In *Women's Leadership in Marginal Posi-
            tions: Explorations Outside the Mainstream,* ed.
            Catherine Wessinger, 151–71. Urbana: Univ. of Illi-
            nois Press.

Falk, Nancy
  1985   "Introduction." In *Women, Religion, and Social Change,*
          ed. Yvonne Yazbeck Haddad and Ellison Banks Findly,
          xv–xxi. Albany: State Univ. of New York Press.
Fauset, Arthur H.
  1971   *Black Gods of the Metropolis.* Philadelphia: Univ. of
          Pennsylvania Press.
Feagin, Joe R.
  1968   "Black Catholics in the United States: An Exploratory
          Analysis." *Sociological Analysis* 29:186–92.
Femia, Joseph
  1975   "Hegemony and Consciousness in the Thought of
          Antonio Gramsci." *Political Studies* 23:29–48.
First Church of Deliverance
  1979   50th Anniversary, 1929–1979, First Church of Deliv-
          erance. Chicago.
Fishman, Robert Gray
  1979   "Spiritualism in Western New York: A Study in Ritual
          Healing." *Medical Anthropology* 3:1–22.
Frank, Jerome
  1973   *Persuasion and Healing: A Comparative Study of Psy-
          chotherapy.* Baltimore: Johns Hopkins Univ. Press.
Frazier, E. Franklin
  1949   *The Negro in the United States.* New York: Macmillan.
  1968   *The Negro Family in the United States.* Chicago: Univ.
          of Chicago Press.
  1974   *The Negro Church in America.* New York: Schocken.
Genovese, Eugene D.
  1974   *Roll, Jordan, Roll: The World the Slaves Made.* New
          York: Random House, Vintage Books.
Gerlach, Luther P., and Virginia H. Hine
  1970   *People, Power, and Change: Movements of Social
          Transformation.* Indianapolis: Bobbs-Merrill.
Geschwender, James A.
  1978   *Racial Stratification in America.* Dubuque, Iowa:
          Wm. C. Brown.
Good, Bryon J., and Mary-Jo DelVecchio Good
  1980   "Spiritualist Realities: A Symbolic Analysis of

Spiritualist Clinical Practice." Paper presented at the 79th Annual Meeting of the American Anthropological Association, Washington, D.C.

Gordon, D.
1987   "Getting Close by Staying Distant: Fieldwork with Proselytizing Groups." *Qualitative Sociology* 10:267–87.

Gordon, David F.
1972   "Getting Close by Staying Distant: Fieldwork with Proslytizing Groups." *Qualitative Sociology* 10:267–87.

Gordon, Milton M.
1964   *Assimilation in American Life: The Role of Race, Religion, and National Origins.* New York: Oxford Univ. Press.

Green, Vera
1970   "The Confrontation of Diversity within the Black Community." *Human Organization* 29:267–72.

Greisman, H. C., and Sharon S. Mayers
1977   "The Social Construction of Unreality: The Real American Dilemma." *Dialectical Anthropology* 2:57–67.

Hall, Arthur L., and Peter G. Bourne
1973   "Indigenous Therapists in a Southern Black Urban Community." *Archives of General Psychiatry* 28:137–42.

Hamilton, Charles V.
1972   *The Black Preacher in America.* New York: William Morrow.

Hannerz, Ulf
1969   *Soulside: Inquiries into Ghetto Culture and Community.* New York: Columbia Univ. Press.

Harris, Marvin
1980   *Culture, People, and Nature: An Introduction to General Anthropology.* New York: Harper and Row.

Harris, Sara
1971   *Father Divine.* New York: Collier.

Harrison, Ira E.
1971   "The Storefront Church as a Revitalization Movement." In *The Black Church in America,* ed. Hart M. Nelsen, Raytha L. Yokley, and Anne K. Nelsen, 240–50. New York: Basic Books.

Haskins, James
    1978   *Voodoo and Hoodoo: Their Tradition and Craft as
              Related by Actual Practitioners.* New York: Stein and
              Day.
Herskovits, Melville J.
    1941   *The Myth of the Negro Past.* New York: Harper.
    1971   *Life in a Haitian Valley.* New York: Farrar, Straus,
              and Giroux.
Holt, Grace Sims
    1972   "Stylin' outta the Black pulpit." *In Rappin' and Stylin'
              Out: Communication in Urban Black America,* ed.
              Thomas Kochman, 189–204. Urbana: Univ. of Illi-
              nois Press.
Hoshor, John
    1936   *God in a Rolls-Royce,* New York: Hillman-Carl. Howe,
              Gary Nigel
    1981   "The Political Economy of American Religion: An
              Essay in Cultural History." *In Political Economy: A
              Critique of American Society,* ed. Scott G. McNall,
              110–37. Glenview, Ill.: Scott, Foresman.
Hurston, Zora
    1931   "Hoodoo in America." *Journal of American Folklore*
              44:317–417.
Hyatt, Harry M.
    1970–74   *Hoodoo, Conjuration, Witchcraft,* 4 vols. Hannibal,
              Mo.: Western Publishing.
Jackson, Jacquelyne Johnson
    1981   "Urban Black Americans." In *Ethnicity and Medical
              Care,* ed. Alan Harwood, 37–129. Cambridge, Mass.:
              Harvard Univ. Press.
Jacobs, Claude F., and Andrew J. Kaslow
    1991   *The Spiritual Churches of New Orleans: Origins,
              Beliefs, and Rituals of an African-American Religion.*
              Knoxville: Univ. of Tennessee Press.
Johnstone, Ronald J.
    1975   *Religion and Society in Interaction.* Englewood Cliffs,
              N.J.: Prentice-Hall.
Jones, Raymond
    1939   "A Comparative Study of Religious Cult Behavior
              among Negroes with Special Reference to Emotional

Conditioning Factors." *Howard University Studies in the Social Sciences* 2(2).

Jordan, Wilbert C.
1975   "Voodoo Medicine." In *Textbook of Black-related Diseases*, ed. Richard A. Williams, 715–38. New York: McGraw-Hill.

Jules-Rosette, Benmetta
1980   "Creative Spirituality from Africa to America: Cross-Cultural Influences in Contemporary Religious Forms." *Western Journal of Black Studies* 4:273–85.

Kaslow, Andrew J.
1979   "The Afro-American Celebration of St. Joseph's Day." In *Perspectives on Ethnicity in New Orleans*, 48–52. New Orleans: Committee on Ethnicity.
1981   "Saints and Spirits: The Belief System of Afro-American Spiritual Churches in New Orleans." In *Perspectives on Ethnicity in New Orleans*, 61–68. New Orleans: Committee on Ethnicity.

Kaslow, Andrew J., and Claude Jacobs
1981   *Prophecy, Healing, and Power: The Afro-American Spiritual Churches of New Orleans*. A Cultural Resources Management Study for the Jean Lafitte National Historical Park and the National Park Service. Dept. of Anthropology and Geography, Univ. of New Orleans.

Keesing, Roger M.
1987   Anthropology as Interpretive Quest. *Current Anthropology* 28:161–69.

King, Kenneth J.
1978   "Some Notes on Arnold J. Ford and New World Black Attitudes to Ethiopia." In *Black Apostles: Afro-American Clergy Confront the Twentieth Century*, ed. Randall K. Burkett and Richard Newman, 49–55. Boston: G. K. Hall.

Kostaerlos, Frances
1995   *Feeling the Spirit: Faith and Hope in an Evangelical Black Storefront Church*. Columbia: Univ. of South Carolina Press.

Kuna, Ralph R.
1974–75   "Hoodoo: The Indigenous Medicine and Psychiatry of the Black American." *Ethnomedizin* 3(3–4): 273–95.

Laguerre, Michale S.
   1980   *Voodoo Heritage.* Beverly Hills, Calif.: Sage Publications.
Lawless. Elaine J.
   1968   *God's Peculiar People: Women's Voices and Folk Tradi-
           tion in a Pentecostal Church.* Lexington: Univ. Press
           of Kentucky.
Leacock, Seth, and Ruth Leacock
   1975   *Spirits of the Deep.* Garden City, N.Y.: Doubleday.
Lewis, Hylan
   1955   *Blackways of Kent.* Chapel Hill: Univ. of North Caro-
           lina Press.
Lewis, Oscar
   1966   "The Culture of Poverty." *Scientific American* 215:
           19–25.
Lincoln, C. Eric
   1961   *The Black Muslims of America.* Boston: Beacon Press.
Lincoln, C. Eric, and Lawrence H. Mamiya
   1990   *The Black Church in the African American Experi-
           ence.* Durham, N.C.: Duke Univ. Press.
Litwack, Leon F.
   1961   *North of Slavery: The Negro in the Free States* 1790–
           1860. Chicago: Univ. of Chicago Press.
Lockley, Edith A.
   1936   "Spiritualist Sect in Nashville." M.A. Thesis, Fisk Univ.
Lofland, John
   1977   *Doomsday Cult.* 2d ed. New York: Irvington Press.
Marble, Manning
   1981   *Blackwater: Historical Studies in Race, Class Con-
           sciousness and Revolution.* Dayton, Ohio: Black Praxis
           Press.
Marx, Gary T.
   1970   "Religion: Opiate or Inspiration of Civil Rights Mil-
           itancy among Negroes." In *Black Americans and
           White Racism,* ed. Marcel L. Goldschmid, 366–75.
           New York: Holt, Rinehart, and Winston.
Marx, Karl, and Frederich Engels
   1964   *On Religion.* New York: Schocken. Mays, Benjamin
           E., and Joseph R. Nicholson.

1933   *The Negro Church,* New York: Institute of Social and Religious Research.

Mbiti, John S.
1969   *African Religions and Philosophy.* Garden City, N.Y.: Doubleday.

McCall, George J.
1963   "Symbiosis: The Case of Hoodoo and the Numbers Racket." *Social Problems* 10:361–71.

McCord, William, John Howard, Bernard Friedberg, and Edwin Harwood, eds.
1969   *Life Styles in the Black Ghetto.* New York: Norton.

McGuire, Meredith B.
1982   *Pentecostal Catholics: Power, Charisma, and Order in a Religious Movement.* Philadephia: Temple Univ. Press.

McGuire, Meredith
1987   *Religion: The Social Context.* Belmont, Calif.: Wadsworth.

McKay, Claude
1940   *Harlem: Negro Metropolis.* New York: Dutton. Maduro, Renaldo J.
1975   "Hoodoo Possession in San Francisco: Notes on Therapeutic Aspects of Regression." *Ethos* 3:425–47.

Mead, Frank S.
1975   *Handbook of Denominations in the United States.* 5th ed. Nashville: Abingdon.

Melton, J. Gordon
1978   *The Encyclopedia of American Religions, vols.* 1, 11. Wilmington, N.C.: McGrath.

Metraux, Alfred
1972   *Voodoo in Haiti.* New York: Schocken.

Mitchell, Henry H.
1975   *Black Belief.* New York: Harper and Row.

Mitchell, Robert C.
1971   "Witchcraft, Sin, Divine Power and Healing: The Aladura Churches and the Attainment of Life's Destiny among the Yoruba." In *The Traditional Background to Medical Practice in Nigeria,* Univ. of lbadan Institute of African Studies, Occasional Publication No. 25.

Mithun, J. S.
1976   "Survival as a Way of Life: Some Adaptive Mecha-
        nisms Contributing toward the Perpetuation of Afro-
        American Culture." In *Ethnicity in the Americas,* ed.
        Francis Henry, 347–63. The Hague: Mouton.
Moore, Sidney Harrison
1975   "Family and Social Networks in an Urban Black
        Storefront Church." Ph.D. diss., American Univ.
Mosely, J. R.
1941   *Manifest Victory: A Quest and Testimony.* New York:
        Harper and Brothers.
Mullings, Leith
1979   "Religious Change and Social Stratification in Labadi,
        Ghana: The Church of the Messiah." In *African
        Christianity: Patterns of Religious Continuity,* ed.
        George Bond, Walton Johnson, and Sheila S. Walker,
        65–88. New York: Academic Press.
Murphy, Robert F.
1979   *An Overture to Social Anthropology.* Englewood
        Cliffs, N.J.: Prentice-Hall.
Nelsen, Geoffrey K.
1969   *Spiritualism and Society,* London: Routledge and
        Kegan Paul.
Nelsen, Hart M., and Anne Kusener Nelsen
1975   *Black Church in the Sixties.* Lexington: Univ. Press of
        Kentucky.
New Orleans City Guide
1938   Federal Writers Project. Boston: Houghton Mifflin.
Parenti, Michael
1964   "The Black Muslims from Revolution to Institution."
        Social Research 31:175–94.
Parker, Robert A.
1937   *The Incredible Messiah.* Boston: Little, Brown.
Parkin, Frank
1971   *Class Inequality and Political Order: Social Stratifi-
        cation in Capitalist and Communist Societies.* New
        York: Praeger.
Parrinder, Geoffrey
1953   *Religion in the African City.* London: Oxford Univ.
        Press.

Peshkin, A.
1986   *God's Choice: The Total World of a Fundamentalist Christian School.* Chicago: Univ. of Chicago Press.

Pinkney, Alphonso
1976   *Red, Black, and Green: Black Nationalism in the United States.* Cambridge: Cambridge Univ. Press.

Pinn, Anthony B.
1998   *Varieties of African American Religious Experience.* Minneapolis: Fortress Press.

Powdermaker, Hortense
1939   *After Freedom.* New York: Atheneum.

Puckett, Newbell N.
1926   *Folk Beliefs of the Southern Negro.* Chapel Hill: Univ. of North Carolina Press.
1931   "Religious Folk-Beliefs of Whites and Negroes." *Journal of American History* 16:9–35.

Raboteau, Albert J.
1978   *Slave Religion: The "Invisible Institution" in the Antebellum South.* New York: Oxford Univ. Press.

Redfield, Robert
1956   *Peasant Society and Culture: An Anthropological Approach to Civilization.* Chicago: Univ. of Chicago Press.

Reid, Ira De A.
1926   "Let Us Prey." *Opportunity* 4:274–78.

Reimers, David M.
1965   *White Protestantism and the Negro.* New York: Oxford Univ. Press.

Reinders, Robert C.
1961   "The Church and the Negro in New Orleans, 1850–1860." *Phylon: Atlanta University Journal of Race and Culture* 22:241–48.

Richardson, James T., Mary W. Stewart, and Robert B. Simmonds
1978   "Researching a Fundamentalist Commune." In *Understanding the New Religions*, ed. J. Needleman and G. Baker, 235–51. New York: Seabury.

Robbins, Thomas, Dick Anthony, and T. Curtis
1973   "The Limits of Symbolic Realism: Problems of Empathetic Field Observation in a Sectarian Context." *Journal for the Scientific Study of Religion* 12:249–71.

Robinson, John W.
  1974   "A Song, a Shout, and a Prayer." In *The Black Experi-
            ence in Religion*, ed. C. Eric Lincoln, 212–34. New
            York: Doubleday.
Rochford, Jr., E. Burke
  1985   *Hare Krishna in America.* New Brunswick, N.J.: Rut-
            gers Univ. Press.
Saxon, Lyle, Edward Dreyer, and Robert Tallant
  1945   *Gumbo Ya-Ya.* Louisiana Writers Project Publica-
            tions. Cambridge, Mass.: Riverside.
Simpson, George Eaton
  1978   *Black Religions in the New World.* New York: Colum-
            bia Univ. Press,
Simpson, Robert Bruce
  1970   "A Black Church: Ecstasy in a World of Trouble."
            Ph.D. diss., Washington Univ.
Singer, Merrill
  1979   "Saints of the Kingdom: Group Emergence, Individ-
            ual Affiliation and Social Change among the Black
            Hebrews of Israel." Ph.D. diss., Univ. of Utah.
  1982   "Life in a Defensive Society: The Black Hebrew
            Israelites." *In* Sex *Roles in Contemporary American
            Communes*, ed. Jon Wagner, 45–81. Bloomington:
            Indiana Univ. Press.
Smith, Joan
  1981   *Social Issues and the Social Order: The Contradic-
            tions of Capitalism.* Cambridge, Mass.: Winthrop.
Smith, Michael P.
  1984   *Spirit World: Pattern in the Expressive Folk Culture
            of Afro-American New Orleans.* New Orleans: New
            Orleans Urban Folklife Society.
Snow, David A.
  1980   "The Disengagement Process: A Neglected Problem
            in Participant Observation Research." *Qualitative
            Sociology* 3(2):100–22.
Snow, Loudell F.
  1979   "Mail Order Magic: The Commercial Exploitation
            of Folk Belief." *Journal of the Folklore Institute* 16:
            44–74.

Spear, Allan H.
 1967 *Black Chicago: The Making of a Negro Ghetto,* 1890–1920, Chicago: Univ. of Chicago Press.
Stack, Carol B.
 1974 All *Our Kin: Strategies for Survival in a Black Community.* New York: Harper and Row.
Staples, Robert
 1976 *Introduction to Black Sociology.* New York: McGraw-Hill.
Stark, Rodney, and William Sims Bainbridge
 1979 "Of Churches, Sects, and Cults: Preliminary Concepts for a Theory of Religious Movements." *Journal for the Scientific Study of Religion* 18:117–31.
 1985 *The Future of Religion: Secularization, Revival, and Cult Formation.* Berkeley: Univ. of California Press.
Sutherland, Robert
 1930 "An Analysis of Negro Churches in Chicago." Ph.D. diss., Univ. of Chicago.
Szwed, John F.
 1971 Preface. In *Black Gods of the Metropolis,* by Arthur H. Fauset. Philadelphia: Univ. of Pennsylvania Press.
Tallant, Robert
 1946 *Voodoo in New Orleans.* New York: Collier.
Taussig, Michael
 1979 "Black Religion and Resistance in Columbia: Three Centuries of Social Struggle in the Cauca Valley." *Marxist Perspectives* 1979:84–116.
Thompson, Daniel C.
 1944 "The rise of a religious cult: The social history of the All National Spiritualist Church of God, Atlanta, Georgia." Thesis, Atlanta Univ.
 1974 *Sociology of the Black Experience.* Westport, Conn.: Greenwood.
Tinker, Edward Laroque
 1930 "Mother Catherine's Castor Oil." *North American Review* 230 (2): 148–54.
Tyms, James Daniel
 1938 "A Study of Four Religious Cults Operating among Negroes." M.A. Thesis, Howard Univ.

Valentine, Charles A.
  1968   *Culture and Poverty: Critique and Counter-Proposals.*
           Chicago: Univ. of Chicago Press.
  1972   *Black Studies and Anthropology: Scholarly and Political*
           Interests in Afro-American Culture. A McCaleb Module
           in Anthropology. Reading, Mass.: Addison-Wesley.
Van Maanen, John
  1988   *Tales of the Field: On Writing Ethnography.* Chicago:
           Univ. of Chicago Press.
Van Zandt, D. E.
  1991   *Living in the Children of God.* Princeton, N.J.: Princeton
           Univ. Press.
Vincent, Theodore G.
  1971   *Black Power and the Garvey Movement.* San Fran-
           cisco: Ramparts.
Wagner, Melinda Bollar
  1983   *Metaphysics in Midwestern America.* Columbus: Ohio
           State Univ. Press.
  1990   *God's Schools: Choice and Compromise in American*
           Society. New Brunswick, N.J.: Rutgers Univ. Press.
Wallace, Anthony F. C.
  1956   "Revitalization Movements." *American Anthropolo-*
           gist 58:264–81.
Wallis, Roy
  1974   "Ideology, Authority and the Development of Cultic
           Movements." *Social Research* 41:299–327.
Washington, Joseph R., Jr.
  1964   *Black Religion: The Negro and Christianity in the*
           United States. Boston: Beacon Press.
  1973   *Black Sects and Cults.* Garden City, NY: Doubleday/
           Anchor.
Weidman, Hazel, et al.
  1978   *Miami Health Ecology Project, vol. I.* Miami: Univ. of
           Miami Press.
Wengle, John L.
  1988   *Ethnographers in the Field: The Psychology of Research.*
           Tuscaloosa: Univ. of Alabama Press.
White, Gavin
  1978   "Patriarch McGuire and the Episcopal Church." In
           Black Apostles: Afro-American Clergy Confront the

Twentieth Century, ed. Randall K. Burkett and Richard Newman, 151–80. Boston: G. K. Hall.

Whitehead, H.
1987　*Renunciation and Reformulation: A Study of Conversion in an American Sect.* Ithaca, N.Y.: Cornell Univ. Press.

Whitten, Norman E., Jr.
1962　"Contemporary Patterns of Malign Occultism among Negroes in North Carolina." *Journal of American Folklore* 75:311–25.

Williams, Melvin D.
1974　*Community in a Black Pentecostal Church.* Pittsburgh: Univ. of Pittsburgh Press.
1980　*On the Street Where I Lived.* New York: Holt, Rinehart, and Winston.

Wilmore, Gayraud S.
1972　*Black Religion and Black Radicalism.* Garden City, N.Y.: Doubleday.
1983　*Black Religion and Black Radicalism.* 2d ed. Maryknoll, N.Y.: Orbis.

Wilson, Bryan
1973　*Magic and the Millennium: A Sociological Study of Religious Movements of Protest among Tribal and Third-World Peoples.* New York: Harper and Row.

Wilson, John
1978　*Religion in American Society: The Effective Presence,* Englewood Cliffs, N.J.: Prentice-Hall.

Winslow, David J.
1969　"Bishop E. E. Everett and Some Aspects of Occultism and Folk Religion in Negro Philadelphia." *Keystone Folklore Quarterly* 14:59–80.

Winter, J. Alan
1977　*Continuities in the Sociology of Religion.* New York: Harper and Row.

Yinger, J. Milton
1970　*The Scientific Study of Religion.* New York: Macmillan.

Index